CHICAGO PUBLIC LIBRARY
400 SOUTH STATE STREET
CHICAGO, IL 60605

BM
660
.H27
1994

Hammer, Reuven.

Entering Jewish
   prayer.

$24.50

DATE			

BAKER & TAYLOR

Entering
Jewish Prayer

Entering Jewish Prayer

A GUIDE TO PERSONAL DEVOTION
AND THE WORSHIP SERVICE

REUVEN HAMMER

Schocken Books New York

Copyright © 1994 by Reuven Hammer

All rights reserved under International and Pan-American Copyright Conventions. Published in the United States by Schocken Books Inc., New York, and simultaneously in Canada by Random House of Canada Limited, Toronto. Distributed by Pantheon Books, a division of Random House, Inc., New York.

Grateful acknowledgment is made to the following for permission to reprint previously published material:

"i thank you God for most this amazing" is reprinted by permission of Liveright Publishing Corporation. Copyright © 1950, 1978, 1991 by the Trustees for the e.e. cummings Trust and in the U.K. by permission of W. W. Norton and Company. Copyright © 1975 by the Trustees for the e.e. cummings Trust. · Quoted passages from *Tanakh: The Holy Scriptures*, some quoted with the author's emendations, are reprinted by permission of the Jewish Publication Society. Copyright © 1985 by the Jewish Publication Society. · Chapter 12 is an expanded version of an article by the author entitled "Tefillin," published in pamphlet form by the Burning Bush Press as part of the Jewish Tract Series. Copyright © 1967 by the United Synagogue of America.

Library of Congress Cataloging-in-Publication Data

Hammer, Reuven.
Entering Jewish prayer : a guide to personal devotion and the worship service / Reuven Hammer.
p.   cm.
Includes bibliographical references and index.
ISBN 0-8052-4117-5
1. Judaism—Liturgy—History. 2. Prayer—Judaism. 3. Siddur.
I. Title.
BM660.H27 1994
296.4—dc20   93-28514

Book Design by M. Kristen Bearse

Manufactured in the United States of America
First Edition
9 8 7 6 5 4 3 2 1

R00970 25740

SOCIAL SCIENCES DIVISION
CHICAGO PUBLIC LIBRARY
400 SOUTH STATE STREET
CHICAGO, IL 60605

To the memory of my grandparents

Berel (Barney) Gordon   Yitzhak (Ike) Hammer
Gitte (Gussie) Gordon   Osne (Annie) Hammer

zichronam l'vracha

Their piety and devotion form my first and finest memories
of prayer.

AND HIS BANNER OF LOVE WAS OVER ME (Song of Songs 2:4). This refers to the Shema and the Amida.

Yalkut Shimoni, Song of Songs, 2

Contents

Preface

The idea of writing a book about Jewish prayer often came to my mind during the past decade while teaching Jewish prayer and worship to both rabbinical students and general audiences in seminaries and congregations in North and South America, England, and Israel. From the questions, comments, and discussions held with these various groups I learned a great deal, and much that appears in this book is a result of this interaction. Wherever I went I found the same reaction: the subject of prayer is of interest and concern because it is so central to participation in Jewish spiritual life. Many people are seeking to find a way that will enable them to feel at home in the synagogue and in the Siddur (the prayerbook). Even those who already participate in prayer frequently feel that there must be more to it than they are currently experiencing. Contemporary Jews want to know the meaning of the prayers. Those who cannot translate all of the Hebrew would like to know the significance of key words and phrases that recur time and time again. They want to understand the concepts embodied in the prayers, the patterns of the service, the reason why we say what we say, and the history of the liturgy.

Participating in a service should not be like attending a theatrical performance. It means being able to be one of the active players. In addition to knowing what the correct page is and finding the passage, we want to understand why we are saying these words and how they relate to the entire service and to being Jewish. Mastering the Siddur enables one to understand many of the basic concepts and beliefs of Judaism. Being able to participate in the prayers enables one to experience the feelings and emotions that they are intended to elicit. The difficulties people face in achieving this are many. They include understanding the language, the references, and the ideas, as well as the world view of those who composed the prayers; appreciating the history of Jewish prayer; and grappling with the clash between the values and beliefs of the modern world and those of the traditional prayerbook. The exhilaration and excitement involved in achieving this and the satisfaction in knowing what one has gained make the difficulties less overwhelming. Once one has gained this knowledge and appreciation, the liturgy, which has so often seemed remote or part of some esoteric or archaic rite, becomes an instrument for self-fulfillment and personal enrichment.

In the course of research and preparation for teaching and then for writing this book, I have read most of the major works written on this subject over the last hundred years or so and have thus learned from the great masters of Jewish liturgy, with their varied approaches to the subject. I have also consulted the classical commentaries on the Siddur and the sources in rabbinic literature that deal with the subject. I should like to acknowledge my personal indebtedness to two great teachers with whom I was privileged to study: Shalom Spiegel and Abraham Joshua Heschel. It was with Professor Spiegel that I first studied the history and meaning of Jewish worship. Professor Spiegel, as anyone who studied with him will testify, was one of the master teachers of our time, whose penetrating insights and dramatic approach were a source of great inspiration. Much that I learned from him is reflected in my approach to the subject. Although I never formally studied prayer with Professor Heschel, his approach to spiritual life and to the importance of worship was evident no matter what the subject he taught and became an important part of my own thinking and feeling. Heschel did more than any other single individual in this century to place the question of prayer on the Jewish agenda once again. It is fitting, then, that while considering what approach to take to the writing of this book, I came across a remark of his which gave me the clue I needed:

Our prayer book is going to remain obscure unless Jewish teachers will realize that one of their foremost tasks is to discover, to explain and to interpret the words of the prayer book. What we need is *a sympathetic prayer book exegesis*. [italics mine] (*Man's Quest for God*, p. 83)

Perhaps that phrase comes as close as possible to explaining the orientation of this book. A "sympathetic" approach intends not merely to convey information but to place that information in a framework that will enhance the capacity of the individual to find a place for prayer within his or her life. I can know everything about who wrote a prayer and when, the various versions of it that exist, and all the manuscript evidence, yet still not be able to pray. But if I sympathetically experience the impulses and the yearnings, the cries and the anguish, the joys and celebrations that led to the creation of that prayer or of those particular expressions, and if I can re-create that spiritual environment in my own life in terms that are both intellectually honest and emotionally meaningful to me, then that information can only enrich the experience of prayer. This is the orientation I seek to create.

In order to achieve this, my book must do many things. It will sketch the history of Jewish worship and give the historical background of individual prayers. I will attempt to explain and interpret the language and literature of Jewish prayer, and deal with the value and importance of prayer, specifically of Jewish communal worship. It is important to present the patterns of prayer—the structure of the service and the way in which it leads us from theme to theme and from one feeling to another. I will also discuss the belief system that created these prayers and show how that system is reflected in them. The problems we face in attempting to make such an ancient document relevant and meaningful to us today will be investigated. Those who are beginning to learn about prayer and to participate in it should find this basic orientation helpful, while those already familiar with the material may find interpretations and explanations that will deepen their insights. I hope obscure passages will take on meaning. Threads and connections should become apparent. All too often the study of prayer becomes like the study of a flower: pulling it apart destroys it forever. That is what I hope to avoid. I am prepared to criticize and to illuminate difficulties, but with the purpose of encouraging the reader to find meaningful solutions. I intend to discuss and explain individual sections, but with the intention of then relating them to the overall scheme. This book will deal therefore not only with the "when" and "where" and "how" questions, but also with the "whys." In this way it attempts to fulfill Heschel's plea for "a sympathetic prayer book exegesis."

Many aspects of these topics are too detailed or lengthy to be included or would distract from the purpose of the work. The reader who wishes to explore specific aspects of the subject further is therefore referred to the bibliography.

Because this book is written for the general reader, I have chosen to depart from the more precise (and more intimidating) scholarly system of transliterating Hebrew words and opted for a system that I think best communicates their pronunciation.

The gutteral letters *chet* ח and *chaf* כ are therefore both rendered as *ch*, except when there is a well-known and commonly accepted spelling in English, e.g., Hanukkah, Hassidism, Rosh Hodesh.

In general, I have omitted the final, unpronounced letter *heh* ה at the end of a word, except again in cases of words with that spelling familiar to the English reader, e.g., Torah, Haggadah, Haftarah, Kabbalah, Rosh Ha-Shanah, *brit milah*.

I should like to express my appreciation to two friends who read early drafts and gave valuable suggestions, Deborah Uchill Miller and Professor Herbert Alexander, and above all to my wife, Rahel, who labored untold hours to help bring clarity out of chaos. It is unlikely that this volume would have reached this stage without the encouragement and helpful insights of Bonny Fetterman, who served as its editor and guided me through more drafts than I care to recall.

Modeh ani . . . I give thanks to the Almighty for this opportunity of occupying myself with matters of spiritual significance and helping to revitalize the words of prayer and praise that constitute the service of the heart.

REUVEN HAMMER
Jerusalem
5753—the year 45 of the State of Israel's independence

Entering
Jewish Prayer

1

What Is Prayer?

To understand prayer, it is essential that we see it in a larger context. Individual prayer may be mainly a way of communicating with God and expressing our feelings, reactions, and needs. When reflected through the prism of Jewish worship, however, prayer is much more than that. It is an integral part of the complete religious life of a Jew—an essential part, but nevertheless only a part. It cannot be isolated from the rest except artificially, for it interweaves with everything else to create the harmonious whole that is Judaism. The other major components of a full Jewish life are study, ritual practice, and moral living. Although prayer is our way of communicating with God, we must remember that it is not the only way. All of these paths lead to God, and all of them are interconnected.

The relationship between study and performance was debated by the rabbis:

> "What is more important, study or performance?" Rabbi Tarfon said that performance is greater. Rabbi Akiva said that study is greater. Everyone present agreed that study is greater because it leads to performance.[1]

The ultimate goal is action, life itself. But one cannot achieve this in an isolated fashion. Study is valuable in and of itself, but its ultimate value lies in its effect upon our entire way of living. This interrelatedness applies to prayer as well. Sometimes it is an end in itself. People want to feel close to God. They want to express their feelings, their fears, their hopes. They want to celebrate their joys in a way that will deepen their intensity. They want to ease their sorrows by placing them within a larger framework of meaning. They want to feel that their life has meaning and that they are part of a historic entity, rooted in the past and with a promise for the future. In that sense Franz Rosenzweig was correct when he said, "The prayer is its own fulfillment. . . . To be able to pray: that is the greatest gift presented to the soul in revelation."[2] But ultimately prayer is also intended to have an effect on the individual and his or her actions. It makes us more aware of the world, of nature, of history, of God's role in history, of the nature of God and His demands upon us. It emphasizes the importance of study and of the performance of commandments, both moral and ritual. One should emerge not only spiritually enriched from prayer but also morally purified, more closely identified with the traditions and beliefs of Judaism, and committed to living according to its high standards of ethics and morality. One who prays should develop sensitivity to all around him and should be highly aware of responsibility toward others. What the Sages said concerning tefillin—"One should not wear the tefillin and then commit a transgression"[3]—applies equally to all forms of worship. When all is said and done, the importance of prayer is its influence upon our lives, which in turn can affect the society in which we live. As Abraham Joshua Heschel wrote:

> Piety cannot consist in specific acts only, such as prayer or ritual observances, but is bound up with all actions. . . . Man's responsibility to God cannot be discharged by an excursion into spirituality.[4]

Prayer has been defined as "the service of the heart" or "in the heart," as opposed to the service that was performed in the Temple, which consisted basically of the offering of sacrifices. The service of prayer is many faceted. In it we address ourselves to God. We may turn to Him in petition, addressing our needs to Him, and needs can be of many sorts. To pray for peace is to ask for our needs as much as is asking for food, rain, or prosperity.

We may turn to God in thankful acknowledgment. We express our gratitude not only for whatever we have but for the very fact of life itself. One of the best-known blessings, recited at special occasions and at every holiday of the Jewish year, blesses God for keeping us alive to enjoy this moment: *"shehecheyanu"*—"Who has kept us alive, sustained us, and brought us to this moment." This life-affirming blessing often stirs deep emotions as we realize how thin is the line separating being from nonbeing and how dependent we are on forces outside of ourselves and beyond our control. Similarly in the Amida, recited three times daily, we publicly proclaim and acknowledge that "You are the Lord our God . . . the Rock of our lives" and that God is the source of the "wonders that are with us daily, evening, morn, and noon."

Often we turn to God in praise. Speaking to Him directly, we call Him "the great, mighty, and awesome God, the Most High God." Or we praise Him variously as the "maker of heaven and earth," the "creator of light and darkness," or He who "brings on the evening." We praise Him through the recitation of numerous psalms that vividly describe His deeds and His creation.

In this "service of the heart" there are also times when the purpose of our words is not to communicate with God but to sensitize ourselves so that we can better speak to Him. Even words addressed to God may have this secondary purpose as their hidden agenda. "Know before Whom you stand" requires a constant resensitization; Jewish prayer is recitation about God, about our history, about our ancestors, about God's deeds, and about God's demands.

The other major component of worship is the opportunity to hear God's message to us. In Judaism, study has always been seen as a form of worship. To study Torah—which includes a wide range of material, from the Torah and the rest of the Bible, through all the Bible interpretations and commentaries referred to as the Oral Torah—is another way of experiencing God. This uniquely Jewish concept has been incorporated into formal Jewish worship. It is reflected in the various instances when Torah is recited. A special part of the service is devoted to reading from the Torah and the Prophets; special occasions call for readings from the Writings; portions of the Torah are recited in the Shema. There are also times when sections of the Oral Torah are recited within the framework of a service. At those times, study and worship are inseparable. Outside the framework of worship, a tremendous emphasis is given to study. One of the points of conflict between modern Hassidim and their opponents, the Mitnagdim, was this very question. Mitnagdim thought that Hassidim spent too much time on prayer, to the detriment of study. As Louis Jacobs has pointed out, Hassidism's elevation of prayer over other duties was an innovation.[5]

The argument over how much time to spend in prayer actually goes back thousands of years, for we find the discussion among the Sages as well. How much should a person pray? The prevailing opinion was "three times a day—and no more," but one Sage said, "Would that a person would pray time and time again all day long!"[6] Nevertheless, human beings cannot spend all of their time in prayer, for if prayer is to be effective it must be not simply an end in itself but a way of enriching our lives and influencing everything we do. If prayer is an expression of our connection with God, that connection, to be meaningful, must be ongoing. Everything we do—all of our lives—must be an expression of that connection. Neither our deeds, our thoughts, our actions toward others, our ethics and morality can be excluded from expressing our relationship to God. Prayer is the conscious expression of that relationship, the moments and hours we devote exclusively to developing that connection: addressing ourselves to God, speaking about God, listening to the words of God. Sometimes that can take a moment—a pause to recite a blessing which transforms even a simple habitual act into a moment of consciousness of the sacred. Sometimes it can be a quarter or half an hour to recite a formal prayer which punctuates the day, calls us from the busy routine to realize the source and meaning of our lives. It could also be a day spent in prayer: Yom Kippur. The rabbis said that it is not the length but the quality of prayer that matters. Moses, they remarked, recited both the longest and the shortest prayers. For forty days he prayed at Mount Sinai, but when Miriam was stricken he prayed for her by uttering only five words: "O God, please heal her!" (Num. 12:13). To pray all the time—in the sense of stopping all else in order to address words or thoughts to God—would be impossible. Never to pray is to starve the soul. As with most things, moderation is the appropriate solution.

The Experience of Prayer

The experience of prayer cannot be uniform for everyone. Each person comes to it out of personal feelings and experiences. To ask, "What does it mean to pray?" is like asking, "What does it mean to speak?" or "What does it mean to think?" At times prayer means to exalt, to rejoice, and to experience exultation and exhilaration. At times to pray means to plumb the depths of one's being and pour out all of one's feelings before God. Prayer may indicate confession—confession of deeds or confession of thoughts and feelings. Prayer may be a desire to give thanks. It may be to exclaim in wonder at the phenomenon of the world or at the mystery of life itself. Prayer may be a way of expressing fidelity and belief. And of course it may be simply what the word "pray" indicates: to ask for something. One need only peruse that magnificent ancient collection of prayers, the Book of Psalms, to see the tremendous gamut of emotions that can bring one to prayer. There are feelings of despair: "In distress I called on the Lord" (Ps. 118:5). There is the experience of overwhelming joy: "Hallelujah. Sing to the Lord a new song. . . . Let Israel rejoice in its maker" (Ps. 149:1–2). Sometimes there is an expression of an almost physical longing to experience the presence of God, without whom life seems to have little meaning: "God, You are my God; I search for You, my soul thirsts for You, my body yearns for You" (Ps. 63:2).

For some, prayer reflects a sense of duty, a requirement placed upon us. Who would dare to address a Being so far superior to ourselves if He did not require us to do so? For others, it comes from a sense of gratitude. How can we experience the good things of this world without expressing our appreciation? Sometimes it stems from a sense of despair. When all is bleak and hope is gone, to whom can we turn if not to God? Prayer can also reflect a sense of wonder. How can I contemplate the vast reaches of space, the unending horizons, the stars too great to number, the wonders of birth and creation, and not exclaim, "How wondrous are Your deeds, O Lord"?

Ultimately prayer is a way of experiencing the reality of God in the world and of relating to that reality. In revelation God reaches out to us, but in prayer we reach out to Him. As Leo Baeck wrote:

> If our life is to be filled with devoutness, we must from time to time abandon the ways of the world so that we may enjoy the peace of God.[7]

Some years ago, experiments began on earth to see if it would be possible to establish communication with other beings in the far-flung reaches of the universe. Even now radio signals are being sent out and receivers are poised to accept any answers. It may seem to us that prayer is similar to this. We are sending out our signals to the universe and saying, Is there anyone out there listening? Reply if You exist! But the difference is that the person of faith finds the reply already inherent in the world and in life. He does not expect God to reply as human beings do. He believes—perhaps even knows—that God hears, and that is sufficient. To be able to speak to God, to be permitted to praise Him, is enough.

> Hillel the Elder once saw people praying and noticed that they were filled with pride. He said to them, "Do you not know that our praise is of no importance? Are there not thousands and hundreds of thousands of angels who serve Him, as it is said: Can His troops be numbered (Job 25:3)? What can our praise add?" He then saw that they became depressed, so he said to them, "Do you not know that although there are thousands and hundreds of thousands of angels, yet He desires not their praise but the praise of Israel, as it is said: The utterance of David son of Jesse, the utterance of the man set on high, the anointed of the God of Jacob, the sweet singer of Israel (2 Sam. 23:1) and [it says]: But You are the Holy One, enthroned upon the praise of Israel (Ps. 22:4)."⁸

The most exalted feeling that can emerge from the experience of prayer is that of having participated in pure praise expressing the wonder of God. It is toward this end that we engage in prayer, but it is not the only experience of prayer. Prayer has many faces. It has been pointed out that the Hebrew word usually translated as "to pray," *l'hitpallel*, is derived from a word meaning "to judge," so that the one who prays is asking for God's judgment upon him. We present ourselves and our needs, with the hope that we are worthy of having our requests answered. Indeed, that Hebrew word, although used in a general way to indicate reciting any prayer, also has the specific and more technical meaning of saying a prayer that is a request. There are many other words for prayer in Hebrew. The Sages once remarked that there are two main types of prayer, as indicated by the verse "To hear the song and the prayer" (1 Kings 8:28). "Song" refers to "the praise of the Holy One," while "prayer" refers to "the needs of human beings."⁹ Sometimes we pray for ourselves. At other times we pray simply to sing God's praises. To these two basic modes—*shevach* (praise) and *bakasha* (petition)—may be added *hodaya:* thanksgiving. The Sages then went on to list ten different Hebrew terms which they found to be connected in the Bible with prayer: cry for help, moaning, song, plea, distress, calling out, prostrating, praying, and beseeching. Of them all, beseeching is the one Moses chose when he prayed to be allowed to enter the Land of Israel. The reason, said the Sages, was that that word implies throwing oneself totally on God's mercy, depending on His nature and not on our own worth. By this they indicated that anything God does for us—any prayer that He answers—is a reflection of His goodness and mercy. As they said, "No creature has a claim upon his maker." To pray cannot be to demand, it cannot be to indicate that one is worthy. Ultimately it is a recognition of dependency upon God and of the free nature of every gift we receive. Life itself, all we have, is not something that is earned but something that is experienced as an act of graciousness on the part of the giver of life.

One of the prayers recited in the preliminary passages of Shacharit, the morning service, raises the entire question of the possibility of prayer. Is it not logically absurd that human beings can speak to the Life of the Universe? Turning directly to God, we first express our feelings of unworthiness.

> What are we? What are our lives? . . .
> What value our righteousness? . . .
> Even the greatest and most valiant
> are as if they did not exist in Your presence . . .
> for most of their deeds are nothing. . . .
> The difference between man and beast is nonexistent.

Although Judaism frequently stresses the exalted place human beings occupy in the universe—"a little lower than the angels"—the crown of creation, at the very moment when we face God in a direct relationship of prayer we suddenly realize how impossibly unimportant and unworthy we are. We are so far below God that we cannot even imagine Him, we cannot begin to grasp His existence. If, as a Sage once said, we cannot even look at the sun, which is nothing but a minor part of His creation, how can we expect to experience and address the creator? In the vastness of His universe—whose measurement we cannot even take—what value can our deeds possibly have? How much wisdom can even the wisest possess? At the very moment of prayer, the dark soberness of our own existence overwhelms us and should, by all rights, bring any attempt at prayer to an absolute halt. But it does not. Instead the prayer goes on to say "But"—and this is one of the most important *but*s one can imagine:

> But we are Your people, Your covenant-children,
> the children of Your friend Abraham
> to whom You swore an oath at Mount Moriah,
> the seed of his only son Isaac, who was bound upon the altar,
> the congregation of Your firstborn son Jacob,
> whom You called Israel and Jeshurun
> because of Your love for him and Your joy in him—
> therefore we are *duty bound* to thankfully acknowledge You,
> to praise You, to glorify You,
> to bless, sanctify, and offer praise
> and thankful acknowledgment to Your name.

To pray is to acknowledge and thank, praise and glorify, bless and sanctify. All of this is an obligation placed upon us because of our ancestry and our history. We *must* do this because God Himself initiated a special relationship with the people of Israel. The possibility of prayer, which just a moment ago seemed such an absurdity, exists because God Himself has opened the door to it. Otherwise, how would we dare? In comparison with God, we may indeed be of no account, but God's concern for us and His desire that we serve Him through prayer invests our lives with meaning and significance. This prayer concludes:

> Happy are we!
> How good is our portion,
> How pleasant our lot,
> How lovely our heritage. . . .

What joy we have in the fact that it is possible, after all, for us to come before God and recite the Shema, the blessings, and the prayers. The ability to pray is a source of rejoicing. It is not a burden, not simply an obligation, and certainly not an absurdity. It is God's gift to the undeserving. The tone is not one of humility—although without humility there can be no prayer. Rather, it is one of exaltation and joy.

According to this prayer, it is our membership in the people of Israel that makes prayer possible. Of course, any human being can come before God and utter praise and petition. Jews were not the first to pray. But there is a different element to prayer when one prays not as a lone human being but as a member of the people Israel. If we accept the fact that we have been called to be "a kingdom of priests and a holy nation" (Exod. 19:6), then worship is part of the duties of this priestly people. It becomes an integral part of that very complex relationship between God and Israel. How are we to express that relationship if we do not take the time to become aware of Him? Thus prayer becomes at the same time a duty and a privilege. It also becomes important for us to pray within a designated framework of the Jewish tradition and not just alone in our own words and thoughts. Jewish worship is more than an experience of God. It is an experience of God through the prism of Judaism.

Prayer is not an exclusively Jewish enterprise. It is an expression of our human status. The impulse to pray comes from basic human needs and desires. The informal words a person addresses to God may well be the same regardless of one's background. The distinctiveness of Jewish prayer is to be found in the concept of the God to whom we pray, a God who is the sole source of life, who can be entreated but not compelled, a God who is father and king at the same time. Formal Jewish prayer utilizes the words others have formulated before us in order to guide us. These words specifically reflect Jewish belief, Jewish ideals, Jewish history, and Jewish hopes for the future. They are based upon uniquely Jewish concepts of God, the nature of God, and our relationship to Him. To pray in the words of traditional Jewish prayer is to be steeped in the thought and value system of Judaism. As Franz Rosenzweig wrote:

> The sum and substance of the whole of historical Judaism, its handbook and memorial tablet, will ever be the Prayer Book. . . . He to whom these volumes are not a sealed book has more than grasped the "essence of Judaism." He is informed with it as with life itself; he has within him a "Jewish world."[10]

Learning about prayer—understanding the liturgy, the history of the Siddur (the daily prayerbook), the structure of the service, and its themes—is a way of helping us to enter the world of Jewish tradition. The Siddur is the best possible introduction into that world. It brings us face to face with Judaism's struggle for an understanding of God, humanity, and the world. Mastery of the Siddur is the key both to the ability to worship as a Jew and to the understanding of the meaning of Judaism. Once we possess it, new vistas open before us.

A full understanding of prayer, however, cannot be gained by studying about prayer or learning about the Siddur or even by discussing the problematics of prayer and the benefits of worship. The text is the Siddur, but the subtext is the art of praying, the action of worship. In the end, that can only be experienced. Just as one may talk and read about love forever and a day, but will never understand it without experiencing love, so it is with prayer. Nothing can compare to the actual experience. On the other hand, to make the experience of prayer meaningful, it is important to gain a basic knowledge of the prayers in our Siddur.

Of course each individual brings to the traditional words of the Siddur his or her own personality, but that personality, in turn, becomes part of the collective personality of the Jewish people. The more we become familiar with the prayers tradition has formulated, the more that vocabulary becomes part of ourselves, and we find that even when we pray informally or spontaneously we use the vocabulary of prayer that comes from Jewish tradition.

Prayer should always be a combination of set words and spontaneous expression. We utilize the magnificent texts that others have written and we add to them, through variations and interpretations and whatever words we wish to add in order to bring our feelings to the fore. Since expression in prayer is so difficult, when geniuses have left us such a rich heritage it seems wasteful not to utilize their words. Even more: human culture is based on the use of creations of the past. Words have echoes. They are enriched by the ways they have been uttered before. Every new text is built on the texts of the past, and the more echoes, the richer the new text. On the other hand, there is a danger in using words simply because they are there, not understanding them or not investing them with meaning. Making meaningless sounds cannot possibly be prayer—it is magic. It is as if we believed that by saying the right sounds we could bring about the effect we want. Such a concept is a regression to paganism in which the gods are subject to the forces of magic and recitation of formulas can force them to do our will. Judaism rejected all of that at the very beginning. We cannot compel God to do anything; we ask Him. Using traditional prayer therefore requires us to bring meaning to the sounds we utter. That meaning can be on the emotional level or the cognitive one, or a combination of both. This is not merely a question of understanding Hebrew. Even if one understands the language, words can be meaningless if they are recited totally by rote or with no attempt to understand them. The more we understand the words and what lies behind them, the greater the opportunity to use them well.

Prayer requires *kavana*, which implies not only concentration but meaning and intention in expressing ourselves before God. The word *kavana* basically means "to aim." There must be intent in whatever we say, an aiming toward closeness to God. What is needed, therefore, is a synthesis of the old and the new. The old is the received text, the words so many others have said and still say. The new is the personal feelings and the individual meaning, which changes every time we say these words, if we say them with fervor and intention, if they are accompanied by *kavana*.

The language of Jewish prayer is Hebrew. Certainly it is permissible to pray in any language. The Sages of the Mishna indicated how important they thought it was that we understand what we say:

> These may be said in any language . . . the recitation of the Shema, the Prayer [the Amida], and the Blessing After Meals.[11]

If that is so, what need is there for the non-Hebrew speaker to pray in Hebrew? Franz Rosenzweig remarked that "the uncomprehended Hebrew gives him more than the finest translation. . . . Jewish prayer means praying in Hebrew."[12] There is an emotional element that reciting prayer in Hebrew can add even to those who do not comprehend every word. There is a feeling of identification with an ancient tradition and with other Jews wherever they may be which enhances the experience of prayer. There is nothing magical in Hebrew, but there is something culturally meaningful that is lost when traditional prayers are said in other languages. Even if one does not understand the words, a glance at the translation will enable one to bring some level of meaning to the recitation, which is then supplemented by the emotional impact of the Hebrew text. Furthermore, by learning about the texts themselves, you can apprehend the sense of the texts, if not of every word.

Obviously, the more one knows the text in its original language, the better. The real meaning of the text lies in its original language. The terms that are used, the multiple meanings and echoes within them, can seldom be fully conveyed in translation.

Languages are also reflections of specific cultures. When God is called *"go'el"* and the English renders it "redeemer," we have entered into another thought-world with connotations not to be found in the Hebrew. For Christianity—and English is a Christian language—redemption means saving someone doomed to perdition because of sin. For Judaism, it means rescuing Israel from the enslavement of foreigners. When we thank God for *"torah u-mitzvot,"* we are not speaking of "law and commandments." "Law" is a set of legal norms. Torah is God's instruction, either in a specific book or in all of Jewish tradition as it has developed until today. "Commandments" has the harsh sound of orders given by a commander. Mitzvot are both actions we are expected to perform and actions of a positive nature which stem from religious convictions. All of this is on the most basic level of semantics. If it is true, as has been said, that reading a work in translation is like kissing through a veil, what shall we say about trying to pray through translation? Beyond the basic level, there is the level of emotion that only the Hebrew can properly achieve.

What are we to do, therefore, when so many Jews do not understand the language? It is fatuous to say, "Learn it!" as desirable as that would be. But we can say, "Learn the vocabulary of prayer." It is possible to study enough about the prayers so that even if you do not understand every word, the main words and phrases will be familiar to you. Glance at the translations as you pray to remind yourself of the meaning, but do not depend on them. For if all translations are interpretations, translations of prayers are even more likely to be explanations and to contain the theology and philosophy of the translator. If you have read about the prayers, you will know enough to assign whatever meaning you feel appropriate at the time you are saying them.

Community Prayer

Hebrew is indispensable if one wishes to participate in communal Jewish prayer in any traditional synagogue. Although Judaism has a rich tradition of individual prayer, it nevertheless places an extraordinary emphasis on community worship. The individual may express himself in whatever words he desires. But when taking part in community prayer, one must also join in the framework that has been accepted by the community. Some prayers have been designed specifically for community use and, according to Jewish tradition, are to be recited only when a community is present. Obviously any of the prayers that are formulated as responses between the leader and the group cannot be said by an individual praying alone. More than that, some of the most important prayers concerning the holiness of God may be recited only in the presence of a quorum. Sanctifying God's name is a public act. Thus those prayers that proclaim the holiness of God, such as the Kaddish and the Kedusha, can only be said in the presence of a minyan, the minimum quorum of ten adults which the tradition has determined constitutes a community.

There is an extra dimension to prayer recited by the community. Tradition teaches that even those prayers the individual is permitted to recite alone have greater impact when uttered as part of the congregation. "In the multitude of the nation is the glory of the king" (Prov. 14:28). The very presence of many people adds glory to what is being done.

> Said Rabbi Abahu, " 'Seek the Lord where He may be found' (Isa. 55:6). Where is He found? In the synagogues and halls of study."[13]

> Abba Binyamin said, "A person's prayer is heard only in the synagogue."[14]

We might well think the opposite. Cannot the presence of God be felt by one person alone on a mountain peak? Where better? Jacob's most intensive experiences of prayer took place when he was most alone, for it was then that he felt the presence of God and experienced the need for God most keenly. There are certainly times when the presence of others even impedes prayer and distracts us from the possibility of concentration. Judaism recognizes this and does not discourage solitary prayer. The presence of God is to be found wherever a person addresses Him. But Judaism is also wary lest such aloneness become the norm and the permanent status of the human being. Religion is not what we do with our aloneness, but what we do with our togetherness. It is not accidental that there is no Jewish ideal of worshiping God by leaving civilization and setting up a lonely cell in the wilderness. That is considered a temptation to be resisted. "Hillel said: Separate yourself not from the community."[15] Formal prayer reflects this as well. To seek God on the mountaintop is the easy way out. If you do it, it should be only in order to return with renewed strength and purpose to the community, for it is in the community that God must be found and made real. We are always seeking that tenth person for the minyan, not because there is something sacred or magical in a group of ten, but because that number represents community for us. The Sages advised that if we cannot pray in a synagogue, at least we should pray at the same time others are praying. In that way we identify ourselves with the group. "When is the time of God's favor? When the community prays!"[16]

The story is told of a great second-century rabbi, Simeon bar Yochai, who, together with his son, had to flee to escape Roman persecution. They went into a cave where they lived for twelve years, watered by a spring, while their food was provided by a miraculous carob tree. Without need to toil, without need for other human beings, they could spend all of their time in prayer and study. When the danger had passed and they left the cave, they had nothing but contempt for human beings who spent their time going about their daily work, declaring scornfully, "They forsake eternal life and busy themselves with things of this life!" The legend relates that whatever they looked upon was consumed by the fire of their rage, so that God commanded them to go back to the cave: "Have you emerged in order to destroy My world?" They came back out only when they had learned that the proper worship of God must be combined with the normal occupations of life.[17]

Prayer that isolates us—prayer that leads us to believe that we need only ourselves and God, and have no need for other human beings and no obligations to them; prayer that regards the community and its needs as unimportant—is destructive prayer. It consumes the world and destroys it.

Community prayer is also a way of strengthening the ties of the individual with the Jewish community. It is not accidental that the most important of our formal prayers are all given in the first person plural. We pray to *"our* God." We ask that God's blessing be "upon *us.*" Even when thanking God, *"we* give thanks" and bless Him for "keeping *us* alive and allowing *us* to reach this time." It is to the events in the history of the Jewish people that we turn in prayer, and it is for the future of this people that we pray. To pray as a Jew, as Heschel put it, is not to turn to Him "as an I to a Thou, but as a We to a Thou."[18]

The Role of Music

Music and ritual have been united since the most ancient times. Even storytelling was accompanied by music. The bards were musicians as well as tellers of tales. Certainly the psalms were songs as well as poems, as the headings of many of them indicate. The religions that sprang from Judaism have all used music and chant as part of the experience of worship, and there is every reason to assume that this was influenced by the practice of the parent religion. Over the centuries, music that accompanies worship has been developed into a high art.

The Talmud teaches that "If one reads [Scripture] without chant or studies [Mishna] without melody, of him is it written, 'I gave them laws that were not good' (Ezek. 20:25)."[19] Melody adds not only to the beauty but even to the quality of the words. To this day, learning in traditional yeshivot is done to the accompaniment of a kind of singsong melody. The Torah is not read during the synagogue service; it is sung. The chanting of the Torah follows notations which were applied by the classical tenth-century Masorites (those who carefully preserved the text of the Torah). Each sign (*trop*—actually from a Greek word, *tropos*, meaning "manner") indicates a musical phrase. There are various melodies for this chanting, differing among the ethnic groups that make up the Jewish people, but there are similarities between them, and all of them help to clarify the way in which the Hebrew words are to be put together. They indicate where a phrase begins or ends, and actually aid in interpreting the meaning of the text. These same signs are applied to all the books of the Bible, but they have different musical values depending on which book is being chanted: the Torah, the Prophets, or different books of the Writings. One must learn to read not only a particular sign but to know how it is sung when found in different texts.

Since there was music in the Temple (the choir of Levites who sang the appropriate psalms accompanied by musical instruments), it is likely that this practice would have been taken over when psalms and other prayers came to be recited in synagogues.

In regard to prayer itself, there are no musical notations in the printed Siddur, but there is a musical tradition called *nusach* which has been transmitted from generation to generation. *Nusach* refers to the musical motifs that are utilized in various combinations when chanting the prayers. The *nusach* sets a pattern for a particular service, much as a leitmotif does for a character in an opera. These musical modes differentiate between one service and another. Weekday *nusach* has one set of tones, the Sabbath another, the holidays yet another, and the High Holy Days a completely different one. There is one tune for the Sabbath day and another for the conclusion of the Sabbath. These tunes reflect the mood of the time. We begin the Sabbath, for example, with exaltation and joy. We conclude with nostalgia and the sadness of parting. The melody creates the mood and reflects the appropriate feeling that should accompany the words. Here too the musical traditions differ from one ethnic division of Judaism to another and reflect the music of the place where each group lived.

When properly understood, *nusach* is a great aid to prayer. A worshiper hears the leader use a certain melody appropriate to Rosh Ha-Shanah, for example, and this helps set the mood for that day. Obviously this depends also on the knowledge that the worshiper brings or the memories he or she has acquired over a lifetime. The one instance with which most of us are familiar is the Kol Nidre melody on Yom Kippur, which seldom fails to stir deep feelings within us, despite the fact that the words of the Kol Nidre are particularly lacking in emotional appeal. In this case it is the melody and the implication of the whole setting that moves us. One would have to go into the psychology of music to know what there is about the combination of tones that so affects the human being, but all of us know its power from personal experience. From the passion of opera to the passion of the most modern expressions of popular music, we see the way in which masses of people can be moved to ecstasy, to tears, to excitement by the sound of music.

The hassidic practice of emphasizing song was part of their method of attaining true prayer. The wordless melody—the *niggun*—was a brilliant method of demonstrating the extrasemantic dimension of prayer. We may even go so far as to say that words can be impediments to the deepest communication, for what words can adequately express our feelings about God? Nor can they truly capture the depths of our emotions at times of grief or of overwhelming joy. In the words of the hassidic master R. Dov Baer, "The ecstasy produced by melody . . . is in the category of spontaneous ecstasy alone, without any choice or intellectual will whatsoever."[20] Words can become idols. They concretize that which cannot be concretized. Ideas can intellectualize experience. Melody is pure soul. One understands why many western congregations have included "readings"—translations of prayers without any melody—into the service. But we would be well advised not to abandon the use of chanting in prayer. We need not turn the service into a performance and the cantor (*hazzan*) into a performer in order to avail ourselves of the musical tradition to enhance our worship. Prayer is not a spectator sport. The role of the *hazzan* is to help us pray, to be the expert we may not be, to inspire us and guide us in a true experience of prayer.

At the time of the Mishna (2d century C.E.) there were no professional prayer leaders. The criteria for leading prayers were that one have a knowledge of the prayers, which was especially important in the absence of written texts, and that one have true *kavana*—concentration in his prayer. In addition, the rabbinic Sages specified that he who goes before the Ark to pray should be skilled in singing, have a pleasant voice, and be well versed in Torah, as well as of good moral character.[21] These guidelines are serviceable today for both professionals and laypersons who lead prayer. There must be a combination of knowledge, talent, skill, and character which will serve as inspiration to those who participate.

There are two basic methods of using melody in prayer: the Ashkenazic and the Sephardic. In the first, most of the prayer is said individually in a singsong pattern, with the leader of the service beginning and concluding each section and leading the chanting of certain appropriate portions. In the second, the congregation chants most of the prayers aloud in unison, word by word, with certain sections chanted by individuals. In either type of service, melody adds an important dimension to the experience of prayer.

Patterns and Themes

When studying the prayers or participating in a service, it is helpful to have a sense of the general patterns and concepts that infuse the entire Siddur. Too often we concentrate on some detail and miss the overall structure, not seeing the forest for the trees. Although each service has its own ambience—the Sabbath emphasizing a tranquil joy, the festivals a feeling of exuberance, the weekdays a greater urgency for comfort and redemption—it is possible to create a general scenario that expresses the basic aspects of Jewish worship, allowing for differences and deviations.

The scenario would begin with preparation for prayer, leading us gradually from the mundane world toward the presence of God through the use of biblical texts that emphasize the goodness of God, His merciful nature, His love for Israel, and His providence toward all mankind. As we encounter more and more of these texts, the exuberance increases. Praise is heaped upon praise. The rhythm and repetition increase, helping to build a mood of joyful expectation. Major events in the history of Israel flash before us, reminding us of our past and acknowledging God's role in that history. All of this preparation leads to the act of blessing, in which we speak directly to God and experience Him as the creator, the revealer, and the lawgiver.

Worship is not only prayer, the human being's reaching out to God. It also includes the opportunity to listen as we recite God's revealed word, accepting the truth of the Torah, pledging faithfulness to God and His decrees, and acknowledging His role in our past redemption.

We are now ready to stand before God, contemplating and praising Him, to come before Him in humble petition, and to leave His presence with a feeling of peace and assurance. It remains for us only to solemnly acknowledge our belief and loyalty and to voice our firm hope in the coming of His kingdom.

Like leitmotifs woven throughout a musical composition, certain themes appear and intertwine with one another to create the symphony of Jewish prayer. Many of these reflect different aspects of our experience of God.

First and foremost is the supreme position of God as the creator of the world. This is especially emphasized in the first blessing before the

Shema and in the numerous poems concerning the creation which have been inserted into it, especially on the Sabbath. It appears in the opening of the Amida as well, where God is called "creator of all" and "creator of heaven and earth." It is emphasized once again in the Alenu, where God is called "master of creation." The creation is an expression of God's power and of His universal nature.

Another aspect is God as revealed in history, and especially in the history of Israel. The constant references to the Exodus from Egypt establish the redemptive power of God. We find it mentioned in the Song of the Sea which concludes the preliminary service, in the third paragraph of the Shema, and in the blessing that follows it. This acknowledgment of His role in the past is complemented by requests for His intervention in history once again, which is the central theme of the middle blessings of the Amida, the Kaddish, and the second paragraph of the Alenu.

A third is God as the giver of Torah and instruction. God has been experienced by Jews as creator and redeemer, but also as the revealer of His will. Whenever we include readings from the Bible in the service, it becomes an opportunity to experience the goodness God has demonstrated in granting to us the most precious gift of all, the revelation of His word. The second blessing before the Shema is devoted to this theme of revelation. So is the Blessing of Torah and the blessing prior to the Haftarah. The theme emerges again not only in the obvious place, the taking out and returning of the Torah, but also in U-Va Le-Tzion Go'el at the end of the morning service, where the words of the Torah blessing are repeated virtually word for word.

Liturgy and History

The traditional liturgy established by the Sages and refined by the Geonim is heavily laden with Jewish history. It cannot be accidental that history runs like a scarlet thread throughout the patterns of prayer. Judaism is a historical religion. It is the saga of a people and of God's actions in seeking and molding that people. Approaching God in prayer becomes an experience of reliving history and anchoring oneself solidly in that history. We stand before God not as individuals but as part of a historical entity, and if we were not conscious of that, the liturgy alerts us to it. It is amazing how many historical periods and events have been crowded into the liturgy. The Patriarchal period forms the basis of the first blessing of the Amida, called Avot (Patriarchs). Egyptian slavery and redemption are referred to time and time again. The giving of the Torah at Mount Sinai is acknowledged when we give thanks for Torah and in the Shabbat Amida. David's kingship is mentioned whenever we pray for the future redemption. During the preliminary service we stand with David as he blesses God at the end of his days. The return from Babylonian exile is recalled in the preliminary service, and we reaffirm the covenant with Nehemiah and the returned exiles. In that passage from Nehemiah we reflect on our entire history, from the Patriarchs to the redemption from Egypt.

One might very well say, then, that to pray is to experience the history of the Jewish people through the eyes of the rabbinical Sages. Every day we relive the way in which Abraham, Isaac, and Jacob are singled out for a covenantal relationship with God, the descent of Israel into Egypt, its enslavement, and its redemption. We journey to Sinai for the revelation and the creation of the new covenant to become a holy nation and a kingdom of priests. In the Blessing of Food we enter the Land of Israel and experience the fulfillment of the divine promise. With the reading of the Torah, the Prophets, and the five *megillot*—Lamentations on Tisha B'Av, Ecclesiastes on Sukkot, Esther on Purim, Song of Songs on Passover, and Ruth on Shavuot—we literally proceed step by step along all of biblical history, through the destruction of the kingdoms, the exile, and the return.

Recurring Verses

There are three verses or sets of verses that are constantly repeated in Jewish worship. The first is "Hear, O Israel, the Lord is our God, the Lord is one" (Deut. 6:4), the beginning of the daily recitation of the Shema. The verse also occurs during the preliminary service in the morning, when the Torah is taken out on Sabbath and holidays, in the Kedusha of Musaf, as a bedtime prayer, and at the prayers to be recited at the time of death, to say nothing of several times during the High Holy Days.

It has been suggested that at least some of these repetitions are the result of censorship. Whenever Jews were prevented from reciting the Shema, they attempted to insert it in other parts of the service.[22] Whatever the cause, the importance of the Shema cannot be overemphasized. But it is not only the declaration of our belief in one God, the monotheistic affirmation, that is intended when we say those words. It is the acceptance of God's kingship, *kabbalat ol malchut shamayim*. This formal act of allegiance is more than a credal recitation. It is the repetition of the acceptance of God as king, which was undertaken by the Israelites at Sinai as the culmination of their emergence from slavery to freedom. The purpose of freedom was to enable us obey God. (The donning of tefillin is also intended to be a concrete expression of this acceptance of God's kingship.) This concept of God as king is expressed again in the second paragraph of the Alenu, where it is seen as the future of all humankind, for all will accept God's kingship. When that happens, "the Lord will be one and His name one." The words of the Shema will become a reality not for the individual alone or the collective people of Israel, but for all the world.

The Kaddish prayer, like the Alenu, is in its essence a prayer for the establishment of God's kingship on earth, the time when God will be recognized and accepted by all. So too the prayer U-Va Le-Tzion Go'el ("A redeemer shall come to Zion") in Shacharit echoes the idea of God ruling forever. Thus the Shema, which is not a prayer but a declaration, expresses a concept that becomes the subject of many petitions asking for its full realization.

Verses from the Song of the Sea, such as "Who is like You, O Lord, among the celestials" (Exod. 15:11) and "The Lord will reign forever and ever" (Exod. 15:18), are also frequently incorporated into the service. Here too the kingship of God is acknowledged. The difference is that in the Shema we proclaim that kingship in the present and pray for it in the future, whereas whenever we quote the Song of the Sea we are giving thanks for the moment when that kingship was first proclaimed, the moment of the first instance of redemption. Redemption is recalled at the end of the Shema and in the blessings that follow it. In addition, the entire Song of the Sea is recited as part of the preliminary service. The past redemption is a promise of the redemption to come.

Another set of verses that recurs frequently is the verses of God's holiness: "Holy, holy, holy! The Lord of Hosts! His presence fills all the earth!" (Isa. 6:3) and "Blessed is the Presence of the Lord, in His place" (Ezek. 3:12). These are embedded in fanciful settings in the various Kedusha prayers of the repetition of the Amida, are recited as part of the first blessing of the Shema, and are repeated again along with their Aramaic translation toward the end of the Shacharit service in the prayer U-Va Le-Tzion Go'el, the Kedusha d'Sidra. Whenever we say these verses we are encountering yet another aspect of God. He is not only the creator to be experienced in the world He has formed, not only the redeemer to be experienced in the annals of our history and anticipated in the future, He is also the mysterious, unfathomable, ineffable God whose awesome presence can be sensed but not explained.

These verses also serve another purpose, and that is the act of *kiddush ha-shem,* "the proclamation of God's holiness." In the technical meaning of the term, these sections are not prayers. They are rather affirmations of belief, liturgical expressions of the act of sanctifying God.

Thus we see that in addition to a variety of aspects of God, there is also a variety of attitudes toward God expressed in the prayers. We are privileged and obligated to praise Him. That praise may take the form of blessing Him, of chanting His praises—hallelujah—of acknowledging and thanking Him. Beyond praise and acknowledgment are the acts of sanctifying His name and of accepting and proclaiming His kingship.

Acknowledgment of God

Acknowledging God is another repetitive theme of Jewish worship. Wherever variations of the Hebrew root *l'hodot* are found, this act is taking place. Such words as *nodeh, modim, modeh,* and *hodu* are forms of it. There is no one English term quite equivalent to the Hebrew. It has the meaning of expressing thanksgiving and also of acknowledging. The term is found in the Bible and was one of the major features of worship during the time of the First Temple. We find it repeated in the Hallel service and in several of the psalms that appear in the preliminary service. In the liturgy it appears most prominently in the Amida, where it serves to bring the prayer to a close: Modim Anachnu Lach—"We thankfully-acknowledge You." Having first praised God and then petitioned Him, we conclude with the acknowledgment of His goodness. It appears in the Blessing of Food, Birkat Ha-Mazon; as a prayer of thanksgiving for the Land, Nodeh Lecha; and in the prayer recited upon arising, Modeh Ani ("I thankfully-acknowledge You"). It is found in the first paragraph of Alenu as well, where we bow and acknowledge the "king of kings of kings." It is likely that the original practice was for the congregation to actually prostrate itself whenever the word was used, an act that has gone out of Jewish practice except on the High Holy Days. Whenever we have undergone an experience of salvation or wish to acknowledge the role God plays in our lives, we do so by this act of thankful recognition.

Blessing God

The predominant motif in the liturgy is praise. Of all the possible Hebrew words that could have been used to express this feeling, the tradition chose the word *baruch*—"blessed." The blessing in its various formulae is the most significant building block of Jewish worship. It is not even possible to cite the number of times it appears. Suffice it to say that the morning service begins with a string of *berachot* (blessings), repeating "Blessed are You" over and over. The service of Pesukei d'Zimra begins with the proem Baruch She-Amar ("Blessed is He who spoke"), leading to a blessing. The morning and evening service both begin with *barchu*— the congregation being called upon to bless the Lord. The Amida begins with a blessing, and every paragraph of it concludes with one. When the Torah is read, each person honored with an *aliya* calls upon the congregation to bless God and does so himself. The Haftarah is surrounded with blessings. The essential part of the Blessing of Food is nothing but blessings of praise. Even the time of death and burial are occasions for blessings. The uniqueness of a blessing is that it is pure praise, asking nothing of God but rather giving us an opportunity to remind ourselves of God's presence and of the ways in which we experience Him in the world. Every moment when we are aware of God, we speak His praise by proclaiming that God is blessed, that He is the supreme being of the universe.

Petitioning God

The other major part of liturgy is the petition, or *bakasha*. Quantitatively it appears far less often than praise. This does not mean that it is unimportant. The word *tefilla* ("prayer") is limited in rabbinic Hebrew to petition. The central part of the Amida is petition. There are many places where blessings are suddenly interrupted by petitions for the redemption of Israel. The individual is also able to ask for his or her own needs officially during the Amida and whenever so moved. In addition, the second paragraph of the Alenu and the repeated Kaddish prayers are all petitions for the establishment of God's kingship.

Our official requests of God, then, are largely for redemption. That which Israel experienced in the past is prayed for in the future as well. Above all we pray for the state of peace, which includes but goes far beyond the absence of war. It is this request that concludes all of our prayers: the Amida, the Kaddish, the Blessing of the Priests, the Blessing of Food. Peace signifies wholeness—wholeness within, wholeness in our relationship to God, wholeness in our relationship with others. It is life without anxiety, it is society without violence, it is a world without enmity. The rabbinic dictum "Great is peace, for all blessings conclude with it"[23] reflects the rule that all prayers must end with peace and expresses the importance of this concept within the values of Judaism.

2

Using the Liturgy

Is there anyone who has never prayed? The answer to that depends upon one's definition of prayer. Everyone has had the experience of crying out for succor, silently or audibly, at one time or another. Since Jewish tradition considers even saying "Amen" an act of prayer, it is unlikely to find anyone who has never done that. It is also rare to find a Jew in America who has never been in a synagogue, never attended a Jewish wedding or a *brit milah* (circumcision) ceremony, never gone to synagogue on Yom Kippur for Kol Nidre, if nothing else. But whether or not these constitute meaningful prayer experiences is a question that only the individual can answer. The difference between meaningful prayer and perfunctory prayer is profound. Prayer implies the intention of communicating with God, a dialogue of which we control only one part and where the answer is not always couched in human language, since the partner in the dialogue is so different from us. It may be going a little far to adopt the hassidic definition that prayer is "making love to the Holy One," but it is at the very least the interaction of the soul with the creator of the soul and of the universe. In Ernst Simon's phrase, it is "the bridge between God and man,"[1] or, as Heschel defines it, "an act which makes the heart audible to God."[2]

Jewish tradition recognizes that it may be difficult to begin such a process. It is not surprising that our liturgy contains prayers to be able to pray—in fact a logical absurdity, for in saying such a prayer we are already performing the act itself. Nevertheless, the central prayer of all services, the Amida, is preceded by the words of Psalm 51:17: "O Lord, open my lips so that my mouth may utter Your praise!" To be able to pray is a special gift, but then so is the ability to perform any human act of importance.

We are all acutely aware of the fact that worship can be a sterile and incomprehensible experience. The reasons for this are many, some connected to ourselves, some to the environment in which we pray, some to the language of prayer—both the use of Hebrew, which many do not understand, and the specific, often archaic, vocabulary of prayer—and some to the difficulty that is inherent in prayer. As Ernst Simon wrote, "Prayer is one of man's greatest but also most difficult arts."[3]

We are disappointed when we make an effort to join in prayer, only to find that when we finish we are no better off than when we started. The experience has not spoken to us. The words seemed meaningless and all in all we feel as if we had entered a maze and never quite found the way out. The important thing is not to give up, but rather to make an effort to remove whatever impediments we can. If we do this, some of the other difficulties may then disappear by themselves.

We can familiarize ourselves with the routine of prayer and with the meaning of the liturgy. We can make the necessary preparations, including the readiness to immerse ourselves in prayer, to open ourselves—heart, mind, and soul—to prayer. We can make the attempt to concentrate, which is connoted by the word *kavana*. With the best will in the world, we will not succeed every time, but we will succeed. How many conversations do we engage in before having one that moves us profoundly? But without the failures and the semisuccesses we can never reach the moments of true intensity.

Each of us may have a different expectation concerning what we hope to experience when we pray, especially when we pray in a synagogue setting. Among the feelings that I seek are a sense of rootedness in the past and comfort and hope for the future. As a part of the Jewish people, I want to experience what it means to belong to that group by viewing myself as a part of its ongoing history, and I want to know that there is more to come. Somehow my life is vastly enriched when I have this experience of being an integral member of a greater whole, one that depends on me and on which I can depend. I also seek to sharpen my sensitivity to the world around me and my appreciation of life itself. When I engage in prayer, I am making use of an opportunity to contemplate my most basic beliefs concerning God, Judaism, and the world, and to affirm them. The distractions of living too often keep us busy with everything but the things that matter. The encounter with the concepts expressed in the Siddur, with my own feelings, and with the experience of reaching out to God challenges me to bring to consciousness the thoughts within me and to refine and strengthen them. The hoped-for results of such contemplation will be that my resolve will be strengthened to live in a way that is morally correct and in accord with the highest ethical traditions of mankind. By making myself sensitive to the world and appreciative of the gifts I am given, I am challenged to be worthy of them and to take nothing, including life itself, for granted. Prayer may take effort, but its rewards are great.

Many of the problems we encounter in regard to prayer are closely connected to the general difficulties we face as Jews when we seek meaning in Judaism in an age and an environment that are largely secular. For many, Judaism is little more than a shadow of some great and vibrant system which once spoke to the Jewish people and sustained us through millennia. Religion in general has lost much of its status. This is a secular world, not only because modern nations are not governed by religion, but because our outlook is predominantly secular. Religion is honored in the western world, but in the same way that a relic of the past is accorded respect. It is not looked to for meaningful advice and guidance. In America, rabbis and ministers give invocations and opening prayers at great state occasions—and at small ones as well. They serve as window dressing and little more. When I served as a chaplain in the United States Air Force, I was once asked to give an invocation at a judo match. I declined, much to the displeasure of the base commander, who could not understand why I saw this as a trivialization of prayer. Prayer should be at the heart of life and not mere trimming. The status of prayer is a reflection of the decline of religion.

Attitudes toward prayer within the Jewish community are as diverse as the community itself. For some Jews, the whole concept of prayer is totally alien. They may never think about it or attempt to experience it. Others attend services, so that prayer is not unknown to them, but they have a variety of reasons for doing so. Some pray because they believe that this is what is required of them as Jews. Some come to the synagogue in order to strengthen their identification with the Jewish people. Coming to the synagogue, which is the central institution of American Jewish life, is a way of gaining a sense of community. Services are also a good opportunity to see friends, to hear a good sermon, to listen to a good cantor, and to feel part of the Jewish community. Many also sense an emotional comfort in religious settings, even if there is no concern with the intellectual or theological content of the services. These are all valid reasons for being part of a congregation. But many of us go to the synagogue also seeking, though often not finding, an opportunity to establish a dialogue with God, to feel His presence or to understand His will. While engaged in prayer, we crave, in the words of Abraham Joshua Heschel, "to sense His presence," feeling intuitively that "all worship and ritual are essentially attempts to remove our callousness to the mystery of our own existence and pursuits."[4]

Why is it that the experience of prayer is so often disappointing? Why do we often come away from a synagogue service without feeling that what we did was meaningful on a spiritual level? Part of the problem may be our difficulties with the belief system that underpins traditional prayer.

Ernst Simon, a saintly man of the spirit who also gloried in logic and rational thinking, enlisting the power of the mind in the service of belief, wrote that there are three suppositions without which there can be no prayer:

1. God exists on the highest level of personality. That is, He shares with man the quality of consciousness, albeit on an infinitely higher level. He is not blind force.
2. God cares for His creation.
3. Man can turn to God with praise and thanksgiving, although prayer has no automatic or magic effect on God.[5]

This definition allows for the possibility of prayer. Those who cannot accept it may view communal prayer as an act of group identification, a sociological phenomenon in which we declare who we are by coming together as Jews in a Jewish setting and reciting words that were relevant in the Jewish past. As meaningful and heartfelt as this may be, it is doubtful if one can really call such an experience prayer.

By all rights, then, any book on prayer should begin with at least a brief discussion of belief in God. It is helpful for us to recall the conclusion of Milton Steinberg after analyzing all the arguments pro and con concerning God's existence. He wrote that while the existence of such a caring God cannot be proved rationally, neither can it be disproved. In this post-Holocaust era, it is even harder to reconcile our belief in a moral God with the terrible events which brought suffering and death to so many millions. Nevertheless, perhaps we can agree with Steinberg that if forced to choose between believing in God—which accounts for the world even though evil is unexplained—or believing in a world in which there is no God—which explains evil but not the world—we should opt for the former. Rejecting belief in a God who is merely man writ large, he arrived at belief in a God who is, as he puts it, "the essential Being of all beings. . . . He is the soul of man whose thought processes are infinitesimal sparks of His infinite fire," with "the entire universe . . . the manifestation of Mind-Energy, of Spirit, or, to use the older and better word, of God."[6]

It is no less an act of faith to believe that the God who exists is a God to whom prayer may be addressed, a God who is capable of hearing. But it is by no means an act of blind and irrational faith. Indeed, if I exist, if I have freedom and personality, why should there not be a higher being with qualities no less than mine? A God who is not more than I am is not a God. Prayer is not only based on such faith; prayer helps us to achieve and strengthen it.

On the other hand, no matter what our belief in God, it is difficult for us today to believe that prayer is going to have an effect on the physical world. Most of us raised in the modern age, with science as the prevailing interpreter of reality, would be at least skeptical about our words having an effect on such a thing as the weather. There are many among us, then, who view prayer as a useless exercise, either because they do not believe that there is a Whom before whom we stand in prayer or because they do not believe that by asking God for something, we are in any way changing what will happen. What is the point of a prayer for rain when we know the physical factors that influence rain or the lack of it? Why pray for health if we do not believe that the progress of a disease can be halted by anything other than medical intervention, according to the laws of medical science as far as we know them? The idea that assemblies of people fasting and imploring God to grant them respite from a plague, from enemies, or from drought, could cause a change in any of those conditions is relegated by many to the realm of superstition.

Our ancestors had some inkling of this problem. The Talmud speaks

about the rain that falls on the fields of the good and the evil alike, so
that "the world continues in its natural way,"[7] that is to say, the physical
laws of nature continue on their own, with no regard to reward or punishment for good or evil. The Mishna also deals with the efficacy of
praying for what has already occurred:

> If one prays concerning that which has already happened, that
> is a vain [useless] prayer. How so? If his wife is pregnant and he
> says, "May it be Your will that my wife bear a male child," that
> is a vain prayer. If one is returning from a journey, hears cries of
> anguish from the city, and says, "May it be Your will that those
> are not from my family," that is a vain prayer.[8]

That which is determined is not a subject for prayer. But our understanding today of what has already been determined would make it difficult
to pray for most things having to do with the physical universe. Perhaps
we must come to view such prayers of supplication (*bakashot*) not as
attempts to interfere with the normal processes of nature, but as the
expression of our hopes and needs, and as our request that God grant us
the power to remedy situations and to overcome difficulties.

Most Jewish prayer is praise and acknowledgment. Furthermore, a
large part of the requests concern hopes for the future, the welfare of
the people Israel, the dawning of the messianic era, the recognition of
God, and the establishment of His kingdom. Thus, even if modern
knowledge and scientific investigation have impinged on one part of
traditional prayer, the main body of prayer remains untouched and valid.
One could argue that such prayer, even if valid, is inferior. Is it not
impertinence on the part of human beings to tell God what they need?
Does He not know before we do? Does He not know better than we?
For hassidic thinkers, the problem was not that God could not or did not
answer prayer, but that asking God for one's needs interfered with true
prayer and made the self rather than God the center of concern. As the
Baal Shem Tov, the eighteenth-century founder of Hassidism, taught,
"For if a man has the intention of waiting for his prayers to be answered,
he introduces something corporeal into his prayers, whereas the proper
thing is for them to be purely spiritual, for the sake of the *Shechina* [the
Indwelling Presence of God] and not for the sake of worldly things."[9] It
is better, then, to understand such prayer as a pouring out of man's needs

before His creator, a cry of the human being in need, and not to expect prayer to be answered in ways that contradict nature.

Moses Maimonides and other great medieval philosophers of Judaism also stressed the aspects of prayer that did not contradict their views of the world. Prayer as intercession, as a request for material goods or for a change in the ways of nature, was far from their basic concept. Without denying these possibilities or changing one syllable of the traditional prayers, they still spoke about prayer in terms that did not require a suspension of their philosophical beliefs. For Maimonides, the basic purpose of prayer was to remind us of God and of the basic beliefs of Judaism. Prayer "prescribes actions which firmly establish the love of God in our minds, as well as the right belief concerning Him and His attributes."[10]

Every modern theologian or philosopher of Judaism has similarly tackled the problem of prayer. Orthodox thinkers are most likely to simply accept prayer as it is, indicating that since nature is God's creation, God can interfere in it as He will. At the other extreme of the religious framework, naturalists such as Mordecai Kaplan seek a new understanding of prayer that is congruous with a naturalist concept of God. Since Kaplan does not believe in a God who is "a self-existent entity . . . who acts in response to any petition,"[11] he would eliminate all prayers, such as those for rain, that contradict this. He suggests that we pray instead for those human abilities that help us to realize or "actualize" the qualities he identifies with "God." Despite the extreme changes he advocates, Kaplan admits that it is impossible to change all the phrases in prayer that reflect ancient, outmoded ideas, so some of the language will have to remain, such as referring to God as "king," but it must be understood only as metaphor.[12]

Others recognize the problems of prayer in a scientific age, but do not go as far as Kaplan in their rejection of a God who is beyond nature. Milton Steinberg, who takes a critical, rationalist stance in his view of God, finds that prayer is not only possible but is the way in which a human being builds a bridge to God, where the human soul has an interchange with its divine source. Thus we should express all of our feelings and needs in prayer, even though we do not expect God to work outside the limits of natural law. We should not seek the impossible, but we should use prayer to orient ourselves toward God and to address Him. Such prayer will also move us to action, for we know that whatever we ask of God we must work for by ourselves as well. It is God who will help us to achieve it.[13]

Emil Fackenheim emphasizes the element of praise in Jewish prayer and states that unless we have "the belief that prayer is 'heard,' Judaism, as it has existed ever since its origins, will come to an end."[14] Of course, experience teaches us that many prayers are not fulfilled, but that does not contradict the faith that prayer is "heard." "A Jew at prayer finds himself situated between Revelation and Redemption in an unredeemed world." He can only hope for an end in which "all worthy prayers are answered."[15]

The modern Jewish thinker who dealt most extensively with prayer was Abraham Joshua Heschel. He too recognized the problem of prayer and nature:

> When a vessel sails into a typhoon . . . it is not the pious man, engrossed in supplication, but the helmsman who intervenes in the proper sphere with proper means, fighting with physical tools against physical powers. What sense is there in imploring the mercy of God? Words do not stem the flood, nor does meditation banish the storm. Prayer never entwines directly with the chain of physical cause and effect; the spiritual does not interfere with the natural order of things. The fact that man with undaunted sincerity pours into prayer the best of his soul springs from the conviction that there is a realm in which the acts of faith are puissant and potent, that there is an order in which things of spirit can be of momentous consequence.[16]

For Heschel, prayer is not so much communication with God but reaching out to Him. It springs from the human being's response of awe to the wonder of the universe. It is the answer to "the inconceivable surprise of living. It is all we can offer in return for the mystery by which we live."[17] Radical amazement stands at the center of Heschel's philosophy of prayer. How is it possible to see what we see, to experience what we experience, to live, and not to be amazed. Yet human beings become indifferent to everything. It is prayer that restores to us the ability to feel, to see, and to appreciate.

Rather than beg the question of the effectiveness of prayer, we need to change our expectations of prayer and openly acknowledge that our understanding of the God to whom we pray is different from the God our ancestors envisioned, in that we do not expect Him to effect changes in the physical universe that defy the laws of nature—because the laws of nature are the laws of God. We are grateful for those laws, because without them there would be no certainty in life. In Einstein's famous words, "God does not play dice with the universe."[18] God is a God of miracles, but the miracles are not breaches of natural law but rather that law itself. As the Siddur expresses it, "Your miracles which are with us daily, morning, noon, and eve"—and that is enough for us. Definitions of God are an absurdity; descriptions of God and His actions are all inaccurate. Whatever we say about God is impossible because any human language about God is false. The description of God as speaking, thinking, wanting, acting is just as absurd as speaking of God's arm, hand, or head; it is just more refined. It is not accidental that the Bible offers no description of God. The prohibition of images seems to extend to word pictures as well. Therefore minimalistic words such as "God is one" serve as the closest we have to an official Jewish definition of God. In formal prayer, too, the words about God are few and carefully chosen. Maimonides' use of negative rather than positive definitions carries this caution to its extreme. What it indicates to us is that we cannot say what God will do or how God's work is performed in the world. It should be enough for us to acknowledge His existence and His care. On that basis, we should feel free to speak of our needs, but our expectations should be realistic. As Franz Rosenzweig said, "No honest man can pray to a God whose existence he denies as a scientist. And whoever prays cannot at the same time deny God."[19] Our understanding and belief in God should be consistent. We cannot place science in one compartment of our lives and belief in another. On the other hand, honesty compels us to acknowledge that prayer has no function if we have no concept of the God to Whom that prayer is addressed.

This does not mean that in order to pray one must have no doubts. On the contrary, there are times when we pray because we have doubts, because we feel the lack of certainty and want to better understand what is happening to us or what our proper response should be. Like Job, we may come before God to protest or to question, not to assent. What we hope to receive then from the prayer is a vindication of our belief. We may come to prayer agreeing with Job that "I know that my

Vindicator lives; in the end He will testify on earth" (Job 19:25), hoping we will emerge feeling that "I had heard You with my ears, but now I see You with my eyes" (Job 42:5).

Is there a place for intellectually honest prayer today, and, if so, what expectations should we have of it? If we are willing to make our prayer consonant with our beliefs, that prayer—including the traditional prayers Judaism has developed—can be of immense help in enriching our religious life. Properly understood, prayer heightens our awareness of the dimension of holiness in the world and of the demands made upon us by the creator. It teaches us to believe that we are not alone in an unfeeling universe, but are the children of a loving parent, that the qualities of love and mercy, justice and right which we feel within ourselves are anchored in a reality greater than ourselves. Prayer reminds us of the wonder of the world in which we live, of the miracle of life which we too often take for granted. In the Japanese film *Ikaru*, the hero, who knows that he is dying, sees the sunset and says, "How beautiful, how beautiful it is! For thirty years I have not seen a sunset—and now I have little time to see another."

Prayer directs our attention to the goals and ideals that Judaism has set for us. It forces us to concentrate on the meaning of our lives and the values of our deeds. It helps us to focus on our place within the world and within the history of our people, giving us a sense of rootedness. In prayer I become more than myself and am afforded the most important opportunity in life—the possibility of finding my connection to God.

The difficulty we have in properly achieving a satisfactory belief system that includes an acceptable concept of prayer is not the only reason that the experience of prayer is often disappointing. For some who frequently attend the synagogue, the very routine of prayer becomes an impediment. Martin Buber tells the story of the Baal Shem Tov, who informed the people in a certain synagogue that the synagogue was "full of prayer." They thought this was a compliment until he explained that prayers that are not said with sincerity, with *kavana*, are like lead balloons. They remain below. After a while, all these heavy prayers fill the synagogue so that there is no room left for any more prayers, making it impossible to pray in such a place.[20] As one of Shakespeare's villains who tried in vain to pray put it:

> My words fly up, my thoughts remain below.
> Words without thoughts never to heaven go. [21]

Routinization is a very common disease. Anything that is done constantly, day in and day out, in a fixed manner can become so much a part of human habit and pattern of action that it is done without thought. It leaves the realm of conscious action and becomes part of automatic functioning. Buber called this "the leprosy of fluency." [22] We can know the words so well that prayer becomes a mere mumbling of words, an outward performance with no inner meaning. Thus prayer turns into words without meaning, sounds without souls.

For others who are less familiar with the Siddur, with Hebrew, and with the routine of the synagogue, the problem is quite different. Lacking knowledge and understanding of the prayers, one cannot be expected to find them of much value. Being unfamiliar with both the "how" and the "why" of prayer, it is difficult not to be discouraged. Prayer is an art, and all art requires effort and even practice. In the realm of music, for example, no one expects to be able to sit down at a musical instrument and simply begin to play Beethoven with results other than noise. First you learn the basics of the instrument, then you learn the techniques, then you practice—sometimes extremely boring scales and dull exercises. Then you learn what music is all about: its codes, forms, and possibilities. Then you learn not only how to play all the passages Beethoven created, but also to understand the inner voices and the deeper meanings of the music. After that, you must continue to practice and perform, and make every attempt to keep your playing fresh and not mere routine. If the answer to the intellectual problem of prayer is a mature concept of prayer and its meaning, then the answer to both the routinization of prayer and the lack of skills and tools needed to practice the art of prayer is the acquisition of such understanding, combined with a conscious effort to achieve a level of mastery. Each person can do this according to his or her own interest and ability. The chapters of this book will attempt to make Jewish prayer intelligible through an understanding of how the prayers evolved and what they can mean to us, thus enabling the reader to participate actively in services as an insider.

. . .

Yes, prayer is a problem, but it is also the answer. It helps me to overcome the first hurdle—to believe that I am not alone in the world. It impels me to find a way to integrate the rational knowledge upon which my life is based with the deeper "knowledge"—in the biblical sense of intimate experience—that there is a dimension beyond all this and that I have been granted the ability and the privilege of addressing myself to God. If I take prayer seriously, I am forced to reinterpret some of the traditional words or patterns into ways that make sense to me. Mastering the art of prayer requires me to accept a certain discipline and to take the steps of study and practice required for effective prayer. Prayer is also an answer because it helps me to become more fully human, to find the correct paths in life, to make my deeds meaningful, and to connect myself with the living force of God that infuses the universe.

There is a difference between the physical functioning of one who, through exercise and correct diet, keeps his body in good condition and that of one who neglects it. There is a difference between one who nourishes and exercises the soul and one who neglects it. Prayer is the exercise and nourishment of the spirit. We neglect it at the peril of neglecting that aspect of life that is most uniquely human.

Prayer is a problem when we have certain simplistic expectations of it, but when we can formulate a belief in God that is neither naive nor contradictory to the evidence of our minds and the faith of our souls, it becomes the answer. We can then begin to understand the importance of prayer and the role it can play in enriching our lives. To borrow another phrase from Heschel, "To worship is to rise to a higher level of existence, to see the world from the point of view of God."[23]

3

Prayer in Early Israel

*U*nderstanding where we have come from helps us to know where we are. If we want to understand Jewish prayer today and the structure and content of the Siddur, we need to gain a historical perspective and go back to the beginning. For Jews, the beginning is always the Bible, a collection of books in which prayer plays a decisive role. Biblical prayer set the stage for all of Jewish worship. Despite all the changes and developments that took place in Jewish prayer over the centuries, the basic patterns, ideas, and even vocabulary of worship stem directly from the Bible. Consider, for example, three phrases from Ps. 146:7–8:

> The Lord sets prisoners free.
> The Lord restores sight to the blind.
> The Lord makes those who are bent stand straight.

All are found in the morning blessings, while the last line of the same psalm is quoted as part of every Kedusha, a prayer recited twice every weekday and three times on the Sabbath and holy days:

> The Lord shall reign forever, your God, O Zion, for all generations. Hallelujah.

A large part of the Siddur consists of sections of the Bible. Entire psalms as well as other biblical passages have been incorporated into the service, and biblical phrases are the basis of almost every prayer. The Siddur could no more exist without the Bible than a child could exist without parents.

Even a cursory glance reveals that major events recorded in the Bible are consistently accompanied by prayer. This led the early Sages (1st century B.C.E.–2d century C.E.) to make the following interpretation of the reaction of the Israelites to their salvation at the Sea of Reeds. Reading Exodus 14:14—"The Lord will battle for you; you hold your peace!"— as a question rather than a statement, Moses said to the Israelites:

> "The Lord will battle for you; will you hold your peace (Exod. 14:14)? Shall you remain silent while God performs miracles and wonders for you?" Israel said to Moses, "Our teacher Moses, what should we do?" He said to them, "You should exalt, glorify, praise, utter song and praise, greatness and glorification to Him who is the master of war."[1]

Confronted by their enemies, their backs to the sea, the Israelites had already "cried out to the Lord" (Exod. 14:10). "Crying out" is the usual biblical term for pleading in desperation for God's help. Just such a cry is to be expected of people facing disaster. What is less natural but more important is that when they experience God's salvation, they acknowledge it by singing His praises. According to the Sages, this is what Moses told them to do: "Do not be silent, but sing God's praises." The Torah records that this was done in a magnificent poem, the Song of the Sea (Exod. 15:1–18), which became the archetype of all songs of triumphant thanksgiving. The poem is quoted in similar prayers in the Book of Psalms[2] and by Isaiah in his vision of a future triumph (Isa. 12:2), and it was eventually incorporated into daily worship:[3]

> Then Moses and the Israelites sang this song to the Lord. (Exod. 15:1)

The song is addressed directly to the Lord:

> Who is like You, O Lord, among the mighty;
> Who is like You, majestic in holiness,
> Awesome in splendor, working wonders! (Exod. 15:11)

It concludes with the proclamation of God's kingship:

> The Lord will reign forever and ever! (Exod. 15:18)

The story of the Exodus is thus bracketed by words addressed to God. The first, the cry to God to save them, is a *bakasha* or request for help. The second, the Song of the Sea, is both the act of praise, exaltation, and glorification, which the Sages called *shevach* (praise), and thanksgiving unto the Lord, proclaiming His sovereignty, known as *hodaya* (thankful acknowledgment). These three elements are the basic components of Jewish prayer for all time.

What is remarkable about this biblical story is that in neither case are these acts of prayer accompanied by sacrifice or other ritual actions or incantations, elements found in every pagan ritual of which we are aware. Even Noah offers sacrifice immediately upon leaving the ark, although he has no words of thanksgiving.[4] The Israelites at the sea, on the other hand, have only words and no sacrifice. Sacrifice comes into play soon enough at Mount Sinai and then when the ritual of the Tabernacle, later the Temple, is described at length.[5] No one can deny the importance of sacrifice in biblical and rabbinic Judaism. Nevertheless, the words of the Sages in the midrash are clear: when God performs miracles and wonders for us, the proper and necessary response is song and praise.

Song and praise come from the heart and the soul of the human being. They express our deepest feelings. They are the proper response to a world of "radical amazement," to borrow Heschel's phrase. As he wrote, "To pray is to take notice of the wonder, to regain a sense of the mystery that animates all beings, the divine margin in all attainments."[6] When we are sensitive to the world, when we appreciate God's actions and His presence, we utter song. This sensitivity, however, is not always as developed as it should be. Because we can ignore even great events, to say nothing of the more routine wonders we experience often, we are bidden to recite praises at appropriate moments and thus re-create the feelings that are expressed in this song. The utterance of song is not only a response, but also a way of sensitizing us to God. To Moses and to the Sages, that was much more important than sacrificial ritual.

By depicting sacrifice as the primary way in which early humans, Cain and Abel, related to the Lord,[7] the Torah is reflecting the ancient origins of sacrifice that anthropology affirms.[8] At the same time, however, from the very first the attitude of the Bible toward sacrifice was totally different from that of pagan religion. Sacrifice was seen not as essential to God nor as sufficient to express the proper relationship of human beings to God. The very first comment that God makes about sacrifice is to explain to Cain why his offering was not accepted:

> Why are you distressed,
> And why is your face fallen?
> Surely, if you do right,
> There is uplift. (Gen. 4:6–7)

The implication is clear. Sacrifice is insufficient. It must be accompanied by doing right. This was a message the prophets of Israel were to spell out in detail time and again.[9]

In general, the relationship of the Patriarchs to sacrifice as depicted in the Torah is obscure. The role that sacrifice plays in the story of their lives is minimal. Abraham erected altars wherever he wandered in Canaan and "invoked the Lord by name" (Gen. 12:8), but there is no mention of him bringing offerings. Only twice is he seen sacrificing. Both times the connection seems to be with legal and covenantal ceremonies. The first instance is when God specifically commands him to do so as part of a mystical covenant ceremony (Gen. 15:9–21). The second is the end of the binding of Isaac, when he offers the ram in place of his son (Gen. 22:13). Neither Isaac nor Jacob is depicted offering sacrifices. Jacob pledges to "set aside a tithe for You" (Gen. 28:22), but even when Jacob returns from his exile and utters a prayer giving thanks and begging further protection, he confines himself to words alone (Gen. 32:10–13). Even his encounter with the divine being when he crosses a stream to meet his brother does not result in sacrifice (Gen. 32:25–33). Considering the later emphasis on the sacrificial system of the Tabernacle and the Temple, this seems strange. Perhaps it can best be understood as an attempt to underscore the idea that sacrifice plays a totally different role in the religion of Israel than in pagan rituals. Long before sacrifice became impossible because of the destruction of the Temple, it had been so totally reinterpreted that it was not an indispensable element of worship, as it was in all of pagan religion.

Sacrifice was divorced from prayer in biblical Judaism and prayer could develop apart from it because of the radically different nature of the religion of Israel. The Bible represents a revolution in mankind's conception of the sphere of the divine. Since all worship is an attempt to communicate with the divine, the way in which we conceive of the divine is going to influence our approach to worship. The great Israeli biblical scholar Yehezkel Kaufmann clarified the nature of the Mosaic revolution in human thought. [10] He demonstrated that the biblical conception of God not only is monotheistic in proclaiming that only one divine power exists, but conceives of that power very differently than had ever been done before. In pagan thought, the gods were not only numerous, they were also limited in their powers. They were powerful but not omnipotent. The mysterious realm of fate controlled them as well. They were in need of food and drink. Being corporeal and therefore subject to physical needs and to the processes of birth and death, they were subject to control through magic. Thus pagan worship was more than an attempt to influence the gods: it was a method of controlling them. Worship was accompanied by gifts which pleased the gods because they needed those gifts. Sacrifices were not symbolic offerings but actual nourishment to be consumed. They were often part of a ritual of magic which, when accompanied by the appropriate spells, could affect the gods and their actions. Paganism's conception of the gods as limited in power and subject to fate and magic meant that human beings could actually compel the gods to do their will if they knew the magic formulas that would bind them. The exact word said at the correct moment could force the divine powers to fulfill the commands of the human being. [11]

In the Mesopotamian flood epic, the character Utnapishtim (the human survivor or "Noah" of that story) sacrifices to the gods when the waters abate, and the gods swarm down "like flies" to consume the sacrifice because they had been without food.

> Then I let out [all] to the four winds and offered a sacrifice.
> I poured out a libation on the top of the mountain.
> Seven and seven cult-vessels I set up,
> Upon their pot-stands I heaped cane, cedarwood, and myrtle.
> The gods smelled the savor,
> The gods crowded like flies about the sacrificer. [12]

Compare this to the biblical story, which confines itself to saying that "the Lord smelled the pleasing odor" (Gen. 8:21)—admittedly an anthropomorphism but hardly to be compared to crowding like flies around a piece of meat! It is no wonder that pagan worship is always sacrificial when we realize that according to pagan belief, man's task on earth was to provide the gods with their needs.

Such paganism exists today. I was once present at a pagan ceremony in Brazil, where ancient African practices still exist side by side with Catholic worship. It began with the ceremonial placing of a dish of food outside the doorway to induce the gods to come and be in attendance.

In contrast, the God of Israel as expounded by Moses is not subject to physical need and not controllable by magic. He has no magic name by which He can be conjured. Instead, the name that God reveals to Moses at the burning bush in itself indicates that no power exists outside of God. *"Ehyeh-Asher-Ehyeh"* (Exod. 3:14): "I Am that I Am"—there is no force that can control Me! This phrase is the source and the explanation of the name of God, the Tetragrammaton, consisting of four letters from the Hebrew root "to be," for which the term "the Lord" is substituted. God responds to Moses, "Thus shall you speak to the Israelites: The Lord . . . has sent me to you: This shall be My name forever, this My appellation for all eternity" (Exod. 3:15).

The God of Israel has no need of food and drink. Therefore the sacrificial system as practiced in ancient Israel became something very different. The outward forms were similar, but the inner meaning was completely revolutionized. There is still a table with food, still an altar for sacrifices of animals, grains, and liquids, but the Lord does not consume the sacrifices. Showbread is placed on the table weekly, and nothing is done with it:

> And on the table you shall set the bread of display, to be before Me always. (Exod. 25:30)

Preexisting forms of worship are retained in a modified fashion and become symbols of Israel's desire to show deference to God and express feelings of thanksgiving or reconciliation, but the ancient kernel that gave impetus to pagan worship is missing.

There is undoubtedly a great deal of historical truth behind the statement by the medieval philosopher Moses Maimonides that the sacrifices were prescribed because it would have been impossible to ask the Israelites not to offer them. They were not ready for such a revolution and would have thought of it as blasphemy and denial of God. The Torah itself hints at this:

> This is in order that the Israelites may bring the sacrifices which
> they have been making in the open—that they may bring them
> before the Lord . . . and that they may offer their sacrifices no
> more to the goat-demons after whom they stray. (Lev. 17:5–7)

Without being bidden to, the Israelites, like everyone else, brought
sacrifices. They needed to be able to do so, but now they would bring
them only to the Lord, whose relationship to and "need" for the offerings
were completely different.

Samuel can ask, "Does the Lord delight in burnt offerings and sacrifices as much as in obedience to the Lord's command?" (1 Sam. 15:22)
because the Lord has no need of the fat of rams. Unlike the pagan gods,
He can threaten to destroy His own Temple and eliminate the offerings
because He has no need of them for Himself.

> Just go by My place at Shiloh, where I had established My name
> formerly, and see what I did to it because of the wickedness of
> My people Israel. And now, because you do all these things . . . I
> will do to the House which bears My name, on which you
> rely . . . just what I did to Shiloh. (Jer. 7:12–14)

The powerful prophetic denunciations of the Temple Cult, which make
it clear that morality is supreme over ceremony and sacrifice, could have
been created only in Israel, for only the God of Israel was not dependent
on His cult.

> You . . . who detest justice . . . because of you Zion shall be
> plowed as a field, and Jerusalem shall become heaps of ruins,
> and the Temple Mount a shrine in the woods. (Mic. 3:9–12)

> I loathe, I spurn your festivals, I am not appeased by your solemn
> assemblies. If you offer Me burnt offerings—or your meal of-
> ferings—I will not accept them. . . . Spare Me the sound of your
> hymns . . . but let justice well up like water, righteousness like
> an unfailing stream. (Amos 5:22–24)

> Will you steal and murder and commit adultery and swear falsely,
> and sacrifice to Baal . . . and then come and stand before Me
> in this House which bears My name and say, "We are safe"?
> (Jer. 7:9–10)

Add your burnt offerings to your other sacrifices and eat the meat! For when I freed your fathers from the land of Egypt, I did not speak with them or command them concerning burnt offerings or sacrifice. But this is what I commanded them: Do My bidding. (Jer. 7:21–23)

From the standpoint of the Bible, it is obvious that sacrifices are not God's need, but a favor He grants the people in order to permit them to feel close to Him. Sacrifices become a method of expressing human emotions, be it guilt and repentance or thanksgiving and well-being. They could not substitute for right conduct and had absolutely no independent value. So the form remained, but the content was changed.

In one respect, even the form had to yield to the new concept of divinity. The most striking feature of the Israelite cult is the fact that although there was music, both instrumental and vocal, in the Temple, the sacrificial service itself was silent. As Yehezkel Kaufmann noted, "The priestly temple is the kingdom of silence. . . . Not only have spells and psalms no place in the priestly cult, even prayer is absent."[13] The attempt to separate Israelite worship from pagan rites demanded the absence of words, since in paganism the word was the essence of the magical rite. Paradoxically, however, the word was freed in Israelite religion to become the true vehicle for communication with God. The word could function by itself, without the accompaniment of sacrifice and without a cultic building or sacred site. Sacrifice was eventually confined to one specific cultic building, the Temple. Prayer was never so confined or limited. Thus the way was opened for prayer as we know it to develop. The God of Israel needed nothing from human beings, but He required much of them—love, mercy, righteousness, and justice: "to do justice and to love goodness, and to walk modestly with your God" (Mic. 6:8). Anyone who followed those precepts could come before Him at any time and in any place with words alone. "Take *words* with you and return to the Lord," says the prophet. "Say to Him: 'Forgive all guilt and accept what is good; instead of bulls we will pay [the offering of] our lips' " (Hos. 14:3).

As a result of this liberating concept, the Bible is filled with personal prayer. Moshe Greenberg, in his extensive study of biblical prose prayer,[14] points out that while the prayers found in the Book of Psalms are professional prayers written by a class of experts, the Bible also records popular, informal prayer, which appears as part of the narrative of the Bible stories. He cites ninety-seven such texts. What characterizes them is that they are free expressions of the human being who comes before God as one person would come before another in conversation. He or she may come to God to ask for personal needs:

> O Lord, God of my master Abraham, grant me good fortune this day, and deal graciously with my master Abraham: As I stand here by the spring and the daughters of the townsmen come out to draw water, let the maiden to whom I say, "Please, lower your jar that I may drink," and who replies, "Drink, and I will also water your camels"—let her be the one whom You have decreed for Your servant Isaac. Thereby shall I know that You have dealt graciously with my master. (Gen. 24:12–14)

—to confess wrongdoing and ask for forgiveness:

> I have sinned grievously in what I have done. Please, O Lord, remit the guilt of Your servant, for I have acted foolishly. (2 Sam. 24:10)

—or to express thankfulness for the bounties one has received:

> Blessed be the Lord, the God of my master Abraham, who has not withheld His steadfast kindness from my master. (Gen. 24:27)

These are the same impulses that characterize many of the prayers of later Jewish worship. They certainly can serve as models for personal prayer even today. In all of these instances there is no need for a cultic figure—priest, Levite, or prophet—to speak for others. There is no person, priest or otherwise, who alone can pray. No offering is made. The person does not have to go to some special shrine in order to speak to God. God is frequently addressed directly. He can be spoken to or appealed to without special formulas, without fixed prayers, at any time that the person wishes to do so. Much of this was incorporated into later Jewish prayer.

In addition to informal personal prayer, the Bible also contains the more formal prayer that existed in ancient Israel. Many of these prayers have been included in whole or in part in the Siddur. The book containing them, the Book of Psalms, was written by a cadre of professional poets and musicians. Although the sacrificial cult was silent, that does not mean that there was no music or prayer in the Temple. We know of the choir of Levites who sang in the Temple, and, although the Torah gives no details about their specific ceremonial function, the writings of the prophets certainly indicate that music, both instrumental and vocal, as well as utterances of prayer took place there. Ironically, the incidental comments of the prophets that testify to this are all negative. However, the opposition is not to music or prayer, but to God's distaste for all worship that is not accompanied by righteous behavior. The prayer of the wicked is no more acceptable than the sacrifice of the wicked.

> Spare Me the sound of your hymns,
> And let Me not hear the music of your lutes. (Amos 5:23)

The prophets mention occasions when masses of people went to the Temple in order to fast, pray, and offer sacrifices in times of danger.

> And when you lift up your hands,
> I will turn My eyes away from you;
> Though you pray at length,
> I will not listen. (Isa. 1:15)

It was specifically on such occasions that the prophets took the opportunity to remind the people that no ritual—prayer included—could substitute for a change in conduct, for a moral reformation.

Second Isaiah, living during the period of the Babylonian exile, speaks about the vision of a future Temple:

> Their burnt offerings and sacrifices shall be welcome on My altar;
> for My House shall be called a house of prayer for all peoples.
> (Isa. 56:7)

This clearly indicates that the function of prayer was neither unknown nor unimportant in the Temple.

In the same vein, the prayer ascribed to Solomon at the dedication of the Temple reflects the importance of prayer:

> May You heed the prayers which Your servant will offer toward this place. And when You hear the supplications which Your servant and Your people Israel offer toward this place, give

heed in Your heavenly abode—give heed and pardon. (1 Kings 8:29–30)

Prayer might be offered outside the Temple or within it, but would be directed toward it since this was the symbolic dwelling place of God. This is the concept underlying the fact that synagogues throughout the world are all oriented toward the Temple site in Jerusalem. Solomon himself recognized that "even the heavens to their uttermost reaches cannot contain You, how much less this House that I have built!" (1 Kings 8:27). God was not in the Temple, but in heaven He would hear all prayers directed toward it.

In this prayer, Solomon also enumerates the circumstances under which one would pray. These include asking judgment against a person who has offended and injured another; praying for restoration after defeat by an enemy; begging relief from natural disasters such as drought, famine, plague, or disease; asking for victory in battle or forgiveness of sin. "May you heed them whenever they call upon You" (1 Kings 8:52).

Since we have no record of a fixed order of service in the First Temple aside from the silent offerings, which are spelled out in great detail, we assume that nothing of that sort existed. What did happen, however, was that use was made of a large repertory of psalms or hymns—poetic prayers sung to musical accompaniment:

It is good to praise the Lord, to sing hymns to Your name, O Most High, to proclaim Your steadfast love at daybreak, Your faithfulness each night with a ten-stringed harp, with voice and lyre together. (Ps. 92:2–4)

These may have been sung when people came to the Temple or after the sacrifices had been offered. Some may have been written for a special event and then entered the available repertory. It has been speculated that certain psalms that emphasize the idea of God's kingship, for example, may have been chanted on the first of Tishre (today Rosh Ha-Shanah, the New Year), which was the celebration of God's kingship over the world.

The Lord is king, He is robed in grandeur. (Ps. 93:1)

The Lord is king! Let the earth exult, the many islands rejoice! (Ps. 97:1)

> The Lord, enthroned on cherubim, is king, peoples tremble,
> the earth quakes. (Ps. 99:1)

We have some specific information about the use of psalms during the days of the Second Temple, but we cannot be certain that the same practices existed earlier. We know, for example, that there was a different psalm designated to be sung each day of the week in the Second Temple.[15] Psalms 113 through 118, known as the Hallel (from the word "to praise"), were chanted in the Temple on the pilgrimage festivals and on Hanukkah.[16]

Reading the psalms, it is impossible to escape the conclusion that many were composed to be sung ceremonially at appropriate times. There are, for example, psalms that celebrate a military triumph:

> Open the gates of victory for me
> that I may enter them and praise the Lord.
> This is the gateway to the Lord—
> the victorious shall enter through it. (Ps. 118:19)

One can imagine these words accompanied by the playing of the ancient equivalent of the triumphal march from *Aida*.

Other psalms may have been sung when people were about to enter the Temple:

> Who may ascend the mountain of the Lord?
> Who may stand in His holy place?—
> He who has clean hands and a pure heart. . . .
> O gates, lift up your heads!
> Up high, you everlasting doors. (Ps. 24:3–4, 7)

Some were chanted as people ascended the mountain to worship:

> I rejoiced when they said to me,
> "We are going to the house of the Lord."
> Our feet stood inside your gates, O Jerusalem,
> Jerusalem built up, a city knit together,
> to which tribes would make pilgrimage. (Ps. 122:1–4)

Many psalms are written in the plural, indicating that they are intended for a group and not an individual. They sometimes call upon the entire people or sections of it to bless or acknowledge the Lord and His actions, leading to the supposition that they were chanted in some antiphonal manner or that there were well-known responses in which the people could join:

> Sing to the Lord a song of praise,
> chant a hymn with a lyre to our God. (Ps. 147:7)

The Book of Psalms reflects various forms of relating to God, different ceremonies appropriate to different moods and circumstances. Three different forms of prayer are signified by the following terms:

> *hodu*—to thankfully acknowledge
> *barchu*—to bless
> *hallelu*—to praise.

To begin with the last of these phrases, no Hebrew word is so well known in all languages of the world as "hallelujah," best translated as "Praise the Lord." The emotional content of the word is so powerful that there was really no way to express it in any other language and no need to translate it. There are no psalms more ecstatic than those that proclaim "hallelujah" or in some way call on people *l'hallel*—to praise Him. Many of these psalms invoke all of nature in one song of praise to the creator:

> Hallelujah.
> Praise the Lord from the heavens. . . .
> Praise Him, all His angels. . . .
> Praise Him, sun and moon,
> Praise Him, all bright stars.
> Praise Him, highest heavens. (Ps. 148:1–4)

> Hallelujah.
> Praise God in His sanctuary;
> Praise Him in the sky, His stronghold. . . .
> Praise Him with blasts of the horn;
> Praise Him with harp and lyre.
> Praise Him with timbrel and dance;
> Praise Him with resounding cymbals;
> Praise Him with loud-clashing cymbals.

Let all that breathes praise the Lord.
Hallelujah. (Ps. 150)

There is an ecstatic feeling to these psalms, with their repetition of the word *hallelu*, their short, staccato phrases, their rhythmic cadences. Words such as these certainly do not suggest quiet, subdued worship. They are more than a description, however poetic, of God. They are a call to the soul, to all creatures, to all parts of the universe, to join in a great rondo of joy at the very fact of being a part of the creation and thus to acknowledge the author of all. Here we have the swirling stars of Van Gogh's *Starry Night* accompanied by Beethoven's apotheosis of the dance at the end of his Seventh Symphony. There is no more exalted joy, no more ecstatic vision of God than this. When reciting such a psalm, one releases emotions, envisions the universe, and feels the pulse of life which invests it.

Blessing God (*barchu*) is an altogether different form of worship. The very notion of "blessing" God or His name seems strange. Blessing is what God bestows upon us. We have no power to grant Him a blessing—such a notion is absurd—and yet we are bidden:

O house of Israel, bless the Lord;
O house of Aaron, bless the Lord;
O house of Levi, bless the Lord;
you who fear the Lord, bless the Lord. (Ps. 135:19–20)

Moshe Greenberg points out that in the Bible the original use of the word "to bless" always referred to God blessing a human being.[17] If one wanted to praise someone, one would proclaim that that person was "blessed unto the Lord" (Ruth 3:10). The reaction to the goodness and worthiness of a human being was to call that person "blessed of the Lord." After a while, this phrase was taken as expressing the highest regard for anyone, including God. Words often change their meaning, and this is such an instance. When Moses' father-in-law, Jethro, wanted to express his tremendous regard for what God had done in freeing the Israelites from Egyptian bondage, he did so by saying,

Blessed be the Lord, who delivered you from the Egyptians and from Pharaoh, and who delivered the people from under the hand of the Egyptians. Now I know that the Lord is greater than all gods. (Exod. 18:10)

Thus, the term "bless the Lord" came to be used as a call to proclaim the praise of God. It means much more, however, than simple praise. To proclaim God as blessed means to acknowledge the greatness and glory of God before all those who hear it. Therefore the response to the call to "bless the Lord" (Ps. 135:19–20) could be:

Blessed is the Lord from Zion,
He who dwells in Jerusalem.
Hallelujah. (Ps. 135:21)

Because of this force of the word, it was eventually chosen from all others to become the basic word of Jewish prayer. Without the blessing, there would be no Jewish worship. If "hallelujah" conjures up feelings of ecstasy, *baruch* engenders a more solemn and majestic mode, in which God's mysterious splendor is proclaimed before all the world.

The third term, *hodu*, means to acknowledge God gratefully because of His deeds. At times this refers to His deeds as seen in nature:

Who made the heavens with wisdom . . .
Who spread the earth over the water . . .
Who made the great lights. (Ps. 136:5–7)

It may also refer to the way in which God supplies the needs of men:

Who gives food to all flesh. (Ps. 136:25)

Most often it refers to acknowledging His deeds in history, such as His rescue of Israel:

Who struck Egypt through their firstborn . . .
Who split apart the Sea of Reeds . . .
Who struck down great kings. (Ps. 136:10–17)

The acknowledgment was made through saying the words, "His steadfast love is eternal," as can be seen in Psalm 136 where this phrase is repeated after every proclamation of one of God's actions. A beautiful example of this kind of ceremony of acknowledgment can be seen in Psalm 118, where a great convocation at the Temple to celebrate the triumph over an enemy who had nearly conquered Israel is described.[18] Israel is called upon to thank and acknowledge what God has done:

> Acknowledge [*hodu*] the Lord, for He is good,
> His steadfast love is eternal.
> Let Israel declare,
> "His steadfast love is eternal."
> Let the house of Aaron declare,
> "His steadfast love is eternal."
> Let those who fear the Lord declare,
> "His steadfast love is eternal." (Ps. 118:1–4)

What follows is a description of the historical event, the danger, and the deliverance, after which the ceremony of thankful acknowledgment is held:

> I acknowledge You, for You have answered me,
> and have become my deliverance. . . .
> This is the day that the Lord has made—
> Let us exult and rejoice on it. . . .
> Acknowledge the Lord for he is good.
> His steadfast love is eternal. (Ps. 118:21–29)

Here gratitude is expressed, the emotion that constitutes a necessary part of the human sense of dependence, but dependence upon God, who is reliable. Often these words of thanksgiving were uttered at the time of salvation, as in the Song of the Sea, but they also became a method of relating these miracles throughout the centuries, as generation after generation repeats the words and re-creates the events and the reactions to them.

All of these modes of relating to God became important in Jewish worship.

As we have seen, many psalms were intended to be chanted in public worship. There are others, however, written in the singular and of a more personal nature. They speak about the events in the life of an individual and not of a nation. Were these intended for public worship or simply the artistic creations of very gifted individuals? Were they taught to the people, so that they could use them when appropriate? Were they sung in the Temple, inasmuch as they express feelings both personal and universal? We cannot answer these questions. In some biblical books we find that psalms evidently composed for purposes of general worship are used as expressions of personal prayer. This is the case of Jonah's prayer (Jon. 2:3–10) and that ascribed to Hannah, the mother of Samuel (1 Sam. 2:1–10). This can mean either that individuals, even as early as the period of the judges, used psalms composed for use in worship in the Tabernacle when they came to pray, or that the later writers of these books put such psalms into the mouths of their speakers when relating earlier events. We should also bear in mind that the first person singular can sometimes represent the entire nation, as it does in the Song of the Sea (Exod. 15), and that some psalms appear in both the singular and the plural, as if they were interchangeable.

One of the psalms that has become particularly important in our liturgy is Psalm 145. It took on so much importance that eventually it came to be recited three times a day. The Sages said of it that anyone who recited it three times a day was assured of a place in the world-to-come.[19] Although it begins with the individual speaking of his personal praise of God, it seems particularly well structured as a community prayer. It combines within itself two ways of addressing God. Sometimes He is addressed directly. At other times, the psalmist speaks about Him. This usage of the second- and third-person forms of address may entail more than questions of politeness or grammar. It takes into account the two aspects of God that we as human beings experience: His transcendent nature—His distance from us—and His imminence—His closeness to us. It is the paradox of God's nature that He can be experienced as both near and far. In later Jewish prayer this ambiguity was duplicated by blessings that first address God as "You" and then proceed to speak of Him in the third person. This also indicates that prayer can have a twofold purpose. It serves both to address oneself directly to God and to proclaim His nature to ourselves and to others, in order to inculcate attitudes and belief about Him. Thus, in Psalm 145 speaking directly to God is alternated with speaking about God.

I will extol You, my God and king, and bless Your name forever and ever.
Every day will I bless You and praise Your name forever and
ever.

Great is the Lord and much acclaimed!
His greatness cannot be fathomed.

One generation shall laud Your works to another
and declare Your mighty acts.
The glorious majesty of Your splendor
and your wondrous acts will I recite.
Men shall talk of the might of Your awesome deeds,
And I will recount Your greatness.
They shall celebrate Your abundant goodness,
And sing joyously of Your beneficence.

The Lord is gracious and compassionate,
slow to anger and abounding in kindness.
The Lord is good to all,
and His mercy is upon all His works.

All Your works shall praise You, O Lord,
And Your faithful ones shall bless You.
They shall talk of the majesty of Your kingship,
And speak of Your might,

To make His mighty acts known among men
And the majestic glory of His kingship.

Your kingship is an eternal kingship;
Your dominion is for all generations.

The Lord supports all who stumble,
And makes all who are bent stand straight.

The eyes of all look to You expectantly,
and You give them their food when it is due.
You give it openheartedly,
feeding every creature to its heart's content.

The Lord is beneficent in all His ways
and faithful in all His work.
The Lord is near to all who call Him,
to all who call Him with sincerity.
He fulfills the wishes of those who fear Him;
He hears their cry and delivers them.
The Lord watches over all who love Him,
but all the wicked He will destroy.
My mouth shall utter the praise of the Lord,
and all creatures shall bless His holy name forever
and ever.

Clearly the psalmist wishes to characterize the Lord in order to bring others to bless and praise Him. The characterization is in itself praise. Note how most of the statements about God begin with "the Lord," followed by some description of His nature and His actions. This form of worship strengthens belief and inculcates the idea of God, leading to universal praise. This twofold purpose is also to be found in the prayers of later generations.[20]

The one thing that does seem certain is that the psalms were not confined to the small circle of professionals who composed them, but became the common property of the entire people. It seems logical to surmise that people who came to the Temple wanting to express their feelings, confess their sins, register their gratitude, or pray for health and prosperity may have done so using these magnificent hymns. The expressions of the longing for God and His nearness, the assurance of His goodness, the praise and description of His ways have all left their mark on Jewish prayer. Although Jewish prayer developed forms that are unknown in the Book of Psalms, without the psalms the Siddur would be a very different work. We cannot even imagine Jewish worship without the basis of the Book of Psalms. It has given us an entire vocabulary as well as basic concepts of what worship is all about. Everything is built upon that.

Aside from the psalms, there are two other formal prayers that were recited in the Temple. The first is the proclamation that was recited when bringing the offering of the firstfruits. Although sacrifices were offered silently, the mere act of bringing the firstfruits of the land was not deemed

sufficient. Words had to be uttered. This prayer not only speaks to God.
It is really a proclamation about Him, declaring His role in the history
of the people of Israel, in order to bring home the lesson that the fruit
of the land is not the result of one's toil and certainly not the gift of
fertility gods, but represents God's promise to the Patriarchs. This fruit
is the end result of God's work in history which transformed Israel from
a wandering tribe to a people living in a fruitful land. At the conclusion,
the person speaks directly to God and acknowledges what He has
given him.

> I acknowledge this day before the Lord your God that I have
> entered the land which the Lord swore to our fathers to give
> us. . . .
>
> My father was a fugitive Aramean. He went down to Egypt
> with meager numbers and sojourned there; but there he became
> a great and very populous nation. The Egyptians dealt harshly
> with us and oppressed us; they imposed heavy labor upon us.
> We cried to the Lord, the God of our fathers, and the Lord heard
> our plea and saw our plight, our misery, and our oppression. The
> Lord freed us from Egypt by a mighty hand, by an outstretched
> arm and awesome power, and by signs and portents. He brought
> us to this place and gave us this land, a land flowing with milk
> and honey. Wherefore I now bring the firstfruits of the soil which
> You, O Lord, have given me. (Deut. 26:3–10)

The other verbal part of the Temple service was the blessing that the
priests bestowed on the people:

> The Lord bless you and keep you!
> The Lord make His face to shine upon you and be gracious to
> you.
> The Lord lift up His countenance upon you and grant you
> peace! (Num. 6:24–26)

It could be said that this magnificent blessing served as a counterbalance
to the sacrifices. The people came to the Temple and brought their
offerings. Before they left, God in turn bestowed His blessings upon
them:

He shall carry away a blessing from the Lord,
A just reward from God, his deliverer. (Ps. 24:5)

This blessing too had a profound impact on the eventual form of Jewish worship and was incorporated into Judaism's basic prayer, the Amida.

Rather than being the central form of official worship, prayer in the Bible is spontaneous and personal. It was the way in which the individual communicated with the Lord whenever so moved. It had no fixed terms, no rules or regulations. During this early period of Jewish history, a more formal type of verbal worship, the biblical psalms, also emerged and found its way into the Temple as an additional element, while the silent sacrifice remained the official worship of Israel. These poetic creations were used in ceremonial ways in order to celebrate or commemorate special events, and they developed a vocabulary of prayer that had highly specific meaning and usage. For all the differences between the psalms and later rabbinic prayer, they nevertheless contained the basic elements of Jewish prayer.

From the very beginning, prayer was divorced from sacrifice. Prayer consisted of an appeal to God, praise of God, acknowledgment of and thanksgiving to God, and confession to God. It was based on the concept of a God who hears, cares, and answers, of a God of love, mercy, and forgiveness. It contained no magic formulations but was rather an attempt to communicate with God and to request Him to help the individual and the nation. It was universal in seeing God as the source of the entire world, the provider for all, the God of mankind but the God of Israel as well, the mover of nature, and the mover of history. It attempted to teach about God in order to bring people to acknowledge Him. It could be sober and thoughtful. It could also be ecstatic. It viewed God as close at hand but yet removed and transcendent. It required sincerity and meaning in order to be effective. All these elements, as well as biblical words, concepts, and phrases, became the foundation for the whole of Jewish worship.

4

The Origins of the Synagogue

*T*he words "prayer" and "synagogue" are linked in our minds, and it is difficult to think of one without the other. Obviously this was not always so. We have seen that independent prayer developed in ancient Israel from the very beginning as the free expression of the individual and that more formal prayer existed within the framework of public worship, separate from sacrificial rites but within the same building, the Temple. During the entire period of the First Temple, which came to a violent end when destroyed by the Babylonians in 586 B.C.E., we hear not a word about a special building or institution created for nonsacrificial public worship. We know both from literary and archeological evidence that such an institution existed by the end of the Second Temple period (1st century C.E.). When and why did it come into being, and when was the link between the synagogue and prayer established? For if Jewish prayer today cannot be understood without knowing its biblical basis, neither can it be imagined without the institution of the synagogue.

There are two main differences between prayer in Judaism today and prayer in the religion of Israel in biblical days. One is that prayer has become fixed in a specific pattern and is an obligatory part of the regimen of Jewish life, rather than being free and spontaneous. The other is that a special community institution exists in which prayer is the central focus. It would be possible to imagine prayer as a purely individual obligation or occupation. There are religions that relate to prayer in that way, but Judaism is not one of them. Individual prayer is possible, but prayer as a community function is constantly preferred and stressed. Since Jewish worship places so much emphasis on the role of the community, the full expression of prayer can come about only in a house of prayer. Perhaps this is what Rabbi Abba Binyamin meant when he taught, "A person's prayer is heard only in the synagogue."[1] This is followed by Rabbi Yitzhak's statement that "the Holy One is found in the synagogue. . . . When ten pray together, the Divine Presence is among them."[2] For all the importance and beauty of individual prayer and spontaneous expression, it is the communal synagogue that sustains prayer and conveys it from generation to generation.

The modern synagogue in the western world goes beyond the traditional role of the synagogue of the past. Synagogues have become comprehensive centers of Jewish life, encompassing education, social life, community affairs, and much more. It is impossible to envision Jewish life in any diaspora community without a synagogue at its center. With its complicated structure and large professional staff, it seems to be different from the traditional synagogue of old. Whatever its original functions have been, however, it is clear that today—and for at least the last nineteen hundred years—synagogues are basically places of prayer. That this may not have been the case at the beginning is a possibility raised by such evidence as the famous Theodotus inscription, which is perhaps the most interesting and striking piece of evidence we have concerning the function of early synagogues. This Greek inscription on the floor of a first-century C.E. synagogue in Jerusalem describes the synagogue building a certain Theodotus built, as a place for

> reading the Law and studying the commandments, and as a hostel with chambers and water installations to provide for the needs of itinerants from abroad.[3]

There is no mention of prayer. Although the argument from silence is never absolute, the evidence is overwhelming that synagogues in the time prior to the destruction of the Second Temple were primarily places for the dissemination of knowledge of the Torah on a popular level and that whatever prayer took place there was either connected to study or secondary to it.[4] After the year 70 C.E., the situation changed drastically: the role of prayer in Jewish life became critical and the synagogue became the focus for this activity.

Even at the beginning, however, the synagogue was a revolutionary institution. It was as revolutionary as Israel's concept of God which made prayer possible in the first place. The synagogue was the place where, for the first time in human history, some sort of communal worship divorced from sacrifice was institutionalized. Never before was there an institution used as a gathering place for religious worship in which sacrifice not only would not but *could not* be offered, an institution that could be housed anywhere, did not have to be in a spot that had some sacred connotation, did not have to conform to some rigid architectual pattern, and was not run by a group of specially sanctified clergy. Whereas the Temple was basically the domain of the priests (*kohanim*) assisted by Levites, all of whom had to be born to the task, the synagogue was an institution of the people. Those who functioned within it, whether as teachers, preachers, or leaders of prayer, could and did come from all sections of the people. Neither birth, ancestry, nor socioeconomic status played any part in determining who could become Sages (eventually known as "rabbis") or who could lead a service.[5] It was not even necessary for a synagogue to have a building of its own. Existing structures could be used, or activities could even be conducted in the open. Eventually the erection of beautiful synagogue buildings became more and more important.[6] Tradition has it that there were hundreds of synagogues in Jerusalem prior to the destruction.[7] Whatever the measure of exaggeration in such a statement, there is no reason to doubt that by that time there were many not only in Jerusalem but throughout the country. Today one can see magnificent ruins of synagogues that have been uncovered throughout Israel, with special emphasis on the northern parts of the country, where Jews flourished in the centuries following the destruction of Jerusalem and after the failure of the Bar Kochba revolt in the second century C.E. The ruins of synagogues in Israel from the second, third, and fourth centuries, with their beautiful stonework, columns, and mosaic floors, indicate that when Jewish communities had the resources, they built beautiful synagogues worthy of their purpose.[8]

Another innovation of the synagogue was that it contained no cultic object, with the exception of the sacred scroll, the Torah, which at the early period was brought out when time came for it to be read and was then removed from the public place. As Shalom Spiegel points out, it is a neutral place, with no merit of its own. It is not the home of God and contains no representation of God. It can be erected and used at any time, in any place, by anybody.[9] This was a Jewish creation that revolutionized human worship and served as the pattern, today taken for granted, for Christian and Moslem houses of worship.

A synagogue was not a shrine. Shrines were erected at places that had some special connection to the gods. In the Bible we find that the Patriarchs erected cultic shrines throughout the Land of Israel, as did Jacob at Beth-El.

> Early in the morning, Jacob took the stone that he had put under
> his head and set it up as a pillar and poured oil on the top of it.
> He named that site Beth-El (house of God). (Gen. 28:18–19)

In this he followed the practice of Abraham who, as we have noted, had erected altars throughout the land that the Lord had promised to him:

> And he built an altar there to the Lord who had appeared to him.
> From there he moved on to the hill country east of Beth-El . . .
> and he built there an altar to the Lord and invoked the Lord by
> name. (Gen. 12:7–8)

In paganism, too, shrines were erected to the various gods wherever that god had appeared or was to be worshiped. In these temples, there were representations of the gods and a presiding priesthood. There were also specific rituals to be performed, which always centered around a sacrificial cult.

In early Israel, following the conquest by Joshua, there were many shrines to the God of Israel. People went on pilgrimage to such sites as Beth-El, Gilgal, and Beersheba.[10] There was, of course, the central shrine which housed the most sacred object of Israel, the Ark containing the Tablets of Testimony. In addition, however, there seem to have been regional shrines in which worship of the Lord took place. They differed from pagan shrines in many ways, but in all of them sacrifice was the central feature, and the priest (*kohen*) was the only permitted officiant. There is some possibility that people gathered around prophets on special occasions without bringing sacrifice, but, if so, we do not know what was done at those gatherings. The story is told, for example, of a woman who goes to find the prophet Elisha when her child has died. She does not reveal to her husband the reason for her trip, and he asks, "Why are you going to him today? It is neither New Moon nor Sabbath" (2 Kings

4:23), which indicates that prophets had held gatherings on holy days at an early period in the kingdom, but we do not know if sacrifices were offered there or not. If not, these could have been early precursors of the institution of the synagogue which came to fruition much later.

The limitation concerning shrines, which was to prove to be extremely significant, was that no shrine to the God of Israel could be erected outside the Land of Israel. That was His sacred soil, and His sacrificial cult was not to be conducted elsewhere. Paradoxical as it may sound, the God of Israel was considered the one, universal God of the entire world, but sacrifices could not be offered to Him anywhere except on the soil that He had chosen for His people.

This accounts for the terrible dilemma of the two and a half tribes—Reuben, Gad, and part of Manasseh—who settled on the other side of the Jordan River, outside the boundaries of the chosen land.[11] Their solution was to erect an altar that was not to be used, an altar that could only be looked at. When word came to the rest of Israel that their brethren had built a altar on the other side of the Jordan, they were incensed at the blasphemy of the act and accused them of treachery and rebellion. Your land, they told them, is unclean. No altar can be built there. The two and a half tribes then explained that they had never intended to offer sacrifices on the altar. Because they were afraid that they and their children would be excluded from the people of Israel and its worship of the Lord, "we decided to provide [a witness] for ourselves by building an altar—not for burnt offerings or sacrifices, but as a witness between you and us, and between the generations to come" (Josh. 22:26–27).

By the time of the Deuteronomic reformation in the days of King Josiah (609 B.C.E.), the exclusivity of the Temple of Jerusalem was firmly established.[12] Not only was it forbidden to build an altar outside of the boundaries of the Land of Israel, it was equally forbidden to build one anywhere in Israel apart from the royal shrine that had been erected in Jerusalem:

> Look only to the site that the Lord your God will choose amidst
> all your tribes as His habitation, to establish His name there.
> There you are to go, and there you are to bring your burnt
> offerings and other sacrifices. (Deut. 12:5–6)

That exclusivity immediately caused problems for the people of Israel. The slaughtering of animals and the eating of meat, for example, had always been connected with sacrificial worship. This was not practical for those who lived far from Jerusalem. Therefore "profane" slaughter—i.e., slaughter for eating and not as a part of worship—was provided for:

> But whenever you desire, you may slaughter and eat meat in any of your settlements . . . but you must not partake of the blood. (Deut. 12:15–16)

Far more problematic must have been the fact that communal worship could no longer take place anywhere outside of Jerusalem. Males were now required to appear before the Lord in Jerusalem at the three festivals:

> Three times a year—on the Feast of Unleavened Bread, on the Feast of Weeks, and on the Feast of Booths—all your males shall appear before the Lord your God in the place that He will choose. (Deut. 16:16)

These pilgrimages were wonderful occasions which, during the period of the Second Temple, became times when thousands upon thousands gathered in Jerusalem from throughout the world. On the other hand, they symbolized the fact that those unable to come to Jerusalem were in effect cut off from personal participation in organized Jewish worship. Such worship had always been connected to the sacrificial shrines and did not exist elsewhere. To erect a nonsacrificial shrine would be a daring innovation.

Some scholars have suggested that the centralization of the cult in Jerusalem might have been the impetus for the creation of the synagogue. The verse "They [the enemy] burned all God's tabernacles in the land" (Ps. 74:8) has been taken to refer to nonsacrificial places of worship created as a reaction to the destruction of all shrines other than the Temple. When the Babylonians destroyed the First Temple, they destroyed these "tabernacles" as well. The suggestion is that in order to offer the people a place to gather—since they could no longer bring sacrifices to local sanctuaries and were too far from Jerusalem to go there regularly—tabernacles were set up for some unspecified type of religious gatherings.[13] Beyond that verse, however, there is not even a hint of such a thing.

All in all, lacking hard historical evidence, it is difficult to know when the synagogue (Hebrew: *bet knesset*—"house of gathering") came into being. Rabbinic tradition, which had no historical scruples, always read current institutions and practices back into the Bible and therefore took it for granted that such institutions as the synagogue and the house of study (*bet midrash*), in which prayer and study were combined, already existed in the days of the Patriarchs. Jacob, they contended, studied in such institutions:

> Jacob was a simple man who dwelt in tents (Gen. 25:27)—in two tents, the *bet midrash* of Shem and the *bet midrash* of Aber.[14]

The tradition that the synagogue was of ancient origin was commonly accepted. Philo ascribes it to Moses,[15] as does Josephus.[16]

What we do know, however, is that the synagogue as an institution and synagogue buildings existed both in the Land of Israel and in the diaspora long before the destruction of the Second Temple in 70 C.E. This is based both on archeological finds and on literary evidence. In the diaspora we have archeological finds that go back as far as the third century B.C.E. In the Land of Israel we have them only from the first century B.C.E.[17] Specific mention of synagogues is found in Jewish writings from the first century before the Common Era, such as Philo, and in references from non-Jewish authors, the earliest being Agatharchides in the second century B.C.E. and Apion in the first century C.E.[18] The Christian Bible also contains numerous references to synagogues.[19]

Among the many suggestions made concerning the time of origin of the synagogue, the most plausible and widely accepted is that it originated during the Babylonian exile following the destruction of the kingdom of Judah in 586 B.C.E. This view is reflected in many rabbinic traditions as well.

> Come and see how precious Israel is to the Holy One. Wherever they were exiled, the Presence of God was with them. They were exiled to Egypt, the Presence of God was with them. . . . They were exiled to Babylonia, the Presence of God was with them. . . . In Babylonia, where [was the Presence of God]? . . . In the synagogue of Huzal and in the synagogue of Shaf-ve-yatib in Neherdea. . . . And I have become to them a minor sanctuary (Ezek. 11:16). Said Rabbi Isaac, "This refers to the synagogues and houses of study in Babylonia." . . . Rava expounded: "O Lord, You have been our refuge in every gen-

eration (Ps. 90:1). This refers to the synagogues and houses of study."[20]

The defeat of the kingdom of Judah at the hands of the Babylonians, the destruction of the Temple of Jerusalem—the only shrine to the God of Israel—and the subsequent exile of the masses of the people to Babylonia constituted a crisis for Israel of traumatic proportions. One of the major problems faced by the Israelites was: How can we possibly continue to worship the Lord in a foreign land? This was given its classic formulation by the Levites, who lamented:

> By the rivers of Babylon, there we sat, sat and wept, as we thought of Zion.
>
> There on the poplars we hung up our lyres, for our captors asked us there for songs, our tormentors, for amusement, "Sing us one of the songs of Zion."
>
> How can we sing a song of the Lord on alien soil? (Ps. 137:1–4)

Since the Levites were the singers of these songs, that was uppermost in their minds. The problem, however, was much more extensive. It encompassed not only songs that had been performed exclusively in connection with the Temple, but the entire cult of worship of the Lord. A sacrificial shrine to the Lord could not be built just anywhere. If the tribes on the eastern bank of the Jordan River were forbidden to build one, certainly Babylon was no place for a temple. In the paradoxical way of history, this seemingly unsolvable dilemma provided the stimulus for a creative solution that revolutionized worship.

The seed of the solution was buried within the problem itself. Had it been possible to offer sacrifices in Babylon, the synagogue might never have emerged. Rather, we would have returned to the pre-Deuteronomic situation of multiple sacrificial shrines, except that they would have existed not only in the Land of Israel but throughout the diaspora as well. That is exactly what had occurred when a group of Jewish mercenary soldiers settled on Elephantine, a small island in the Nile. Sometime at the end of the seventh century or the beginning of the sixth century B.C.E. they built themselves a temple on Egyptian soil, where they established a complete cultic ritual, including priests and sacrifices. That temple functioned while the Temple in Jerusalem was in existence, during the exile, and even after the return from exile and the rebuilding of the Jerusalem Temple. It was destroyed only in 411 B.C.E. by the order of the Persian governor who had been bribed by Egyptian clergy.[21] Obviously the traditions of this maverick group concerning the worship of the Lord on foreign soil were different from those contained in the mainstream of biblical doctrine. What was done at Elephantine was unthinkable for the Jews in Babylonia. No one even suggested it. According to the Book of Deuteronomy, which was accepted as authoritative by those who were exiled, sacrifices were forbidden anywhere other than Mount Zion in Jerusalem, much less outside of the Land of Israel.

Exile was a religious problem for Israel as well as a national and personal problem. For the individual, the problem was the need to adjust to life in a new land and a new culture, and to find a way to support oneself. Unlike popular supposition, the Babylonian exile was not like the slavery of Egypt. The Babylonians transferred whole populations from one conquered land to another or to Babylon in order to make it less likely that there would be a rebellion against their rule. They did not, however, enslave them. The Judeans exiled to Babylon were free to live their lives there and establish their homes.[22] Jeremiah had told them to do just that:

> Build houses and live in them, plant gardens and eat their fruit. . . . Multiply there, do not decrease. (Jer. 29:5–6)

Although Jeremiah did not intend this to be the beginning of a permanent community, inasmuch as he prophesied that in seventy years God would bring them back to their own land (Jer. 29:10), they were so successful in following his advice that the vast majority of them remained there when the opportunity arose to return.[23]

In the pagan world, if one went to another land, the common practice was to worship the gods of that land. That is undoubtedly what was done by those non-Israelites who eventually came to be called Samaritans, who were settled in the northern kingdom of Israel after its defeat in 721 B.C.E. They soon began to think of themselves as Israelites, even though they were not accepted as such later by the returning Jews.[24] Theoretically this solution was available to the individual Judean, but not if he or she wished to remain true to the religious traditions of Israel. For worshipers of the Lord, then, that option was not viable, although some thought about trying it. They came to Ezekiel, the prophet of the Babylonian exile who was the spiritual and religious authority of the exiles, and made such a suggestion, which he vehemently rejected:

> And what you have in mind shall never come to pass—when you say, "We will be like the nations, like the families of the lands, worshiping wood and stone." (Ezek. 20:32)

They themselves realized that to worship the gods of Babylonia would mean worshiping that which did not exist, but what were they to do, in view of the fact that it was impossible to worship the God of Israel in any organized fashion because they were in Babylonia and not Jerusalem? The terrible destruction prophesied in Deuteronomy had taken place:

> The Lord will drive you, and the king you have set over you, to a nation unknown to you or your fathers, *where you shall serve other gods, of wood and stone* [italics added]. (Deut. 28:36)

This was their punishment. They would not be able to worship the true God but would have to serve idols.

> For only on My holy mountain, on the lofty mount of Israel— declares the Lord God—there, in the land, the entire House of Israel, all of it, must worship Me. There I will accept them, and there I will take note of your contributions and the choicest offerings of all your sacred things. (Ezek. 20:40)

Ezekiel made it clear to them that the sacrifices would be accepted in Jerusalem, but not in Babylonia, and that that would not come about until the exile was over and the people returned. But by then those who had come to Ezekiel would be dead. Was there any way in which they could continue to worship the Lord?

From the very beginning, the religion of Israel had recognized that the Presence of God (later to be termed the *Shechina*) was indeed every-where and was with them in Babylonia. Ezekiel asserted this in his famous vision of God leaving the Temple in Jerusalem.[25] God could no longer be worshiped in the gloriousness of His Majesty—there could be no Temple in Babylonia—but the Divine Presence, as it were, would be somewhat of a sanctuary for them.

Theoretically, nothing in the Torah or Prophets contradicted the worship of God without sacrifice even on foreign soil. He created, rules, and is present everywhere. As for sacrifice, the God of Israel, unlike the pagan gods, was not dependent upon it. Not to be able to sacrifice to Him was a punishment for the people. It deprived them of a gift God had given them, the ability to fully express themselves to Him and to feel His presence, but the lack of sacrifices had no effect on Him. The destruction of His sanctuary did not mean to the Israelites what such a destruction would have meant to pagans, namely, the defeat of the god of that sanctuary. On the contrary, they believed, following the prophets, that the Lord Himself had brought it about as a punishment for disobedience and would see to its restoration as a reward for repentance.

What seems likely, then, is that during the years of the exile, gatherings of the Israelites took place under the auspices of leaders such as Ezekiel, who was both priest and prophet, but whose duties in the exile were limited to those of a prophet. If prior to the exile there existed a tradition of going to prophets on holy days, it would have certainly made sense to utilize that in the exilic situation, where no other form of worship of the Lord existed.

What would be done at such gatherings, held on the Sabbath or a festival? Perhaps the traditions and teachings of Moses and the other prophets were read and expounded. Perhaps psalms were chanted or other prayers recited. The prophets were, after all, well versed in prayer. Part of their function was to pray for the people. From the time of Abraham on, we see people coming to prophets for intercession. Thus, when King Abimelech takes Abraham's wife, Sarah, having been told that she was Abraham's sister, God says to Abimelech, "Restore the man's wife— since he is a prophet, he will intercede for you—to save your life" (Gen. 20:6). Similarly, Pharaoh says to Moses, "Forgive my offense just this once, and plead with the Lord your God that He remove this death from me" (Exod. 10:17). When the Lord is angry with Israel, He commands the prophet Jeremiah: "Do not pray for this people, do not raise a cry of prayer on their behalf, do not plead with Me; for I will not listen to you" (Jer. 7:16).

The prayer of the prophet was not offered at the Temple or as part of a sacrificial ceremony. On the contrary, the prophet was far removed from Temple ceremonies. Although there were prophets who functioned as part of the royal court and the official establishment, the greatest of them were individuals who owed their sole allegiance to God and had no connection with the organized center of worship. In the exile, however, there was no such center, and the people looked to leaders such as Ezekiel for help in maintaining their connection with the God of Israel. Gatherings in which prophets or other leaders taught the traditions of the religion of Israel and possibly offered prayers connected to these or prayers for the welfare of Israel may well have been all that bound the people together. It may have seemed then a poor substitute for the magnificence of the Temple and its worship, but it was to prove more durable and become one of Judaism's most important contributions to civilization. In the words of Shalom Spiegel, "The Jews were the only people of antiquity who succeeded in divorcing prayer from sacrifice, and so were the first to evolve the modes and manners of public worship as the world knows them now."[26]

Although after the return we hear nothing of synagogues until a few hundred years later, the supposition is that this concept continued to live in the diaspora community and found its way back to Judea with the returning exiles as well. As pointed out above, the main function of synagogues during the period of the Second Temple clearly was the dissemination of Torah. Just as during the exile deportees had gathered to hear the traditions and the explanation of them, so the synagogues established in the Land of Israel served as centers of Torah study. The Torah would be read, as would passages from the Prophets, and those capable of doing so would expound upon what had been read.[27] Prayers may have been recited before and after these readings, similar to the blessings recited today following the reading from the Prophets.[28] The description of the magnificent synagogue of the Jewish community in Alexandria in Egypt bears this out:

> Said R. Judah, "Whoever has not seen the double colonnade of the synagogue in Alexandria in Egypt has never seen the glory of Israel. It was in the form of a huge basilica, with one colonnade within another. At times it contained double the number of people who left Egypt at the time of the Exodus. There were seventy-one golden thrones representing the seventy-one elders, each one of which contained twenty-five myriads of gold. In the

center there was a wooden platform. The *hazzan* of the synagogue
stood upon it with scarves in his hand. When they began to read
[the Torah], he would wave the scarves and [the congregation]
would respond 'Amen' to each blessing. [When prayers were
recited] he would wave the scarves and they would answer
'Amen.' "[29]

It is not surprising that such elaborate structures did not exist in Judea.
The Temple in Jerusalem, whose magnificence is no less praised by all
the sources,[30] sufficed for Jews in the homeland. There was no need and
no desire to build rival structures. This may also explain the fact that we
have found earlier ruins of synagogues in the diaspora than in Israel. It
is also interesting that one name used for synagogues in the diaspora was
"house of prayer." Perhaps the presence of the Temple in Jerusalem and
the absence of any such ritual structure in the diaspora made the role of
prayer more central abroad and less important in Israel.

Early synagogues, especially in the diaspora, were gathering places
for the Jews of a community; there they could collect funds both for their
own needs and for sending to Jerusalem. In some, sacred community
meals were held.

Greek was the language of diaspora synagogues, while in the Land
of Israel, Aramaic, the vernacular, was used along with Hebrew, which
was no longer the spoken language of the people. The reading of the
Torah outside of Israel was conducted in Greek, using the Greek translation, the Septuagint. In Israel, a free Aramaic translation accompanied
the reading. The Sabbath was probably the main day on which synagogues were used. The term *sabbateion*, a Sabbath house, was applied
to some of them. Regardless of the diversity, what all of the synagogues
had in common was "a cult based on communal study or prayer."[31]

It has been suggested that the limited role of prayer in pre–70 C.E.
synagogues may have been a deliberate attempt on the part of the religious leadership to avoid establishing any institution or practice that could
be interpreted as a rival to the Temple worship.[32] The Dead Sea Scrolls
are the scripture of a sect that had separated itself from the Temple and
considered the service there to be improper and contaminated; it developed official prayers because it had no such compunctions.[33] The
activities of the early synagogue, on the other hand, probably centered
around Scripture with a minimal element of prayer.

During the period from the return from exile until the destruction of the Second Temple, prayer continued to develop, but not necessarily within the confines of an organized structure. The Book of Ben Sira, for example, records many prayers that are similar in theme and vocabulary to our prayers today.[34] The Christian Bible, which reflects Jewish life in the first century C.E., also demonstrates that prayer was a normal activity.[35] We also find that prayers for groups were discussed prior to the destruction of the Temple,[36] and we have the traditions of groups who would gather to pray and meditate for hours, the so-called "early pious ones."[37] It remained for the era following the destruction of the Second Temple to bring about the full development of prayer and its connection to the synagogue.

The synagogue was not the preserve of any one group of people. It was a layman's institution. It reflected the same democratic tendency as had the creation of a rabbinate, which usurped the place of the hereditary priests as the main teachers of God's instruction. It was the possession of the community and run by community leaders. The house of study, the *bet midrash*, was the main institution of the Sages. The synagogue really belonged to the people.

With the destruction of the Second Temple, it was only natural that the synagogue would assume an even more important role than before. Prayer itself became more prominent and, as prayers acquired a more fixed pattern, the role of prayer in the synagogue also became more important. If during the first exile the people had no solution to their religious dilemma, in the intervening six hundred and fifty years the synagogue had emerged as a major feature of Jewish life everywhere. Nor was the situation of exile completely strange, as it had been in Babylonia, for in the interval Jewish life in the diaspora, far from the Jerusalem center, had become a normal and regular part of Jewish existence. There the synagogue had functioned as a true center and gathering place of the Jews and as a place where study and worship could take place.

It cannot be overemphasized that the synagogue had never been perceived as a rival to the Temple. During the period of the Second Temple, both served the purpose of worship of the Lord, but they did so in different ways. The Temple was "service" through a sacrificial rite. The synagogue encouraged "the service of the heart." The synagogue was revolutionary in this concept, but it never implied that the Temple was outmoded. It arose out of need, not out of a desire to change, and the Sages had only the greatest appreciation for the Temple, even though they recognized the flaws in some of the priests who served in it. The synagogue represented another way of serving God, one with a much more educational function than the Temple. The lack of rivalry is indicated by the fact that after the destruction of the Second Temple, prayers for its rebuilding were incorporated into the synagogue ritual. Furthermore, rabbinic tradition went so far as to teach that at the end of days, when all Jews would return to the Land and the Temple would be rebuilt, the synagogues of the diaspora would continue to exist and would play a special role:

> Said Rabbi Eleazar Ha-Kappar, "In the future the synagogues and houses of study which are in Babylonia will be removed and reestablished in the Land of Israel. As it is said, For Tabor among the mountains and Carmel by the sea shall come (Jer. 46:18). Now is this not a matter of logic: if Tabor and Carmel, who had but briefly offered themselves as places for teaching Torah, are to be reestablished in the Land of Israel, certainly synagogues and houses of study in which Torah is read and expounded will be reestablished in the Land of Israel!"[38]

How fitting it is that when the exile comes to an end, instead of disappearing as places whose usefulness has been outlived, the institutions established in order to provide a solution to the religious problems of the exile will be established forever within the Land of Israel.

5

The Creation of the Siddur

The Siddur, the Jewish prayerbook, is the key to understanding and experiencing the meaning of Judaism. There is no better text for acquiring a sense of what it means to be a Jew. As Abraham Joshua Heschel wrote, "The liturgy is our creed in the form of a *spiritual pilgrimage*. Our liturgy is no mere memorial to the past; it is an act of participating in Israel's bearing witness to the unity, uniqueness, love and judgment of God. It is an act of joy."[1]

The material that appears in the Siddur was created over a period of thousands of years and has not yet stopped growing. Nevertheless, it is possible to say that there are two elements that characterize the Siddur and differentiate it from all that came before. The first is that the Siddur is exactly what its name proclaims, "an order of service." The Hebrew root of the word means "order." In the Bible, we have a record of prayers that were recited by individuals or by the entire people at specific times, but they were not part of an order of service to be recited on a regular basis. The Book of Psalms is a collection of prayers for either the individual or the group, but a collection is not an order. The closest we have to a public order of service prior to the year 70 C.E., when the Second Temple was destroyed, is the group of psalms known as the Hallel, which, according to our sources, was recited in the Temple on every major festival. Individuals undoubtedly prayed, but there is nothing to make us think that there was a certain collection of prayers formulated for them to recite daily or even on every Sabbath or festival. Once it is determined that people are to recite certain prayers at certain times in a specific order, we have a *siddur*.

The second new characteristic is that the recitation of the order of prayer is a matter not of choice but of religious obligation. The positive commandment to recite certain prayers at certain times is no less incumbent on the Jew than the offering of sacrifices had been or observance of the regulations of the Sabbath and festivals.

These two factors were superimposed upon material that may have originated much earlier in one form or another. Today, if we add to the Siddur or change prayers, we are not altering the fundamental nature of Jewish prayer but only continuing a process that has been going on for millennia.

The origin of specific prayers and their authorship are questions that have always intrigued us. Some early rabbinic Sages ascribed the prayers to the Patriarchs.[2] Others spoke of the role of the legendary "elders" or "Men of the Great Assembly" in establishing the pattern of prayer.[3] Attributing our order of prayer to such early figures was a way of adding prestige and importance to it, but this need not be seen as factual. The growth of many of the prayers was so gradual and organic that it is impossible to speak of anyone as having originated it. On the other hand, we do know when the major component of the Siddur, the Amida, was fixed and made obligatory, but it was not until after the destruction of the Second Temple.[4] Even in this case we cannot say who "authored" the prayer, but only who arranged and ordained that it be recited. Many of the later liturgical poems, called *"piyyutim,"* that are recited today on the High Holy Days have authors whose names are known to us, as are similar poems for the festivals or Sabbath worship which are no longer commonly used. In the case of the central sections of the liturgy that form its basic core, the Shema and the Amida, we have no such information.

The Earliest Order of Prayer

The earliest reference we have to an order of prayer is found in a section of the Mishna, Tamid 5:1. It is the record not of a public service but of a private one conducted by the priests alone. The Mishna, the authoritative collection of Jewish norms, was edited and published as an official text around the year 200 C.E. by Rabbi Judah the Prince. A descendant of Hillel, he was the most important Jewish figure of his time. He served as patriarch and was recognized by the Romans as the head of the Jewish community in the Land of Israel. His edition of the legal and philosophical traditions and sayings became the final authoritative collection of the early Sages (the Tannaim) and the basis for all later Jewish law. The Mishna contains material that originated hundreds of years before that final redaction. The order Tamid, which describes the sacrificial ceremonies of the Temple, is considered to be the oldest section of the Mishna and reflects traditions recorded either prior to the destruction of the Second Temple or immediately thereafter.[5]

Describing the way in which the daily morning sacrifice, the *tamid*, was offered, the Mishna tells us that after completing the sacrifice the priests left the sacrificial court and went down to the Hall of Hewn Stone, a chamber in the Temple complex which was used for large gatherings, including the meetings of the Great Court (the Sanhedrin). This room was not part of the sacred area of sacrifice or the public courts in which people stood to witness the ritual. The text continues:

> The leader said to them, "Recite one blessing," and they blessed. They recited the Ten Declarations, "Hear," "And it shall come to pass," "And He said . . .". They blessed the people with three blessings: "True and Steadfast," "The service," and the Blessing of the Priests.

In other words, sometime prior to the year 70 C.E., there already existed an order of prayer—a *siddur,* if you will—for a service that was recited daily by the priests.

Unfortunately, we do not have a similar record of an order of service for laymen, nor did laymen participate in this service. It was private, exclusively for the priests. No one else was present. Therefore we cannot say if it reflected similar prayers uttered by Jews elsewhere or not. Perhaps this was the service from which nonpriests later copied their liturgical order, expanding it for more general needs. In any case, this service was in no way part of the sacrificial order. If anything, it interrupted the sacrifices, since it was only afterward that the priests returned to the Temple proper to offer the incense and conclude the Temple service by reciting the Priestly Blessing (Num. 6:24–26) for the benefit of the public that was in attendance. Were it not for the fact that the authorities felt it necessary to record the exact way in which the priests conducted themselves at the daily sacrifice, we might never have known of this ancient ritual.

Whatever the relationship of this service to nonpriestly services, it had enormous significance for the history of Jewish worship and the development of the Siddur. Let us, therefore, examine its contents and their meaning.

The service can be divided into three main sections: (1) the call to recite a blessing; (2) the reading of four selections from the Torah; and (3) the recitation of three blessings for the benefit of the people of Israel.

In the first section, the leader called on the priests to pronounce a blessing, which they proceeded to do. The Mishna does not give us the text of the blessing—it does not even give us a hint as to what it was. This has led to speculation and numerous proposals as to its content. Later talmudic authorities suggest that it was one of the two blessings found at the beginning of the service of their time, either the one concerning the light or the one concerning the Torah.[6] The most likely explanation, however, is that they were being asked not to recite some specific blessing but to proclaim God's blessedness, much as is done today when the leader of the service says, "Bless the Lord who is blessed," and the congregation responds, "Blessed is the Lord who is blessed for all eternity." We have already seen that "to bless" was one of the many forms of praising God which existed in the days of the First Temple, mentioned over and over in the Psalms. There the people respond by saying, "Blessed is the Lord who dwells in Zion" (Ps. 135:21). This response is similar to the call to bless God, the Barchu, in present-day services. It is, however, very different from the more elaborate blessings with which we are familiar, all of which have a very specific formulation, blessing God in connection with a particular action or something we see or experience. It is rather a general proclamation that God is blessed, i.e., He is the highest of all beings. As Brevard Childs has written, "To bless God entails a special sort of praise. It acknowledges in thanksgiving that one's trust in God's care—*chesed*—has been fully vindicated."[7] Thus we find that when David addressed the people, he proclaimed about God, "Blessed are You, Lord, God of Israel our father, from eternity to eternity" (1 Chron. 29:10). All David says in this blessing is that God is blessed. Later, when he finishes his address, David turns to the people and asks them to do the same thing: " 'Now bless the Lord your God.' All the assemblage blessed the Lord God of their fathers" (1 Chron. 29:20).

An even more striking parallel to our service can be found in the story of a great assembly called by Ezra:

> Ezra opened the scroll in the sight of all the people, for he was above all the people; as he opened it, all the people stood up. Ezra blessed the Lord, the great God, and all the people answered, "Amen, Amen," with hands upraised. (Neh. 8:5–6)

Thus, at the ceremony that may have provided the model for the daily reading of sections of the Scripture, God was proclaimed blessed prior to the reading. We also find that later on, when the people were to renew the covenant, that ceremony began with a blessing:

> Rise, bless the Lord your God who is from eternity to eternity: "May Your glorious name be blessed, exalted though it is above every blessing and praise!" (Neh. 9:5)

In the service described in the Mishna, then, the priests began by blessing the name of the God in whose Temple they served.

A reading from the Torah follows. The Mishna deliberately uses the word "read" (*karu*) and not "prayed" or "blessed," since "reading" always indicates a recitation from Scripture, which in Hebrew is called "a reader" (*mikra*). Jewish tradition took great care to distinguish between the Bible, which was written and therefore was to be read from, and everything else: Mishna, midrashim, and even prayers were Oral Torah and not written down. Therefore they could never be "read," only memorized and recited. Not until hundreds of years later was permission given to write down some of these things and to "read" them. At this early time, the only written text was the Bible and "reading" was a technical term indicating a recitation of Scripture. That was the central feature of this ancient service.

Scriptural reading is one of the most ancient features of Jewish ceremonial gatherings. It is first mentioned in the Torah itself, where the practice of gathering the people together once every seven years for a public reading of the Torah is described:

> Every seventh year, the year set for remission, at the Feast of
> Booths, when all Israel comes to appear before the Lord your
> God in the place that He will choose, you shall read this Teaching
> aloud in the presence of all Israel. (Deut. 31:10–11)

The purpose of this was so that everyone—"men, women, children, and
the strangers in your communities—. . . may hear and so learn to revere
the Lord your God and to observe faithfully every word of this Teaching"
(Deut. 31:12). We do not know if the intent was to read the entire Torah,
or only the Book of Deuteronomy or parts of it. In any case, it was an
occasion for impressing upon the people the importance and sacredness
of the Torah. Later generations had experienced neither the theophany
at Sinai nor the direct teaching of God's word by Moses. Hearing the
teaching of Moses read aloud to them at the Temple, which itself substituted for and represented Sinai, the mountain of God, would not only
teach them what was expected of them but would instill in them reverence
for God.

Similarly, we have noted that in 444 B.C.E., when Ezra the Scribe
wished to establish the rule of the Torah as the official constitution of
the Jewish people who had returned from exile in Babylonia, he called
a great assembly at the gate of the rebuilt Temple on one of the important
festival days, the first of Tishre (Rosh Ha-Shanah), and had the entire
Torah read aloud to them.

> He read from it . . . from the first light until midday, to the men
> and the women and those who could understand; the ears of all
> the people were given to the scroll of the Teaching. (Neh. 8:3)

Not only was the Torah read, it was also explained and expounded in
language the people could understand. The conclusion of this ceremony
took place later in the same month, when the Israelites confirmed the
Torah as God's word and renewed the covenant made at Sinai to be God's
people and obey His commands.

These public readings of the Torah differentiated the religion of
Israel from other religions of the time, which viewed the rules and regulations of the cult as a secret mystery revealed only to the priests. The
priests were the keepers of knowledge and shared it with others only as
needed. From a very early time Judaism taught that all the people should

be instructed in Torah. Hearing the Torah read was both a cultic act—a reenactment of the Sinai revelation—and a way of informing and inspiring the people of Israel.

Torah reading thus formed an integral part of the early service of the priests, as it does of all Jewish worship to this day. In the dialogue of worship, reading from the Torah is hearing God speak to us. We have seen that reading and expounding Scripture was the main function of the early synagogue. Here we find it prominently featured in the earliest recorded order of service.

The selections to be read must have been carefully chosen. Because of its length, it would have been impossible to read the entire Torah every day. Therefore certain passages were designated, which represented the Torah and were also important for specific teachings. The first of the four passages is the Ten Declarations (usually but less accurately called the Ten Commandments). Presumably the passage read was Exodus 20:1–14. The other three were Deuteronomy 6:4–9, Deuteronomy 11:13–21, and Numbers 15:37–41.

The reading of the Ten Declarations is an obvious choice: the theophany at Sinai is unique in that God spoke directly to all the people, without an intermediary. The other three selections are known to us by the title they acquired later—the Shema—and are still read twice daily as part of the evening and morning services.[8] They contain the basic doctrines of belief in one unique God, reward and punishment, and redemption. Thus they constitute both a paradigm of the entire Scripture and a basic creed that could be recited daily.

It seems strange that while the last three sections became the unit of the Shema and retained their place of prominence in Jewish worship, the first section—the most distinguished of all—should have disappeared. According to rabbinic tradition, its very importance was the reason for its disappearance. It was eliminated, records the Talmud, because of the "claims of the heretics."[9] These heretics claimed that only the Ten Declarations were sacred, that they alone represented the word of God, while the rest of the Torah and its commandments were not holy. In order not to give credence to these arguments, the Talmud suggests, the Sages eliminated the public recitation of the Ten Declarations. In this way they denied that section any special sanctity or status. All of the Torah is divine. Although some believe that the heretics referred to here

were the early Jewish-Christians, it seems more likely that they were
heretical groups, possibly within Judaism, known as gnostics, who
stressed the duality of the powers of good and evil.[10]

Prior to the elimination of the Ten Declarations, these four selections
formed one unit, and their unity was emphasized by the fact that they
began and ended with nearly identical verses, beginning, "I the Lord
am your God who brought you out of the land of Egypt, the house of
bondage" (Exod. 20:2), and concluding, "I the Lord am your God, who
brought you out of the land of Egypt to be your God: I, the Lord your
God" (Num. 15:41). By beginning and ending with God's direct address
to the individual, this declaration of faith became the embodiment of
the direct experience of "I and Thou." The experience of standing at
Sinai, of hearing God speak directly to each person, is re-created. It is
particularly appropriate that in the first selection the Hebrew word "you"
is in the singular form, while at the end it is in the plural. Thus we are
initially addressed as individuals, but we soon take our place as part of
the people Israel. We stand before God as individuals responsible for
our own actions, but we are strengthened by our membership in this
people.

Following these readings, the third section of the ancient service
consisted of three blessings or prayers for the people. Although no
one aside from priests attended this service, this would not have prevented the priests from saying prayers on behalf of the people of Israel
whom they served and in whose name they served the Lord.[11] Unfortunately, the Mishna does not give us the text of these prayers. Instead,
it identifies them briefly, as if they were well known to all. We do know
of prayers that bear the same designations. They are part of our services
today and are also mentioned frequently in other sections of the early
rabbinic writings. The first, "True and Steadfast," is a prayer that follows
the recitation of the Shema. The second, "The service," is the designation of one of the paragraphs of the Amida which asks for the acceptance
of the prayers and service of Israel. The third, the Blessing of the Priests,
is the concluding prayer of the Amida, a paraphrase of the Priestly Blessing. We cannot be certain, but it is possible that there was some resemblance between the blessings of the ancient service and the prayers we
know by the same names today.[12]

"True and Steadfast" is an assertion that the words of Torah just read are indeed true, an affirmation and acceptance of what has been said. The texts we have conclude with a prayer for redemption, so this would very likely also have been a prayer for the redemption of Israel. Even before the destruction, Israel considered itself to be in need of God's salvation, the ultimate expression of which would be the coming of the Messiah and the transformation of all human society.

Regarding the second prayer, "The service," it would have been most appropriate for the priests, who had just concluded the offering of the daily sacrifice on behalf of the entire people, to petition God to look favorably upon that people and accept their offering.

The third prayer, based on the words of the blessing found in Numbers 6:24–26, would also have been entirely appropriate, since the priests would shortly return to the sacred precincts and conclude the morning ceremony by reciting that blessing. A similar prayer has been found in the writings of the Dead Sea sect. [13]

Two of the three petitions offered, then, were closely linked to the priesthood and its task: offering the sacrifice and bestowing God's blessing on the people. In the first, they represent the people to God; in the second, they represent God to the people.

The service we have described was well suited to the priests. Having offered the daily sacrifice, they proclaimed the blessedness of the God whom they served and in whose sanctuary they officiated. They read from the words of that God, reenacting the ceremonies of acceptance of God, His word, and the basic doctrines of Torah. They proclaimed their belief in the truth of Torah, after which they prayed that God accept the service of the people and bless them with the blessings promised in the words they would shortly pronounce over the people.

Thus we have come full circle. The sacrificial service had been totally devoid of the spoken word. But the force and importance of the word divorced from sacrifice as a method of communicating with God had become so important by the period of the Second Temple that the priests themselves, the very guardians of the sacrificial rites, sought to incorporate it into their own daily experience. It was as if the sacrificial ritual was insufficient if performed by officiants who did not make clear that they accepted God and His Torah or who did not petition the Lord for the good of Israel.

Although well suited to the specific needs of the priests, this service also contains the basic elements of every Jewish worship service. It begins with praise of God, continues with Torah, and concludes with petitionary prayer. Praise, Torah, and petition describe all of Jewish worship.

The Crisis of Destruction

If the synagogue can be said to have emerged from the crisis of the destruction of the First Temple and the exile of the Judeans to Babylonia, the destruction of the Second Temple may be seen as the catalyst that brought about the creation of the Siddur and the entire system of Jewish worship that has informed Judaism until today.

The Temple with its sacrificial order had been the focal point of Judaism and the Jewish people from the time of their return from exile in 538 B.C.E. until its destruction. Whatever its place in the days of the First Commonwealth, it was even more important during the Second Commonwealth. With no legitimate king of the lineage of David, it was the Temple that served as a symbol of Jewish unity and of the Jewish people's devotion to God. It is difficult for us to imagine what it must have meant for the structure to be destroyed and for the institution of sacrifice to be eliminated from Jewish life. But crisis often brings with it creativity, and Judaism was blessed with great leaders who were able to find ways of coping in the wake of the catastrophe.

How providential it was for the future of Judaism that the healing balm existed before the injury took place. Postexilic Judaism had created the synagogue, prayer unconnected to sacrifice, communal study, and a nonpriestly group of leaders and teachers, all of which had coexisted with the Second Temple. These now stepped in to fill the void left by the absence of the cultic center. It was done, however, not by denigrating the importance of the Temple, but by symbolically incorporating the Temple and its service into the newly enhanced synagogue and its pattern of prayer and study.

For example, the Sages taught that the reading of the biblical portions describing the sacrifices could substitute for them when the Temple no longer existed. Thus, according to the Talmud, Abraham had asked God for assurance that should Israel sin and not be able to offer sacrifice, He would not punish them as He punished the generation of the flood. God replied:

> I have already ordained for them the "order of the sacrifices." When they read them before Me, I account it as if they had brought them to Me and I forgive their sins.[14]

This accounts for the fact that on holidays the biblical portion describing the sacrifice for that day is read as part of the Torah service and is also incorporated into the basic prayer, the Amida.

Prayers for the restoration of the Temple were also composed, and the daily psalm that had been recited by the Levites in the Temple became part of the daily prayer service. From a psychological point of view, the synagogue service filled the same religious needs the Temple had answered.

It is clear that after the destruction of the Second Temple, when sacrifices and the Temple service were lost, prayer in general began to play a much more important role than it had previously and the synagogue service flourished in the vacuum that had been created.[15] The Sages were interested in stressing the connection between sacrifice and worship. In this way the importance of prayer could be emphasized. Prayer was raised to the level of sacrifice, which was of highest sanctity and had been ordained by the Torah. When the Temple no longer existed, this became even more important, for although prayer was not merely a substitute for sacrifice, having an importance of its own, it was a reminder of it. Thus the rabbis taught:

> To serve Him (Deut. 11:13). This refers to prayer . . . and just as service at the altar is called "service," so is prayer called "service."[16]

It is easy to understand that when the Temple was destroyed, some way had to be found to enable the Jewish community to continue a life of worship and acknowledgment of God. Having groups come together to pray was an excellent method of strengthening Jewish life in a period of chaos and lack of central institutions. Although individuals had not attended every sacrificial service at the Temple, and indeed had not been required to do so, each person felt that the daily communal offerings were being brought for him or her and that God's gifts of love and forgiveness were being obtained for each member of the community of Israel.

Around 100 C.E., shortly after the destruction of the Temple, the order of the eighteen prayer paragraphs—called "blessings" because each one concludes with a blessing formula, or *hatima*—was formalized and accepted by Rabban Gamliel II in Yavneh:

> Simeon Ha-Pakuli arranged eighteen blessings according to the proper order before Rabban Gamliel in Yavneh.[17]

Rabban Gamliel determined that the institution of a mandatory daily recitation of these Eighteen Blessings, also called the Amida, by each individual would provide the needed framework for a life of Jewish piety. He decreed that prayer, which had previously been a matter of individual choice, would become a religious requirement and determined the text of the main prayer to be recited, the Amida. Thus, the two main sections that comprise Jewish worship now existed: the Shema and the Amida.

Many attempts have been made to trace the earliest precursors of the Amida, if not its actual origins. Experts are not in agreement as to when it began, but many have found similarities of both language and content in prayers that were written during the two centuries prior to the beginning of Christianity. Chapters 36 and 51 of the extracanonical Book of Ben Sira, which stems from the third century B.C.E., contain similarities to the Amida and use some of the same phrases.[18]

In any case, it seems possible that at least some of the sections of the Amida (probably the first three blessings and the last three) predate the destruction of the Temple. Some scholars believe that an official prayer containing at least some of the sections was recited as an act of community worship although not as an individual prayer.[19] Others think that prior to the destruction of the Temple, there may have been pious individuals who recited certain prayers regularly, but that there was no official order of service and certainly no required individual prayer.[20]

Under Rabban Gamliel's supervision, the text of the prescribed blessings was determined and the rules for their recitation were enacted. Some rabbis felt that it was not necessary or even possible for everyone to recite the exact formula, and a certain flexibility was maintained. Thus the Sages argued about the specific requirements for the individual in reciting the Amida (also known simply as the Prayer), but all agreed that it was now to be a part of the daily regimen of life:

> Rabban Gamliel says: One should recite the Eighteen Blessings daily.
>   Rabbi Joshua says: —an abbreviated Eighteen.
>   Rabbi Akiva says: If he is fluent in the Prayer, he should recite the Eighteen Blessings. If not—an abbreviated form.
>   Rabbi Eliezer says: If one makes the Prayer into a fixed routine, it is not a request for mercy.[21]

Rabban Gamliel was convinced that everyone was well enough acquainted with the Prayer to be able to recite a complete version of it, and he required them to do so. Rabbi Joshua required only a brief version. Such an abbreviated version still exists today and is used when there is not enough time to recite the full text; it contains a brief restatement of the main idea of each paragraph.[22] Rabbi Akiva believed that the recitation depends on the individual: if one can recite it completely, one should; if not, the shorter version will do. Rabbi Eliezer disagreed: one should never simply recite a fixed text, for then the Prayer lacks the element of true pleading before God, which is the very essence of the Amida.

There were, in fact, many Sages who urged that each person say something novel whenever praying. It is reported of Rabbi Eliezer that "he would recite a new prayer every day" so that "it should not be like reading a letter."[23] Others said that a completely fixed prayer text was unacceptable prayer, and in order to avoid it one should always "make an innovation."[24]

The Amida was not intended as a substitute for sacrifice, since the desire to resume the sacrificial system remained strong. Although most Jews felt that the Temple service had been necessary for the achievement of atonement and found it difficult to adjust to the new situation, the rabbinic leadership assured them that even now atonement could be achieved—interestingly enough, not by prayer, but by appropriate deeds:

> Once, as Rabban Yohanan ben Zakkai was coming forth from Jerusalem, Rabbi Joshua followed after him and beheld the Temple in ruins.
>   "Woe unto us!" Rabbi Joshua cried, "that this, the place

where the iniquities of Israel were atoned for, is laid waste!"

"My son," Rabban Yohanan said to him, "be not grieved; we have another atonement as effective as this. And what is it? It is acts of loving-kindness, as it is said, For I desire loving-kindness and not sacrifice." (Hos. 6:6)[25]

Even though Rabban Gamliel seems to have adopted a fixed text for the Amida,[26] we do not have any copy of it nor can we be certain that everyone agreed to use his text word for word. Only the names of the blessings are recorded.[27] Flexibility undoubtedly continued at least until the ninth century, under the Geonim of Babylonia, when the exact text was fixed and required.[28] Even then, total uniformity was not achieved. This was especially true because of the prohibition against writing down prayers and blessings—they were part of the oral tradition—so that no one used a written text when praying, not even the leader of the service.[29] As late as the fourteenth century, it was taken for granted that there were no two communities in which the text of the Amida was exactly the same.[30]

Rabban Gamliel's decision altered the nature of the synagogue. Prayer now took its place alongside study as an integral part of what was now the central institution of Judaism.

The pattern of nonsacrificial worship that developed after the destruction of the Second Temple was to recite sections of the Torah—the Shema—with blessings before and after, upon rising in the morning and before retiring at night. The Prayer—the Amida—was recited by itself three times daily, presenting one's petitions before God evening, morning, and afternoon. The decision to combine the two into one unit was made sometime in the third century, when Rabbi Yohanan, basing himself on earlier pietistic traditions, urged that one should always recite the Prayer immediately after the last blessing of the Shema, thus joining the Prayer to the blessing of God's salvation, while others argued that the evening Shema should be recited after the Prayer and not before.[31] Once Rabbi Yohanan's suggestion was adopted, the basic components of today's worship service were in place: the Shema and the Prayer are recited together in the evening and the morning, and the Prayer, the Amida, is recited by itself, in the afternoon service, as it was originally.

The Blessing Formula

Another important development that reached its climax in the centuries following the destruction and made the creation of the Siddur and Jewish liturgy possible was the evolution of a new literary formula, the *beracha*. This change in the way in which one addresses God took place during the rabbinic period. It is impossible to understand Jewish worship without appreciating the meaning and importance of the *beracha*, or blessing, the basic formula of Jewish worship.

It is important to differentiate between "blessing" and "prayer." Although we commonly use "prayer" to refer to everything in the service, in Hebrew "prayer" (*tefilla*) also has a specific meaning: petition. "Blessing," on the other hand, refers to the praise of God, proclamation of His greatness. According to Solomon Zeitlin, "A prayer is a plea for something in the future, while a blessing is an expression of thankfulness for something past or present."[32]

Anyone who has ever participated in any traditional Jewish ceremony has heard blessings recited. Weddings consist of a series of blessings. So does a circumcision ceremony. A bar mitzva or bat mitzva consists of blessings over the Torah and the reading of the Prophets. Even a funeral is built around a set of blessings. One says a blessing before eating and then recites more after the meal. A Passover Seder consists of readings interspersed with the appropriate blessings. Take away the blessing, and Jewish worship falls apart. Yet we find no blessings in the technical sense in that great work of early Israelite worship, the Book of Psalms, or anywhere else in the Bible. Once, in the Book of Chronicles, we find the opening of the rabbinic blessing formula. Instead of "Blessed is the Lord," which is the common biblical terminology, David is quoted as saying, "Blessed are You, Lord" (1 Chron. 29:10), a phrase that eventually became the key to worship.[33]

Blessings come in many forms. The briefest, as we have already seen, is the proclamation of God as blessed: "Blessed is the Lord." The blessing formula, however, comes into being when, instead of speaking about God, we address Him directly, as in the words attributed to David. The blessing developed by the rabbinical Sages went much further. Eventually they determined that, to qualify as a liturgically acceptable blessing, it must not only contain the Tetragrammaton—the name of God, which we pronounce as *Adonai* (the Lord)[34]—but also the designation "our God" (*eloheinu*). Thus the opening formula becomes "Blessed are You, O Lord our God" (*baruch ata Adonai eloheinu*). The model for this phrase may have been the first line of the Shema, "Hear, O Israel, the *Lord our God*, the Lord is one" (Deut. 6:4). The conjunction of the two words had great significance when Moses uttered it, containing as it does the proper name of God. The Tetragrammaton was revealed to Moses at the burning bush and defined, as it were, the essence of the God of Israel: He is the very existence of the universe and causes all to exist. The Hebrew word derives from the root "to be." When Moses asked God to reveal His name,

> God said to Moses, "I Am that I Am." He continued, "Thus shall you say to the Israelites, 'I Am sent me to you.' " And God said further to Moses, "Thus shall you speak to the Israelites: The Lord [in Hebrew this is a third-person form of the first-person *I am*] . . . has sent me to you: This shall be My name forever, this My appellation for all eternity." (Exod. 3:14–15)

Whenever we recite a blessing, no matter what the subject, we are re-affirming that our God, the being we worship as supreme, is the Lord, without whom there would be no existence.

When a blessing closes a paragraph of a prayer, it consists of that opening formula plus some statement about God, His nature, or His deeds. For example:

> Blessed are You, O Lord our God, who has redeemed Israel.

> Blessed are You, O Lord our God, shield of Abraham.

> Blessed are You, O Lord our God, the healer of the sick of His people Israel.

> Blessed are You, O Lord our God, who blesses His people Israel with peace.

These are typical of blessings that are not self-contained but are recited as the conclusion of an entire prayer.

All other blessings contain the phrase "king of the universe" (*melech ha-olam*), which, according to the third-century authority Rabbi Yohanan, must be included in any blessing.[35] These are short, one-sentence blessings said when experiencing an important event in one's life or when seeing something unusual, or blessings recited prior to eating. They always start with the formula "Blessed are You, O Lord our God, king of the universe" (*baruch ata Adonai eloheinu melech ha-olam*). Thus we have seen that the earliest form, "Blessed are You, O Lord" (*baruch ata Adonai*), expanded to "Blessed are You, O Lord our God" (*baruch ata Adonai eloheinu*) and then to "Blessed are You, O Lord our God, king of the universe" (*baruch ata Adonai eloheinu melech ha-olam*).

The following are examples of blessings related to some experience:

Blessed are You, O Lord our God, king of the universe, who removes sleep from my eyes and slumber from my eyelids.

Blessed are You, O Lord our God, king of the universe, who made the great sea.

Blessed are You, O Lord our God, king of the universe, who has given of His wisdom to human beings.

Blessed are You, O Lord our God, king of the universe, truthful judge.

Blessed are You, O Lord our God, king of the universe, who has kept us in life, sustained us, and brought us to this season.

Some examples of blessings for food are:

Blessed are You, O Lord our God, king of the universe, who brings forth bread from the earth.

Blessed are You, O Lord our God, king of the universe, creator of the fruit of the vine.

Blessings that come at the beginning of a prayer must also contain this phrase. For example, in the first blessing prior to the morning Shema:

Blessed are You, O Lord our God, king of the universe, former of light and creator of darkness, maker of peace and creator of everything.

The longest formula is for blessings that are recited in conjunction with the performance of a commandment, a specific *mitzva*. It adds the phrase

"who sanctified us with His commandments and commanded us to . . ."
(*asher kideshanu b'mitzvotav v'tzivanu*). Before lighting Sabbath candles,
one recites:

> Blessed are You, O Lord our God, king of the universe, who
> sanctified us with His commandments and commanded us to
> kindle the Sabbath light.

Before eating matza on the first evening of Passover, we say:

> Blessed are You, O Lord our God, king of the universe, who
> sanctified us with His commandments and commanded us con-
> cerning the eating of matza.

All of these occasions are opportunities for blessing God. Although we
recite a blessing over bread and wine, the blessing is not imparted to the
bread or the wine. We do not "bless" the wine in the sense of imparting
some holiness to it that it did not possess before. We bless God who
made these things, not the things themselves. The blessings we say over
food have been likened to the act of paying for what we consume.[36] Prior
to the blessing, everything belongs to God. After appropriately acknowledging Him, we have permission to consume it. But a blessing goes far
beyond that. Saying a blessing upon seeing something new or experiencing something mundane or unusual, good or bad, is a way of helping
us to appreciate the world and what God does for us. We become aware
of what is around us and what is happening to us, and we acknowledge
the divine dimension in every aspect of life. Thus, in the most normal
and natural way possible, we continually experience God. Blessings provide us with occasions for proclaiming that God is blessed.[37]

Max Kadushin aptly characterized the blessing as an embodiment of
rabbinic Judaism's attitude or mode of "normal mysticism." Whereas
mysticism attempts to create an immediate, sensory experience of God
(and in non-Jewish mysticism even to achieve union with God), rabbinic
Judaism regarded this level of intensity as beyond the capability of most
people and as something that, at best, could not be sustained on a regular
basis. What are we to do with the everyday experiences of life? Why not
attempt to turn those ordinary moments into the experience of the presence of God? Thus the blessing calls our attention to God in both unusual
and usual things. Even eating is transformed from a physical act into one

that carries with it the experience of God by the recitation of the accompanying blessing.[38]

These formulas are a creation of the religious genius of the Sages of Israel. They were not arrived at overnight. They emerged after a long period of fluctuation in which many different forms were used by individuals within the community of Israel and even within the rabbinic group itself. In the Dead Sea Scrolls, for example, we find that the members of that sect used the formula "Blessed are You, my God," which the rabbis would not permit.[39] The extracanonical Book of Ben Sira contains many prayers that use the term "acknowledge" (*hodu*), as do many passages in the Dead Sea Scrolls.[40] Of the various biblical terms that could have been utilized—*hodu*, *hallel* ("praise"), or *barech* ("bless")—Pharisaic Judaism singled out "blessed" as the favored term and eventually created the blessing formula. We should not take this for granted but appreciate it for the marvelous creation that it is. As Kadushin comments, "It was nothing short of religious genius first to have achieved the *beracha* formula, and then to have made it the basic element of the prayers."[41]

The genius of the blessing consists of the way in which, within a few words, it contains so much of what is vital to Jewish worship and belief, as well as in its flexibility. It is the perfect way to begin a prayer, to concretize a feeling or an experience, or to conclude a unit of prayer. By chosing the direct form of addressing God—"Blessed are You"—it emphasizes the closeness of the relationship between the human being and God. There is something rather daring about human beings, with all of their foibles and weaknesses, speaking directly to the ultimate power of the universe. At a time when kings and emperors were addressed in the third person, as is still occasionally the case today, the Sages decreed that we were to talk not about God but directly to Him. The God of the Siddur is not the God of the philosophers. He is not the God about whom one speculates. He is not an abstraction but an immediate presence to whom we speak and whose name we bless at every available opportunity. The Sages said that a person should recite one hundred blessings a day.[42] How better to bring about a sense of closeness to God than to speak to Him directly, and especially to do so when there is an experience that concretizes His presence and His work. Everything we see thus becomes an occasion to remember the creative work of God. Eating becomes the time to remember that everything we have stems eventually from Him. The changes of times of day become opportunities to remember His works and bless Him for them. The performance of commandments becomes not a dry routine but a moment to voice praise for God and to recall the purpose of what we are doing: to sanctify us, to elevate us toward the holy.

The wording of the blessing formula has particular significance. We have already noted that the name "the Lord" was required because of its meaning and its historical associations with the very beginnings of Mosaic monotheism. The following phrase, "our God," is in the plural, thus emphasizing the importance in Judaism of the role of the community. Jewish identity is expressed within the context of the group. Each of us addresses God not merely as an individual but as a member of a people, of the Jewish group, with all the historical and contemporary connections that implies. Perhaps the worst of all human emotions is the feeling of being alone. The sense of "I am alone, I have no one," which accompanies deep depression, is all too common today. Judaism's ultimate answer to this is not only that one is not alone because of the presence of God, but also that one is not alone when connected to the people of Israel. Prayer alleviates aloneness in this double fashion—therefore we say "our" God, not "my" God.

The next phrase, "king of the universe," may seem old-fashioned to us. It is imagery taken from the era of the Persian kings, who designated themselves "king of kings." Kings are not very important today and at best they sit upon shaky thrones, but the image can still be a powerful one, for we all know what it means. It represents absolute rulership, complete ownership. It is a phrase that has ancient resonance. Yochanan Muffs has pointed out, however, that it is not solely an image of power. In ancient days the king was viewed as the symbol of "the benign uses of power. He was a father, a mother, a nurturer. . . . Kingship . . . is an expression of kindness rather than severity."[43] Many of Judaism's most sacred prayers and ceremonies, such as the recitation of the Shema or the Alenu, involve proclaiming God our king, the ultimate power to whom we owe sole allegiance, as opposed to any natural or human force. This is known as *kabbalat ol malchut shamayim*, taking upon oneself the yoke of the kingship of God. With every blessing we thus announce our allegiance to God and proclaim Him king not of a limited kingdom but "of the universe." Once again Judaism's combination of the particular and the universal is evident. He is "our God," i.e., the God of Israel, but He is also the king of "the universe." He rules all humankind, all nations, as surely as He rules the people of Israel, even if other nations do not yet acknowledge it.

One of the most unusual features of the blessing formula is the jarring switch from second to third person. At first we address God directly— "Blessed are *You*"—but we immediately change the person and speak *about* Him—"who sanctified us by *His* commandments"—using the third person in defiance of all rules of grammar and literary style. This is so awkward that many translations gloss over it and use the second person throughout, obscuring this unique formula. Regardless of what appears in a translation, be aware that whatever follows the direct address to God is always in the third person. It is "He created," not "You created." It is always "His people" and not "Your people." It is unlikely that this is a matter of a lapse in style. There must be a reason for it.

In a sense, this mixture of direct and indirect address did not originate in the blessing; it can be found in the psalms as well. We have noted that some psalms speak directly to God, some speak about Him, and some do both. Both the psalmist and the rabbis are attempting to tell us that although we have been given the great privilege of addressing God, He nevertheless remains beyond our experience and our ken, and most of the time we can only speak about Him. In the eleventh-century work *Machzor Vitry*, the author took note of the anomaly of the blessing:

> When a person mentions the name of the Holy One, he says, "I am ever mindful of the Lord's presence" (Ps. 16:8), and he must make himself feel that he is standing before Him; and since he stands before Him, he addresses Him directly. But when reciting the blessing after mentioning God's name, one says, "Blessed is the glory of the Lord, in His place" (Ezek. 3:12), and recites it as if through an intermediary.[44]

God is both near and far, imminent and transcendent; we experience Him simultaneously as being in our presence and as existing in some other sphere which we cannot comprehend. He is both awesome and loving. Lest "king" be seen only as harsh, we use Rabbi Akiva's phrase. He is both "our father" and "our king." This is another way of referring to the two qualities that form the basis of the Jewish concept of God, "the quality of justice" and the "quality of mercy." As the Talmud puts it, "Wherever you find God's might, there do you find His humility."[45] To have been able to express these two experiences of God in one brief formula, in defiance of both grammar and logic, was the genius of the creators of this formula.

The Emergence of the Siddur

During the period following the destruction of the Second Temple, a time of great creativity for rabbinic Judaism, Jewish prayer developed fully and crystallized the formula of the blessing, determined the daily Amida recitations, created the structure of the Shema and its surrounding blessings, and decreed the themes of these recitations, without specifying word by word what was to be said.

The beauty of these basic prayers and blessings is seen in their classic simplicity. Utilizing phrases and vocabulary from biblical verses, they expressed the concepts determined by the Sages with a minimum of verbiage and in language people could appreciate, understand, and re- member. Since it was forbidden to write down the prayers, such simplicity was important for both practical and theoretical considerations. Attempts at fanciful elaboration were frowned upon and even considered offensive. A story is told of a person who led the prayers and, instead of confining himself to the few praises of the Lord contained in the first paragraph of the Amida, added several of his own. Rabbi Hanina was present and stopped him by remarking sarcastically,

> Have you exhausted all the possible praise of the Master? Were it not that they were written by Moses in Scripture and affixed to the prayer by the Men of the Great Assembly, we would not even dare utter those three [descriptions], and you go on adding all of this? It may be compared to a human king who had thou- sands upon thousands of gold coins, and people praised him for owning silver. Would that not be a terrible slight toward him?[46]

There is something to be said for reticence.

Nevertheless, the creative human spirit seems to enjoy the exuberance of the romantic or the baroque, not only the simplicity of the classical. From the early times of the talmudic age, poets began to cast the basic themes of the prayers into more elaborate patterns. Eventually some of these poems, known as *piyyutim*, became part of the accepted text.[47] Later, *piyyutim* were written as expansions of already accepted texts or even as substitutes for them. It has been suggested that while the individual worshiper would recite the simple text he knew, the prayer leader was expected to elaborate on the theme.[48] In this way the public service was not a mere repetition of what everyone knew, but continually changing and dependent upon the ability of the poet (the *paiytan*).

The best known of the early *paiytanim* lived in the Land of Israel. They were Yose ben Yose, Eleazar Kalir, and Yannai. The dates of these gifted writers are not certain, varying between the third and sixth centuries. Later, others appeared in Rome and Spain, as well as throughout all of Europe. Although they wrote poems for both the Sabbath and festivals, thousands of which are in existence, few are recited today except on the High Holy Days, when the services are elaborated through their use.[49]

The next and determining phase of the development of the contents of the Siddur was the period of the Geonim, beginning in the ninth century, when the specific text and rules of prayer were standardized in a way that was not disturbed until the modern era. The rule preventing the writing of prayers and therefore the creation of a real prayerbook was no longer observed by the geonic period. Prayerbooks were written and used by the eighth century, but a multiplicity of texts and customs made it difficult to determine exactly what was correct practice and what was not. It was only logical for the authoritative leaders of the time to set down in writing a specific formula for all these liturgical works and to finalize a specific framework and rules of prayer—to create a true Siddur. The Babylonian tendency, unlike that of the community in the Land of Israel, was to look toward authoritative, centralized leadership and to reduce disparate customs. "Gaon," meaning "the pride of," was the title given to the heads of the major Babylonian academies, whose influence over the Jewish world was great. The Geonim were recognized throughout the world as major authorities on Jewish law and practice. In 856 C.E.,

Amram Gaon, the head of the academy at Sura, was asked by Spanish Jewry for help in determining the correct order of prayer. His *responsa* became the basis of the Sephardic rite of prayer, and he compiled the first "authoritative" Jewish prayerbook. Unfortunately, over the years the text of his *responsa* was frequently modified in such a way that very little of the text of his writing as we have it is exactly what he wrote.[50]

The great philosopher Saadia Gaon (882–942) built on this and produced his own prayerbook a century later. It consisted of text, rules, and commentary, and represented an elaborate attempt to restructure and reinterpret the liturgy according to Saadia's philosophical system.[51] In the eleventh century, Simcha ben Samuel, a pupil of Rashi, produced his work on the prayers in Vitry, France. It was known as *Machzor Vitry*. He utilized the work of Amram Gaon and the decisions of his own teacher, creating a comprehensive volume that gave the liturgy as practiced in his part of the world along with complete explanations of the meaning and reasons for the prayers. This work thereafter served as the basis for the Ashkenazic rite.

By this time, flexibility in prayer was a thing of the past. An individual could have a Siddur of his own transcribed and need not depend only on memory. The text was to be recited exactly as determined by the rabbinic authorities, although some still continued to permit the addition of appropriate *piyyutim*, even though such an authority as Maimonides condemned this practice as likely to cause people to take the prayers too lightly, compromising their feelings of devotion.[52]

Originally there were two major rites, that of the Land of Israel and that of Babylonia. The former retained its flexibility longer than the latter, but it also lost its influence on the Jewish world as the Jewish community of the Land of Israel diminished in importance compared to that of the diaspora. Were it not for the discovery of the Cairo Geniza by Solomon Schechter in 1896, we would know little of the prayers of the Land of Israel. Babylonian versions became the basis for both the Spanish (Sephardic) and European (Ashkenazic) rites. These in turn were further differentiated according to location and, later, according to theological trends. Thus, modifications were made in the sixteenth century by the mystics of Safed, in the Land of Israel, led by Isaac Luria (known as the Ari), and in eighteenth-century eastern Europe by the founders of Hassidism.

What is most amazing about this development is that, for all the disparities among the various versions, the differences remain insubstantial in comparison to the amount of agreement. The basic components, the major themes, the important phraseology and biblical quotations are the same. There are differences in regard to what is said at what point in the preliminary and concluding sections of the service, to say nothing of differences in the way in which the service is conducted and in the melodies used. A person used to worshiping according to a particular Ashkenazic rite would feel confused in a service conducted by Yemenites, for example, but he would easily recognize that the underlying structure is the same. The last two hundred years have produced a variety of modifications of the traditional prayerbook on the basis of ideological differences, first in central and western Europe, later in America and Israel. Even the most radical prayerbook, however, follows at least partially the outlines of the service as determined by the rabbinic authorities and codified by the Geonim, so that an understanding of any Siddur, regardless of the movement that produced it, depends upon the study and development of these ancient formulations.

We have traveled a long way from the brief service of the priests in the Hall of Hewn Stone two thousand years ago or more to the traditional services of today, which grew out of the core concretized by the Geonim. Whatever changes have taken place, the pattern that we glimpsed there can still be seen today. It is a combination of study and prayer, of praise and petition, based primarily on the themes of the Shema and its blessings and the benedictions of the Amida.

6

The Daily Order of Prayer

*P*articipating in Jewish worship, especially within the setting of a synagogue service, is very different from praying as an individual. Instead of addressing God personally—expressing our individual feelings, needs, or desires in our own way—we are required to enter into a framework that others have devised, utilizing words others have composed. It seems that, instead of using our own thoughts of the moment, we are expected to communicate through someone else's thoughts, most of which were composed in entirely different situations over a thousand years ago. In place of speaking spontaneously, we are expected to repeat the same words we have recited innumerable times before and will say again in the future. No wonder many of the rabbis remarked that one must include something new at every service. Of course, the main thing that is "new" is oneself. Depending on my thoughts, my mood, my feelings, my existential situation of the moment, what I say, no matter how many times I have said it before, takes on new meaning. In addition, each individual is encouraged to add his or her own prayers to the required recitations. This will make the old words new and add substance to the new by connecting it to all that has come before.

Participating in worship within a formal framework may require one to repeat time and time again the same words and even to listen to the repetition of prayers that at that moment are not particularly pertinent to his situation, but it does have positive advantages. It is often surprising how pertinent ancient words can sometimes be, how suddenly a phrase that meant nothing before can take on significance. Expressing one's thoughts is liberating, but it is also confining because an individual's perspective is always limited. Joining with others not only makes us part of a community but also widens our concerns. Suddenly I am thinking not only of myself and not only of the moment, but of the Jewish people, of humanity, of the distant future as well as of today. My words are emerging not only from my limited experience but from the experience of a people that reaches back thousands of years. Thus, my life becomes part of the life of the Jewish people, my needs and concerns part of theirs. I draw strength, hope, and inspiration from something much more extensive than myself. I learn to absorb the values of Judaism within myself and to let them guide my thoughts and ultimately my actions.

Repetition has definite advantages. It is enough to read most books once, but the Torah can be read again and again, always with new insights. The same is true of the Siddur. I do not need new words every time I pray, and I doubt if I would be capable of creating them. The old ones have lasting potency. They only lose their meaning when I lose my ability to concentrate and to absorb them anew. I especially need them when I do not know what to say. Further, entering into a familiar routine can be very comforting. With proper preparation, it is possible to find the balance between the old and the new, between the constant and the novel, between myself as an individual and as part of a group.

It is true that public prayer in Judaism may seem overwhelming, chaotic, and complicated to one who is not familiar with it. It may even be confusing to those who have some measure of acquaintance with it. "What page are we on?" is probably the most frequently asked question in the synagogue. I have childhood memories of my father signaling with his fingers to my mother, who was up in a women's gallery, to help her find the page. Some services tend to be lengthy, especially those of the festivals and High Holy Days, and if one is not conversant with the structure of the service and the Siddur, attending a service can be rather like going through a maze and wondering if you will ever find the way out. The problem is not only finding one's place in the Siddur but understanding what is happening—knowing what these words mean and why we are saying them. Therefore it will probably raise eyebrows to say that the pattern of Jewish prayer is quite simple—but it really is. Before discussing the various sections of the Siddur and the individual prayers, it will be helpful to have a general overview of that pattern.

Prescribed Jewish worship consists of three daily services: Arvit or Maariv (evening), Shacharit (morning), and Mincha (afternooon). On the Sabbath and holy days, the Musaf (additional) service follows Shacharit. At the beginning of the Sabbath, Kabbalat Shabbat (Welcoming the Sabbath) precedes Arvit. Each service contains an Amida (the central prayer recited while standing). The Amida is read silently and individually, and is then repeated out loud by the *shaliach tzibbur* (leader of the service), except at Arvit. There were disputes among the Sages as to the status of the evening service, which was considered by some to be optional. Therefore the evening service contains no public recitation of the Amida.[1] At Arvit and Shacharit services, the Shema (a recitation of three sections of the Torah) and its blessings are recited prior to the Amida. The main thing to remember is that the Amida is recited three times daily and the Shema is recited twice.

Shacharit is preceded by a preliminary service consisting of Birchot Ha-Shachar (morning blessings) and Pesukei d'Zimra ("verses of song"), a collection of biblical prayers from the Book of Psalms and elsewhere. The Mincha service also has a preliminary section, but it is very brief— just one psalm and a few verses. Following the Shacharit and Mincha Amida, the Tachanun (prayers of supplication) are recited on weekdays. At Shacharit, they are followed by some psalms and the Kedusha d'Sidra (a prayer of sanctification). The different sections of the service are separated by recitation of the Kaddish, a brief prayer for the establishment of God's kingdom. It is said at the end of the preliminary service, after the reading of the Torah, after Shacharit, and after Musaf.

On Mondays, Thursdays, the Sabbath, and holidays, the Torah is read after the Shacharit Amida. On special holidays, the Hallel (psalms of praise) is recited after the Shacharit Amida but before the Torah reading. Every service concludes with the Alenu, the prayer for the universal recognition and kingship of God. The following is the basic outline of the major parts of the services:

Weekday Arvit	*Shabbat Arvit*
Shema	Kabbalat Shabbat
Amida	Shema
Alenu	Amida
	Alenu

Weekday Shacharit	*Shabbat Shacharit*
Preliminary Service	Preliminary Service
Shema	Shema
Amida	Amida
Tachanun	(Hallel on festivals)
(Hallel on festivals)	Kriyat Ha-Torah [Torah reading]
	Haftarah
Kriyat Ha-Torah (Mondays and Thursdays) [Torah reading]	
	Musaf
Kedusha d'Sidra	Amida
Alenu	Alenu

Weekday Mincha	*Shabbat Mincha*
Preliminary Service (Ashrei)	Preliminary Service
	Kriyat Ha-Torah [Torah reading]
Amida	
Tachanun	Amida
Alenu	Alenu

Although the specific content of the prayers varies with the occasion, they will always consist of the three major types of prayer: *shevach* (praise), *hodaya* (thanksgiving), or *bakasha* (petition). Every prayer can be designated as one of these three. The Shema is a declaration of the acknowledgment of God's kingship and the acceptance of His commands. The services also contain the element of hearing God's instruction (Torah), so that a dialogue is created: on the one hand, we express ourselves and speak to God through our prayers; on the other, God speaks to us through His revealed word, be it the Shema, which consists of three sections of the Torah, or the reading of the Torah or the Haftarah (Prophets). That is the basic structure of public prayer; all the rest is commentary, but the commentary is extensive.

7

Preparation for Prayer

*O*ne of the most beautiful parts of the service is the preliminary section that leads up to the two main units of worship, the Shema and the Amida. This service grew over the years almost without planning as more and more need was felt for proper preparation for prayer. People hesitated to plunge into the heart of the matter without taking time to make certain they were ready to concentrate on the serious business at hand. They realized that, like anything else worthwhile, prayer requires preparation. Preparation implies training and understanding of what one is going to do, but it also requires a gradual warm-up period before undertaking the task itself. Even after intensive training, no athlete begins a race before limbering up to make sure that the body is properly prepared. No musician begins to play or sing without first exercising the voice or warming up the fingers. The feeling of having to clear one's mind, of needing some preparation for the service, has always accompanied Jewish worship and has resulted in more and more additions to the service, all of which are preliminary to the required order of prayer itself.

The Mishna tells us that one must prepare one's mind properly before reciting the required prayer, the Amida, and cites the practice of an unidentified group of pietists sometime prior to the destruction of the Second Temple who did this by quiet meditation:

> One should not stand to recite the Prayer unless one is in a serious frame of mind. The pious men of old would pause for an hour

and then pray so that they might direct their hearts toward God. Even if a king greeted them, they would not respond, nor would they stop if a serpent was coiled at their heels.[1]

Over the years this advice was reflected in the addition of many preliminaries to the morning service. Instead of the quiet meditation recommended here, prayers, blessings, and readings from the Psalms and other books of the Bible were suggested, all to the same purpose: "directing the heart" toward God. Eventually some meditations that had been recited informally by individuals became part of the official service, and some prayers and blessings that people had recited in their homes were taken over into the synagogue service.

There has always been much controversy over exactly what was to be said, what was actually required and what was not. Different communities added various readings and hymns, so that the first impression is of a haphazard collection of prayers, blessings, and biblical readings. On closer examination, however, we can see that beneath all these additions and variations the preliminary service has a firm structure. It is composed of two major sections: the "blessings of the morning" (Birchot Ha-Shachar) and the "verses of song" (Pesukei d'Zimra). The core of the Birchot Ha-Shachar is a list of morning blessings concerning activities performed upon arising. The core of the Pesukei d'Zimra is the reading of the last chapters of the Book of Psalms, encapsuled in blessings appropriate for recitation before and after reading biblical words of praise.

The following is an outline of the most important sections found in traditional Ashkenazic Siddurim today:

1. Birchot Ha-Shachar
   A prayer concerning the restoration of the soul
   A series of brief blessings concerning daily activities
   A prayer concerning the ability to pray and including the first verse of the Shema
   Readings from the Torah and from rabbinic writings
   Kaddish recited after studying rabbinic passages
   Psalm 30
   Mourner's Kaddish

2. Pesukei d'Zimra
   Baruch She-Amar (opening blessing)
   Blessing before the biblical passages
   Biblical passages:
      1 Chronicles 16:8–36 (David brings the Ark to Zion)
      Various verses from psalms on God's mercy and protection of
        Israel
      Psalm 100 (thanksgiving)
      Various biblical verses on God's kingship
      Psalm 145 (Ashrei)
      Psalms 146–50 (last psalms of the Book of Psalms)
      Verses beginning with the word *baruch* ("blessed") serving as
        an introduction to—
      1 Chronicles 29:10–13 (David's blessing of God)
      Nehemiah 9:6–11 (the history of Israel until the rescue at the
        Sea of Reeds)
      Exodus 14:30–15:18 (Song of the Sea)
      Verses emphasizing the kingship of God
   Blessing following the biblical passages (Yishtabach)
   Partial Kaddish

In reverse order to their appearance in the service, the "verses of song"
became a part of the regular service first. The "blessings of the morning"
were incorporated later, mainly to make certain that these benedictions,
originally intended for the individual alone, would be said by all. These
blessings also provided an appropriate introduction to the "verses of
song." It seems that even preliminary sections need preparation!

The tone of the preliminary service is very different from that of
the statutory prayers, the Shema and the Amida. The contrast is akin to
that between baroque art or architecture and the classical school. The
basic material utilized in these sections comes from the Bible, thereby
predating the central prayers composed by the rabbis, but the choice of
selections and the new material that was added depart from the simplicity
of line and form, the subdued vocabulary and quiet rhetoric of the formal
service. With its accumulations upon accumulations, material added at
different times and places, the end product is less strict in its logic, freer
in its forms, and more exuberant in style. Psalm follows psalm, verses
from different psalms are woven together, historical events are re-created,

words weighted with powerful connotations are repeated. Like baroque architecture, which delights in curves and extravagant decorations, or baroque music, which is filled with elaborate digressions, so these prayers are intricate and, if not excessive, certainly not reticent in style.

The effect of this style can be very powerful, appealing directly to the emotions and creating a mood of enthusiasm which is very welcome as one prepares for the seriousness of the central prayers to follow. It is not unlike a concert where the first piece is a lively overture which delights the audience and creates an atmosphere of enthusiasm and good feeling so that they will accept the more serious tone of the classical symphony to follow.

This deliberate effect can be experienced best in Sephardic synagogues, where every word is chanted aloud by the entire congregation, as opposed to the Ashkenazic custom of having the leader chant the first few words of each selection aloud, then plunge into silence, and emerge at the end of the section to recite the last few words. Granted that it takes longer, but the effect of the Sephardic style is to feel the accumulated momentum and the resulting enthusiasm more intensely.

The Morning Blessings

Birchot Ha-Shachar, the morning blessings, became part of the public service after it had become customary to recite the "verses of song." Today they form the first part of the morning service, consisting of a collection of hymns, psalms, and sections of the Written and Oral Torah, as well as the blessings from which they derive their name. Most of these are prayers and meditations that were originally intended as private devotions to be said at home before coming to the synagogue. The exact selections and their order differ from one rite to another. We shall discuss the central ones that appear in most prayerbooks in use in the western world today.

The Talmud prescribes a particularly beautiful and meaningful prayer to be recited upon arising:

O my God,
the soul You have placed within me is pure.
You created it,

You formed it,
You breathed it within me,
You guard it within me,
You will take it from me in the future
and will restore it to me in the future-to-come.
As long as the soul is within me
I thankfully acknowledge You,
O Lord my God and God of my fathers,
Master of all deeds,
Lord of all souls.
Blessed are You, O Lord, who restores souls to the dead.[2]

In rabbinic parlance, sleep was considered "one-sixtieth of death." Consciousness is surrendered; the body enters a state of minimal animation. There is no way of knowing if awareness will be regained and physical activity restored. Therefore, to wake to life in the morning is to experience a foretaste of resurrection. It requires us to give thanks to the creator of our soul and our consciousness, and to bless God for life itself.

The blessings that follow have their origins in sayings found in the Talmud and in the Tosefta, a fourth-century work containing material from the mishnaic period. We read there that "a person must recite three blessings each day." In the Tosefta the blessings are: "Blessed is He who did not make me a gentile; . . . who did not make me an ignoramus; . . . who did not make me a woman."[3] The Talmud reads: "who made me an Israelite, who did not make me a woman, who did not make me an ignoramus." One of the Sages suggests substituting "a slave" for "an ignoramus."[4] The current text in traditional Siddurim is: ". . . did not make me a gentile . . . a slave . . . a woman," with women saying: "who made me according to His will," but other versions exist. A Geniza manuscript, for example, reads: ". . . made me an Israelite and not a gentile."[5] Although it is frequently assumed that the reason for these blessings is that a Jew is thankful that he belongs to groups who are obligated to perform *mitzvot*, which these are not, that would not explain the blessing concerning the ignoramus. The Tosefta explains that it is because "an ignorant man does not fear sin." It is more likely that these expressions reflect feelings of pride and thankfulness that the Jew felt for being what he is. Prayers have been found in which Greeks thanked their gods for making them Hellenes and not barbarians.[6] Because of the possible misunderstandings and the offense implied, Siddurim of the Conservative Movement have revised these blessings into a positive mode: ". . . who has made me an Israelite, a free person, in His image."

The other blessings in this litany were originally reactions to the normal actions connected with getting up.[7] A blessing is said when hearing the cock crow: ". . . who gave the cock discernment to differentiate night from day." A blessing is said when first opening one's eyes: ". . . who opens the eyes of the blind." There is a blessing recited when getting dressed: ". . . who clothes the naked" and so on. When the list is completed and we have prayed that we not encounter evil or temptation during the day ahead, we bless God "who performs acts of loving-kindness for His people Israel." The simple acts of waking up, opening our eyes, rising, dressing, and preparing to meet a new day are transformed into a recognition of God's gift of life to us. No one should take life for granted. Each new day is a divine gift.

These blessings were formalized as part of the preliminary service in order to make certain that they would be recited, but it must be admitted that they are much more meaningful when attached to the specific actions of rising, dressing, et cetera. On the other hand, the recitation of each blessing immediately after the other has its own emotional power. This comes not so much from the content of the individual blessings, but from the repetition of the opening words of each of them: "Blessed are You, O Lord our God. . . ." The effect of such repetition is mesmerizing and certainly helps to launch our prayer with a cumulative acknowledgment of the existence of God, the Blessed One. In this respect there is a resemblance to prayers in other parts of the service, such as the poetic proem to the "verses of song": Baruch She-Amar ("Blessed is He who spoke") and Baruch Adonai L'Olam ("Blessed is the Lord forever") toward the end of the preliminary service; the latter two also feature a hypnotically rhythmic repetition of the word "blessed."

By the ninth century these blessings were recited in the service in many places in Spain, even though that did not become the universally adopted practice until much later. It has been noted that in many versions there are eighteen such blessings. It is unlikely that this would have come about accidentally. Rather it seems that an attempt was made to anticipate the recitation of the Eighteen Blessings—the Amida—in the regular service.

We then recite a prayer that was said by Rabbi Judah the Prince when he completed his recitation of the Amida.[8] In it, he prays to be saved from "those who are arrogant and from arrogance, from an evil person, an evil companion, and an evil neighbor," as well as from evil or punishment generally.

Also included in this opening section is a blessing of Torah, readings from the Torah about the sacrifices, and selections from rabbinic literature. In this way the importance of study is emphasized, and even those who cannot devote themselves to intensive daily study have at least minimally fulfilled that obligation.

The prayer concerning the obligation and privilege of praying, Ribon Kol Ha-Olamim ("Master of all worlds"), is a confession originally used on Yom Kippur.[9] In accord with the sense of sinfulness which epitomizes the Day of Atonement, it expresses the lack of worth of the human being:

> What are we, what is our life, what our faithfulness, what our
>   righteousness—
> What is our strength, what our might—
> What can we say before You, O Lord our God?

This section, which was discussed above (see pp. 9–10) also contains the recitation of the line "Hear, O Israel," and in some versions the entire first paragraph of the Shema. This may have been done in order to make certain that the Shema was recited early enough to conform to its prescribed time (from the first light until the end of three hours of daylight).[10] Even the first line by itself was deemed sufficient; Rabbi Judah the Prince considered pausing and saying that one verse a fulfillment of the command to take upon oneself the yoke of the kingdom of God.[11]

The preliminary section includes other hymns intended to be said when entering a synagogue. Among these are the well-known poems Adon Olam ("Master of the universe"), which dates from the fifteenth century, and Yigdal ("May He be magnified"), a poetic version of Maimonides' creed of faith written by Daniel ben Judah in the fourteenth century. Both of these poems have become popular closing hymns as well. Another is Ma Tovu ("How goodly are your tents"), found also in the Siddur of Amram Gaon. This is a compilation of verses beginning with the words uttered by the prophet of the nations, Balaam, who had been hired to curse Israel and wound up blessing it instead:

How goodly are your tents, O Jacob,
Your dwellings, O Israel! (Num. 24:5)

"Tents" was usually interpreted by the rabbis to mean synagogues, so the verse was particularly appropriate. To it were added other verses that speak about coming before God:

But I, through Your abundant love, enter Your house;
I bow down in awe at Your holy Temple. (Ps. 5:8)

O Lord, I love Your Temple abode,
the dwelling-place of Your glory. (Ps. 26:8)

As for me, may my prayer come to You, O Lord,
at a favorable moment;
O God, in Your abundant faithfulness,
answer me with Your sure deliverance. (Ps. 69:14)

The Verses of Song

These prayers and meditations have prepared us for the Pesukei d'Zimra, the verses of song. *Zimra* ("song") refers to the ancient liturgical songs of the Bible, the Book of Psalms. The heart of this section is the recitation of Psalms 146–50, the last five chapters of the Book of Psalms. In some versions of the service, additional psalms were recited as well; some contain as many as thirty-five in all. In our current version, many more psalms are recited on the Sabbath and holidays, when time permits and the atmosphere is more relaxed and festive, than on weekdays. The concluding psalms of the Book of Psalms may have been chosen deliberately in order to symbolize the ancient practice of reading the entire book daily. The second-century sage Rabbi Yose ben Halafta prayed that his portion might be with those who complete the Book of Psalms every day.[12] Since there are one hundred fifty psalms, that would be a difficult though not impossible task. Just as the "early pious ones" meditated for a long period of time before prayer, some of the Sages may have taken it upon themselves to prepare for prayer through the regimen of reciting the entire Book of Psalms. Obviously such a recitation would not be practical for most people; therefore reciting the last psalms in the book came to be a symbolic way of adhering to Rabbi Yose's advice. One "finishes" the book daily—even if one has not completed it.

These final five psalms also form a unit of their own, which is well suited to the task of preparing for worship by meditating on the praise of God. All five begin and end with the word "hallelujah" ("praise the Lord!"). Whatever function these psalms may have served in the period of the First Temple, when taken together they build in intensity to an ecstatic climax of praise. This derives from both the general subject matter and the repetition of the word "hallelujah." Psalm 146 uses this expression four times in all and is a relatively calm description of God as the righteous creator, protector of the weak. Psalm 148, on the other hand, uses the term ten times, and every verse calls on the entire universe and all human beings to praise God.

> Praise Him, all His angels. . . .
> Praise Him, sun and moon. . . .
> Praise the Lord, O you who are on earth,
>   all sea monsters and ocean depths,
>   fire and hail, snow and smoke . . .
>   youths and maidens alike,
>   old and young together.

Psalm 150 is short but intense. Every verse repeats the word *hallel* ("praise") twice.

> Hallelujah!
> Praise God in His sanctuary;
> praise Him in the sky, His stronghold.
> Praise Him for His mighty acts;
> praise Him for His exceeding greatness.
> Praise Him with blasts of the horn;
> praise Him with harp and lyre.
> Praise Him with timbrel and dance;
> praise Him with lute and pipe.
> Praise Him with resounding cymbals;
> praise Him with loud-clashing cymbals.
> Let all that breathes praise the Lord.
> Hallelujah!

As if that were not ecstatic enough, tradition dictates that the last line be repeated. The medieval commentator David Abudraham suggests that it may have been the custom to signal the conclusion of a book by repeating the last line.[13] The word "hallelujah" itself does not mean praise; rather, it is the command *to* praise. This is then carried out by reciting the words of the psalms.

This group of psalms, to which have been added other biblical sections, is enclosed within a set of blessings written by the Sages. These blessings are appropriate for saying when reciting psalms or passages of praise. The opening blessing is preceded by a proem, a poetic introduction, known as Baruch She-Amar ("Blessed is He who spoke").[14]

Blessed is He who spoke and the world came into being.
Blessed is He.
Blessed is He who created the world.
Blessed is He who speaks and acts.
Blessed is He who decrees and fulfills.
Blessed is He who is merciful toward the earth.
Blessed is He who is merciful toward all creatures.
Blessed is He who faithfully rewards those who revere Him.
Blessed is He who lives forever and exists for all eternity.
Blessed is He who redeems and saves.
Blessed is His name.

The traditional Jewish practice is that whenever God's name is recited in a blessing, the congregation responds, *"Baruch hu u-varuch sh'mo"* ("Blessed is He and blessed is His name"). If we combine the second and the last lines of this proem, the result is this response. Not a formal blessing in itself, the proem proclaims God's praise in terms of His role as creator of the world, as described in the first chapter of Genesis. It also stresses the rabbinic value concept of God's quality of mercy. The world, taught the Sages, was created with mercy and kindness, not with strict justice. The repetition of the word *baruch*—blessed—is deliberately calculated to prepare us to recite the blessing that follows:

Blessed are You, O Lord our God, king of the universe,
the God,
the merciful father,

praised by the mouth of His people,

glorified and honored by the tongue of His faithful servants.

We will praise You, O Lord our God, with the songs of Your
    servant David.

With praises and songs [*zemirot*] will we magnify, adore, honor,
    and proclaim Your name,

And we shall crown You as our king, our God,

the only one,

the life of the universe,

king, adored and honored

whose name is everlasting.

Blessed are You, O Lord, king who is praised through
    adorations.

In this elaborate paragraph, which begins and ends with the blessing
formula, one verb is deliberately piled upon another to emphasize the
magnitude of the praise that is due to God. The themes ring out clearly:
we are about to perform the act of praise and adoration and to proclaim
God as king, through the words of David.

The words of praise themselves begin with a long citation from First
Chronicles 16:8–36 describing the ceremony of thanksgiving held by
David when he brought the Ark of the Lord into Jerusalem and set up
a tent there as a sanctuary to God. The key word is *todah* ("thanks"):

Give thanks [*hodu*] unto the Lord;

Call on His name;

Proclaim His deeds among the peoples.

This thankful acknowledgment is made for God's kindness to the people
of Israel in the course of their history, beginning with the covenant of
Abraham, which was fulfilled with the entrance into Canaan, and cul-
minating with the creation of this sanctuary in Jerusalem. The passage
concludes:

And all the people said, "Amen" and "Praise [*hallel*] the Lord."

Thus our praise begins by recapitulating an ancient act of praise and
thanksgiving, reminding us that our worship is a continuation of that
which has been done throughout the ages.

This is followed by a collection of verses from various psalms on the theme of God's mercy, asking His salvation from our oppressors. What the compilers of these verses have done here is quite remarkable. Without adding a word of their own, they have created a new sequence entirely out of verses taken from various places in the Book of Psalms, a sequence that becomes an actual dialogue between God and Israel.

> Show us, O Lord, Your faithfulness;
> grant us Your deliverance. (Ps. 85:8)

> Arise and help us,
> redeem us, as befits Your faithfulness. (Ps. 44:27)

God replies:

> I the Lord am your God
> who brought you out of the land of Egypt;
> open your mouth wide and I will fill it. (Ps. 81:11)

Israel responds:

> Happy the people who have it so;
> Happy the people whose God is the Lord. (Ps. 144:15)

> But I trust in Your faithfulness,
> my heart will exult in Your deliverance.
> I will sing to the Lord,
> for He has been good to me. (Ps. 13:6)

This serves as a perfect introduction to Psalm 100, which is headed "A psalm of *todah* [thanksgiving]." *Todah* is also the name of the sacrifice brought to acknowledge God's kindness. A rabbinic midrash connects this psalm with that sacrifice:

> Enter His gates with thanksgiving [*todah*], His courts with acclamation. Give thanks to Him! Bless His name! (Ps. 100:4). . . . In the world-to-come, all offerings will cease except the thank-offering [*todah*]: this will never cease. All prayers will cease except the prayer of thanksgiving: this will never cease.[15]

To acknowledge God's goodness is equivalent to offering that sacrifice before God:

> For the Lord is good;
> His steadfast love is eternal;
> His faithfulness is for all generations. (Ps. 100:5)

According to the Sages, both the prayer and the sacrifice are eternal, for even in the perfection of the world-to-come, when there will be no need and no sin, we will still want to express our gratitude to God. In some places the custom grew up of not saying this psalm on the Sabbath or other times when the thank-offering was not sacrificed in the Temple.

Psalm 100 is followed immediately by a poesy of verses, mostly ones from the Book of Psalms with a few verses from other books of the Writings. Words from one verse are echoed in the next. These recitations of praise for God lead to the most famous of all liturgical psalms, Psalm 145, known as Ashrei.

Whenever it appears in the Siddur, this psalm is preceded by the two verses that give it its name, since they both begin with the word *ashrei* ("happy"):

> Happy are those who dwell in Your house;
> they forever praise You. (Ps. 84:5)

> Happy the people who have it so;
> happy the people whose God is the Lord. (Ps. 144:15)

The latter verse is the conclusion of the psalm that proceeds Psalm 145. The former is obviously appropriate to recite in a synagogue, even though the "house" originally referred to was the Temple.

Psalm 145 had already been singled out for liturgical use by the Talmud, which interprets the word "dwell" or "sit" to mean that one should sit for some time in the synagogue prior to prayer. Regarding the psalm itself, the Talmud states:

> Whoever recites "A Psalm of David" three times a day is assured of a place in the world to come. . . . It is both alphabetical and says, "You open Your hand and feed every creature to its heart's content." (Ps. 145:16)[16]

Rabbi Yohanan then adds that an additional reason for reciting it is that this psalm, in which each verse begins with a consecutive letter of the Hebrew alphabet, is missing a verse for the letter *nun* and that *nun* is the first letter in the word *nofel* ("to fall"). By deliberately avoiding that unhappy letter, the psalm indicates that Israel will not fall—it will not be defeated. There may be some connection between the idea of reciting Ashrei three times and the threefold repetition of the word "happy" which precedes the psalm in the liturgy. In any case, the talmudic saying was taken literally, and Ashrei is recited here in the "verses of song," later in the Shacharit service, and yet again as the preliminary reading for the Mincha service.[17]

The Ashrei is followed by the group of psalms from the end of the Book of Psalms. They form the heart of this section.

A brief collection of verses from Psalms, all of which begin with the word *baruch* ("blessed"), now serves to introduce the final section of the Pesukei d'Zimra.[18]

Blessed is the Lord forever;
Amen and Amen. (Ps. 89:53)

Blessed is the Lord from Zion,
He who dwells in Jerusalem.
Hallelujah. (Ps. 135:21)

Blessed is the Lord God, God of Israel,
who alone does wondrous things;
Blessed is His glorious name forever;
His glory fills the whole world.
Amen and Amen. (Ps. 72:18–19)

The first and last of these verses are also the respective conclusions of the third and second sections of the Book of Psalms, where they serve the same purpose that they serve here: bringing the collection to an appropriate and enthusiastic conclusion. The hypnotic repetition of *baruch* leads to a blessing, in this case David's proclamation of the blessedness of God to all the people (1 Chron. 29:10). Once again, we see that a historical section has been inserted, describing a ceremony at which David, by tradition the author of the psalms, presided.

We next recite Nehemiah 9:6–11, in which the pledge of the people to renew the covenant of Sinai and accept the Torah is quoted, once again rehearsing the history of Israel, this time from Abraham until the splitting of the Sea of Reeds. The reading breaks off at that point so that it can serve as an introduction to the recitation of the Song of the Sea (Exod. 14:30–15:18).

The recitation of this section is mentioned in the period of the Geonim. In view of the place of the Song of the Sea as *the* song of praise—the archetype of all praise—its recitation here is entirely appropriate. Since all that has been recited is intended to introduce the ceremony of the acceptance of God's kingship—the Shema—the reading is stopped at the verse "The Lord will reign forever and ever" (Exod. 15:18).

Other verses are then appended that specifically stress the theme of kingship:

> For kingship is the Lord's
> and He rules the nations. (Ps. 22:29)

> For liberators shall march up on Mount Zion to wreak judgment on Mount Esau; and the kingship shall be the Lord's. (Obad. 1:21)

> And the Lord shall be king over all the earth; in that day the Lord shall be one and His name one. (Zech. 14:9)

The importance of the verse from Obadiah can best be understood when we remember that after the destruction of the Second Temple, the rabbis used Esau as a symbol of the Roman Empire, while later Esau and Rome were naturally identified with the Christian Church which superceded it. Thus this verse is not a historical reference but a prophecy yet to be fulfilled, that of Judaism's eventual victory over its rivals and persecutors. The final verse, which Zechariah may well have based on the first verse of the Shema (". . . the Lord is our God, the Lord is one"), serves as an additional preparation for the recitation of the Shema.

Having concluded the recitation of these scriptural passages of praise, we close this service with the blessing known as Yishtabach, "to be adored" or "to be praised":

> May Your name be adored forever, O our king,
> *the* God,
> the great and holy king over heaven and earth!
> For unto You, O Lord our God and God of our fathers,

song, adoration, praise, melody [*zimra*], strength, rulership,
eternity, greatness, power, praise, glory, holiness, kingship, blessings, and thanksgiving
are fitting from now until all eternity.

The concluding blessing (*hatima*) is:

Blessed are You, God, king, who is greatly praised, God who is
thankfully acknowledged, master of wonders, who loves the
songs of melody [*zimra*], king, God, life of the universe.

Here too the language is extravagant and poetic, in contrast to the spare
language of the fixed prayers surrounding the Shema and the Amida.
This rhetoric is closer to the free, poetic language used commonly in
midrashic literature. For example, in the Tannaitic midrash to the Book
of Exodus, the Mechilta, when Moses asks God what he should be doing
in the face of the enemy at the Sea of Reeds, God replies:

You should be exalting, glorifying, adoring, uttering song and
praise, greatness, wonder, thanksgiving and praise [*hallel*] to Him
who controls battles.[19]

The vocabulary and phraseology are very similar to those of these blessings of song.

Although it may have started simply as a method of helping the individual
to prepare for prayer by directing the heart toward God, the preliminary
service has taken on a life of its own far removed from the quiet meditation of the "early pious ones." It has acquired its own character and
purpose, well expressed in the blessings that open and close it. It is
intended to be a unit of praise, adoration, melody, and song, based on
the work of the legendary "sweet singer of Israel," David, proclaiming
the wonder of the "king who is praised through adorations." There was
need for a unit of prayer that dealt not with the needs of Israel, nor with
the dogmas Israel must accept and believe, but with the enthusiasm of
worship, the wonder of the world, the appreciation of God's deeds in
nature and in the history of Israel—an unrestrained affirmation of the
beauty of life itself. The feeling engendered by it is strikingly similar to

that captured in a poem by the twentieth-century American poet e.e. cummings:

> i thank You God for most this amazing
> day:for the leaping greenly spirits of trees
> and a blue true dream of sky;and for everything
> which is natural which is infinite which is yes
>
> (i who have died am alive again today,
> and this is the sun's birthday;this is the birth
> day of life and of love and wings:and of the gay
> great happening illimitably earth)
>
> how should tasting touching hearing seeing
> breathing any—lifted from the no
> of all nothing—human merely being
> doubt unimaginable You?
>
> (now the ears of my ears awake and
> now the eyes of my eyes are opened)[20]

It is not always easy to achieve such emotion or to rise to such a pitch of passionate involvement. The preliminary sections of the Siddur can help us to do this and prepare us for the statutory prayers that form the center of Jewish worship.

8

The Shema

AN OPPORTUNITY TO LISTEN

The Shema is undoubtedly Judaism's most famous prayer. Its opening verse, "Hear, O Israel! The Lord is our God, the Lord is one," is common knowledge. Yet, as its full name, Kriyat Shema—the Declaration of Shema—implies, it is not a prayer at all. A prayer is addressed to God. It is an attempt by human beings to speak to the creator, an expression of human feelings, human wants and desires, human desperation or exaltation. Jewish worship, however, has always consisted of both the utterance of the human being and of the opportunity for that human being to hear in return the words directed toward him or her from Heaven. *Shema*—"hear": listen. To listen is as important as to speak, perhaps more so. To hear is as vital to human life as to express oneself. Any dialogue consists of both speaking and listening. Dialogue becomes pointless when one of the parties ceases to listen to the other. The dialogue of worship too becomes pointless when either party turns a deaf ear to the other. We cannot speak for God, but Judaism affirms many times that God "hears prayer." Does the worshiper hear Him?

One of the ways in which God speaks and we listen is through the words of the Bible:

You yourselves saw that I spoke to you from the very heavens. (Exod. 20:19)

However one understands the concept of revelation and the divine character of the Bible, Judaism continues to affirm that, within the Bible, the voice of God can be heard. Because of this, listening to the words of the Bible is one way of listening to God. By including these words within worship, worship becomes a dialogue, even if an indirect and rather stylized one.

The Shema consists of three portions of the Torah—the most sacred section of the Bible—surrounded by blessings composed by the Sages of the rabbinic period and augmented by later poets. Although today these readings and blessings are part of a larger service, they really form a remarkable, self-contained unit. The blessings begin with a call to proclaim the blessedness of God. We praise Him as the creator, as do the celestial beings, and proclaim His kingship. We thank Him for His love, which He bestowed on us through making us His people and giving us the Torah and commandments. We read three paragraphs from that Torah, sections that proclaim the oneness of God and our obligation to love and serve Him, reward and punishment, and redemption. In so doing, we take upon ourselves the yoke of the kingship of God and the yoke of His commandments. The concluding blessings affirm these teachings and recall the redemption of Israel at the Sea of Reeds, looking forward to the redemption yet to come. At night we add a prayer asking for God's protection.

Not only is the Shema the most famous part of the Jewish prayerbook, it is also the most ancient. As we have seen, it was recited daily by the priests as part of their devotions in the Temple. In addition, references to it in the writings of Josephus and in the Gospel of Luke provide evidence of its antiquity.[1] Its Torah sections were recited twice daily by pious individuals during the Second Temple period, at least as a private devotion.

Reading sections of the Torah was an expression of the importance of listening to the word of God. Because of its length, it would be impossible to read the entire Torah every day. So, to make it possible to include the Torah in the daily devotion, selections were taken from it and placed within the context of the service. These selections would both represent the whole and present certain concepts that the Sages felt it essential to stress. So strong was the belief that these sections represented the entire Torah that the Sages taught that anyone who read them each day was considered to have fulfilled the command to study Torah day and night.[2] Nevertheless, they hesitated about informing the populace of this, lest it diminish their commitment to study.[3] To understand why these particular selections were chosen, let us look carefully at the essential ideas they represent.

The Nature of God   The first Torah section, Deuteronomy 6:4–9, is part of Moses' farewell address to the people of Israel. Using the unique name of God—for which we substitute the title Lord (*Adonai*)—twice within the same verse, Moses attempts to crystallize in a few words the essence of his revolutionary doctrine:

Hear, O Israel! The LORD is our God, the LORD is one!

This name of God, the Tetragrammaton YHVH, ceased to be pronounced at all after the destruction of the Temple in the year 70 C.E. For many years before that, it had not been pronounced except at specified times during the Temple service. This name, consisting of four Hebrew letters stemming from the Hebrew root "to be," was revealed to Moses during his initial encounter with God at the burning bush. As that story indicates (Exod. 3:13–15), the name is to be understood as the condensation of the phrase *Ehyeh-Asher-Ehyeh*, variously translated as "I Am that I Am," "I Will Be what I Will Be," "I Am who I Am," or even "I Am Present." This appellation, unlike other earlier names of God, divides the Israelite belief in God from all others. It indicates that God is the being of the world, without whom nothing else exists; the presence which cannot be influenced by magic; the essence of all that is, was, and will be.

What can we know about such a God? Virtually nothing, which is why the Torah is remarkably silent about Him and His essence while very verbal about His demands and requirements. In this one verse Moses attempts to tell Israel as much as they can and need to know: 1) The Lord is our God. A god is that which one worships. Israel is to worship and obey the Lord. 2) The Lord is one. This can also be translated and understood as "the Lord alone"—i.e., He is the only one. If He is the only one, there are no others. Whatever else exists in this universe, He is the only divinity. There is only the Lord, and everything else is *not* the Lord; everything else is that which He created. Pantheism and polytheism are false. He has no rivals. There are not two gods, as Persian religion taught, with its duality of good and evil; nor are there three gods or many gods—but there is God, there is a divine power and ruler of the universe, and He is the Lord, with all that this implies. This powerful, brief assertion cannot be rivaled as the essence of the teaching of Moses. No wonder it became the watchword of Jewish belief.

This first section contains much more. It continues by demanding not only belief in the Lord, but that we love Him:

> You must love the Lord your God with all your heart and with
> all your soul and with all your might.

This demand borders on the absurd. Can anyone command love? We should remember that this is the speech of Moses, not of God directly telling the people that they should love Him. Nevertheless, the assumption is that behind the word of Moses stands the will of God. How does one love God? In what ways? The early Sages themselves pondered this and found no answer except to assert that, of all possible motivations for worshiping God and doing His will, love was the highest and most desirable. Fear, awe, and respect may be part of the human attitude toward God, but love is the strongest motivation and the one that will endure even under the most difficult circumstances.[4] How one achieves it is another question. The Sages thought that constant reiteration of the words of the Torah might help and that the proof of love was to be found not in abstract feeling but in the conduct of life:

> Take these words to heart, for thus you will recognize Him who
> spoke and the world came into being, and you will cling to His
> ways.[5]

The demand that this love be with "all your heart and with all your soul and with all your might" serves to emphasize its rigorous nature. In biblical usage, the heart is the seat of thought rather than of emotion. In today's language we would speak rather of the mind or consciousness. The Sages interpreted the word to mean: with both your good and bad inclinations, or with all the feelings and impulses that you possess. It means to turn them all toward God in total dedication.[6]

The soul means life. Thus the Sages saw the word here as the demand that one be willing to give up life itself because of love of God:

> Even if God takes away your soul, love Him until the last drop
> of life is wrung out of you.[7]

"Might" has been variously interpreted to mean either one's material possessions or, as Rabbi Akiva said,

> Whatever measure God metes out to you, whether of good or of punishment—love Him.[8]

The section continues with the command to study and recite "these words" at all times and to teach them to the following generation. They are also to be placed upon the arm and the forehead, and inscribed on the doorposts and the gates. By "these words," did Moses mean the entire Torah, the speech he was giving, or the verse teaching that God is one? Whatever the answer, later Jewish tradition understood it to mean that this paragraph should be recited daily. This became the basis for reciting it evening and morning as the first part of the Shema and including it in the phylacteries (tefillin) and the mezuza, the container affixed to all doorways.

Reward and Punishment   The second section of Torah readings, Deuteronomy 11:13–21, repeats the demand to love God completely, as well as the command to study these words, teach them, and bind them on the hand and forehead—certainly a good enough reason to have selected this section for daily repetition. It also contains ideas that, while possibly problematic, are basic to Jewish belief:

> If, then, you obey the commandments that I enjoin upon you this day, loving the Lord your God and serving Him with all your heart and soul, I will grant the rain for your land in season. . . . Take care not to be lured away to serve other gods and bow to them. For the Lord's anger will flare up against you, and He will shut up the skies so that there will be no rain. (Deut. 11:13–17)

They are problematic in that in this day of scientific knowledge and greater understanding of the causes of rain or drought, it is difficult for us to believe literally that the presence or absence of rain is an indication of divine favor or disfavor. There is also the moral dimension to consider: is it indeed true that rain ceases when there is disobedience to God or that the presence of rain is an indication that those who receive it are

living according to the divine will? The rabbis of the Talmud may have
had this problem in mind when they coined the phrase "The world
pursues its natural course." They used the illustration of stolen wheat:

> If a man stole a measure of wheat and then sowed it in the ground,
> it is only right that it should not grow—but the world pursues
> its natural course.[9]

Indeed, nature seems totally oblivious to good and evil.

As anyone who is familiar with Israel knows, the presence or absence
of rain there makes a powerful impression. The paucity of natural water
sources makes the Land of Israel almost entirely dependent on rainfall.
With it, the crops grow and the land flourishes. Without it, everything
perishes. It is easy to see, therefore, why both the Torah and later Judaism
seized on rain as the visible symbol of God's reward or punishment. The
rabbis went so far as to imply that He deliberately made the Land of
Israel heavily dependent on the rains in order to assure that people would
be conscious daily of their need for God and grateful for His gifts.

> Rabbi Simeon ben Yochai says by way of a parable: A human
> king had many children and servants who were fed and sustained
> by him. The keys to the storehouse were in his hands. When
> they did his will, he opened it and they ate until they were
> satisfied, but when they did not do his will he locked the store-
> house and they died of starvation. Thus it is with Israel: when
> they do God's will—"The Lord will open for you His bounteous
> store, the heavens, to provide rain for your land" (Deut. 28:12);
> but when they do not do His will, what does it say? "For the
> Lord's anger will flare up against you, and He will shut up the
> skies so that there will be no rain" (Deut. 11:17).[10]

Human beings depend on God for everything. The question is how to
make them aware of it. Larger concepts—such as human life requiring
the ever-present heat and warmth of the sun or the presence of oxygen—
are rather abstract. The rain as a symbol of our dependency is immediately and easily graspable. (In these days of environmental awareness,
we know that human actions indeed can affect the rain and climatic
conditions. Lack of rain may not be a direct result of moral laxitude, but
the ruination of nature can be a result of evil conduct and human greed.)

In biblical language, then, rain represents reward and punishment, and this second paragraph of the Shema affirms that reward and punishment do exist. If the first paragraph is an assertion of the existence of the one God, the second is an assertion that He is a just and concerned God. He is not the divine watchmaker who creates the mechanism of the universe but then departs from it and has no concern with it or with the conduct of human life. Nor is He the capricious god of paganism who toys with human beings that Shakespeare described in *King Lear:*

As flies to wanton boys, are we to the gods;
They kill us for their sport. [11]

The rabbis, recognizing the difficulty of asserting justice in light of experience, were nevertheless unwilling to give up the idea, and they engaged in lengthy and complex discussions of the issue, its relationship to what happens to us in this world, and what may be expected in some world-to-come. They best summed it up in this statement:

It is not in our power to explain either the prosperity of the wicked or the suffering of the righteous. [12]

The Shema asserts that there is a God, a statement that cannot be proved or disproved, an act of faith which may be based on reason and reasonable assumptions but which ultimately requires a decision of belief. The second paragraph further asserts that there is reward and punishment, understand it as you will. The Jewish definition of atheism is: "There is no judgment and no judge." [13] The assertion of these two sections is exactly the opposite: There is a judge and there is judgment. Human actions do not go unnoticed.

The God of Redemption   The third paragraph, Numbers 15:37–41, is mainly concerned with the command to make fringes on the corners of garments. In biblical times these fringes, or tzitzit, were not worn on some special garment, as they are today, but were attached to the corners of everyday garb where they could easily be seen.

That shall be your fringe; look at it and recall all the commandments of the Lord and observe them, so that you do not follow your heart and eyes in your lustful urge. (Num. 15:39)

One cannot see God. In Judaism, one is not even permitted to make a symbolic representation of the Lord. How, then, is one to remember that the God who is concerned with our actions is indeed present? How can one be made aware of His commandments and thereby helped to resist the temptations to evil which are a constant part of human life? The fringes contained a thread of deep blue (until the secret of how to make the dye was lost), a symbol of divine royalty, comparable to the purple of the Roman nobility. Seeing them reminds us of how we are supposed to live in the sight of God. The fringes are a commandment whose only importance and meaning is to remind us of all the commandments. Thus, one way to understand the importance of this section and its inclusion in the daily reading is to see it as the substitute for reading each and every one of the commandments, which, according to the tradition, are 613 in number.

Something else that may explain the presence of this section in the Shema and which certainly adds to its importance is its very last verse:

> I the Lord am your God, who brought you out of the land of
> Egypt to be your God: I, the Lord your God. (Num. 15:41)

The mention of the Exodus from Egypt adds the idea of redemption, another critical assertion which may be said to complete the fundamental ideas the Sages wanted us to affirm twice daily: God is one, the only one; He rewards and punishes; and He redeems.

The Daily Proclamation

The Shema was compiled sometime during the Second Temple period in order to provide an opportunity to listen daily to God's word through chosen paragraphs from the Torah which both represented the whole and presented three basic dogmas about Judaism's belief in God. It soon acquired additional levels of meaning as well.

We know, for example, that the ancient method of saying the Shema was quite different from our own. At a public service, in the presence of a quorum of at least ten adults, the Shema was not merely read; it was "proclaimed" (*pores al shema*).[14] The leader of the ceremony would proclaim to the people that crucial first line: "Hear, O Israel! The Lord is our God, the Lord is one!" At that point, he may have dramatically opened a scroll on which that passage was inscribed and held it up before the people. This proclamation was a reminder and an imitation of the first time Israel was addressed with those words. Just as Moses proclaimed them to the people, exhorting them to attend and live according to them, so the leader takes the role of Moses and speaks to the current people of Israel. In this way the verse became not merely a familiar ritual phrase but an important message, as if it were being heard for the first time:

> They should not be in your eyes like some antiquated edict to which no one pays any attention, but like a new edict which everyone runs to read.[15]

In the ancient town square, a messenger would proclaim an edict of the ruler and affix it to a wall or post. Something that had hung there for a long time grew stale. The Shema was to be proclaimed twice each day as if it had never been heard before.

Upon hearing that verse, the people would respond, using the response that was then commonly used whenever the name of God was recited:

> Blessed be the name of His glorious Majesty forever and ever![16]

This response appears in every Siddur and interrupts the reading of the biblical passages. The appearance of those words right in the middle of the Torah selection has always seemed strange, but it is understandable when seen as a response to a proclamation. The worshipers would then continue with the recitation of the rest of the Shema.

This method of proclaiming the Shema was abandoned, possibly as a result of the Roman persecutions in the second century C.E. when public practice of Judaism was forbidden. Jews continued to say the Shema, but quietly. Once the practice of proclaiming the Shema stopped, the purpose of the response was no longer valid. There can be no response when nothing is said. When everyone recites the first verse of the Shema individually and quietly, or when, as in our day, the entire congregation says it together, a response is out of place. However, it had become such an accepted part of the Shema that it was retained. The only difference was that now it was said quietly, so as not to interrupt the passage from the Bible, rather than being recited out loud. Legends grew up to explain this strange practice. The best known is that it was Jacob's response to his sons when they assured him of their belief in the one God.

> Jacob called his children together when he was about to depart this world and said to them, "Do you have any doubts within your hearts about Him who spoke and the world came into being?" They said to him, "Just as you have no doubts in your heart about Him who spoke and the world came into being, so we have no doubts in our hearts about Him. Rather—Hear, O Israel! The Lord is our God, the Lord is one!" Jacob gave thanks that no unworthy children had come from him and said, "Blessed is the name of His glorious Majesty forever and ever!" The Holy One said to him, "Jacob, all your life you wanted this—that your children should recite the Shema morning and evening."[17]

This ancient rabbinic legend adds a very human and poignant dimension to what otherwise appears a rather austere public declaration. Not so, says the legend: "Israel" means not the people of Israel but the father Israel—another name for Jacob. Jacob, the first of the Patriarchs to have more than one child who would carry on the tradition, had the worries of every father. What will my children be like? Will they be decent human beings? Will they live up to the standards of our faith or—like Ishmael and Esau, the wayward children of my father and grandfather—will they turn away from the true belief? All his life he was troubled by this, but only at the very end did he dare to ask the question: Do you believe wholeheartedly or not? He left this world with a sigh of relief and an utterance of thanksgiving when assured that they would carry on his ways and that they had no doubts. Thus too, implies the legend, every Jew when reciting the Shema morning and evening turns to his ancestor Jacob, the embodiment of all the generations of Israel who have gone before, and assures him: our belief is firm. The Lord is our God, the Lord alone. He is one and unique.

Another legend explained the presence of the nonbiblical response as being words stolen from the angels. Moses, ascending to heaven to receive the Torah, overheard the angels praising God with that sentence. He then taught it to the people of Israel but told them that they must not say it aloud because it did not belong to them. It may be compared, said the rabbis, to someone who steals a precious diadem and gives it to his wife. He tells her, "Everything I have given you I bought with my own funds and you may wear in public; but this I stole. Therefore you may not wear it outside of the house." On the Day of Atonement, the legend continues, the words are said out loud because on that day there is no difference between us and the angels. Then we too are free of sin and free of dependence on bodily needs.[18]

The Yoke of God's Kingship

Yet a third layer of meaning was added to the Shema when the first two sections were interpreted as embodying two rabbinic concepts:

· the acceptance of the yoke of the kingship of Heaven (*kabbalat ol malchut shamayim*);
· the acceptance of the yoke of the commandments (*kabbalat ol ha-mitzvot*)

The Shema became a pledge of allegiance, an oath of loyalty to God the king, followed by a pledge to obey the laws of the king.

The Israelites accepted God as their king at Mount Sinai. The biblical account speaks of God telling them:

If you will obey Me faithfully and keep My covenant . . .
you shall be to Me a kingdom of priests and a holy nation.
(Exod. 19:5–6)

The willingness of the people to accept God as their king was then followed by their willingness to accept the terms of the covenant as enunciated in the Ten Declarations and other laws given by God through Moses.

This may be likened, taught the Sages, to a king who wished to rule over a city. First he had to come to the people and ask if they accepted him as king. They would accept him, however, only after he had proven that he could do things for them. Thus God came to Israel and reminded them that he had taken them out of Egypt and saved them from their enemies. Immediately they accepted Him as their king.[19]

Another parable tells of a king who once came to a city and wanted to proclaim his laws. His advisors told him: Do not proclaim laws until

they have accepted you as king, for they will not obey them. So he asked
them if they would accept him, and when they did so, he told them,
"Now accept my decrees." Thus, once the Israelites accepted God as
their king—the acceptance of the yoke of the kingship of Heaven—they
then accepted His decrees—the acceptance of the yoke of the
commandments. [20]

> Why does [recitation of] the paragraph "Hear, O Israel" precede
> the paragraph "If, then, you obey the commandments"? So that
> we should first accept the yoke of the kingship of Heaven and
> then accept the yoke of the commandments. [21]

The rabbis saw the daily recitation of the Shema as a repetition of the
ceremony at Sinai. Here too the people of Israel accept God's kingship
and His laws. They accept His kingship when reciting the first line of
the Shema. Although that verse does not even contain the word "king,"
the idea is obviously embedded in it. If one acknowledges that the Lord
is our God and there is none other, then one is accepting God's kingship.
The response, "Blessed is the name of His glorious Majesty forever and
ever," specifically mentions kingship in order to make that meaning
explicit. As a matter of fact, this acceptance became so central that
rabbinic law specifies that unless one concentrates and mentally accepts
God as king when reciting those words, one has not fulfilled the commandment of reciting the Shema. [22] Patterning ourselves after the practice
of Rabbi Judah the Prince as recorded in the Talmud, we cover our eyes
with our hand when saying the first line, thus allowing us to concentrate,
to shut out all else, in order to think of God as our king. [23] Similarly we
are to prolong the utterance of the word "one" long enough to mentally
extend His kingdom to all points of the compass. [24] In our days, knowing
what we do of the extent of the universe, that could be a long "one"
indeed!

The daily recitation of the Shema, therefore, plays many roles in the
liturgy and occupies a place of supreme importance in the pattern of
religious life. Judaism affirms that God speaks to man through the verses
of the Torah. To emphasize that, we listen daily to His word, studying
His book through selected passages that both represent the whole and

emphasize the most important ideas upon which Judaism is built: the existence of the one God, reward and punishment, and redemption. These verses, especially the first one, also serve as a declaration of our belief. In the face of the messages from other groups that there are many gods or none, we are daily told: Remember—the one God exists. He is a God without image, for He cannot be captured or controlled; nor can He be described in plastic terms. Even our verbal description of Him cannot be taken as more than hints at His reality. To succumb to idolatry is to create gods and then worship them, to imagine that whatever we have set up represents the ultimate truth. The worship of the one God of the Shema is to reject all of those ideologies and idolatries, and subject ourselves to the greater reality over which we have no control but whose demands have been made known to us. In addition, the act of reciting these paragraphs serves as the oath of loyalty, the acceptance of God's sovereignty over us and of the set of regulations He has given to us.

Sanctifying God's Name

One more layer of meaning has developed over the centuries, and that is the connection with death and martyrdom. Tragically, through the press of catastrophic events, this meaning has become all too common.

The interpretation of the words "with all your might" as meaning that whatever measure He metes out to you, you must acknowledge Him, and of the words "with all your soul" that you must be willing to give up life itself for the sake of God,[25] undoubtedly created the basis for reciting the Shema before death.

The practice of reciting verses from the Torah at the time of martyrdom is recorded in the stories of the very first religious martyrs at the time of the Maccabean revolt.[26] Other contemporary stories that told of the Roman decrees against Judaism in the second century C.E. frequently included the recitation of a verse by the martyred person as an act of *kiddush ha-shem*, the sanctification of the name of God.[27] It is an indication of the martyr's faith in the justice of God. In the words of Job, "Though He slay me, yet will I trust in Him" (Job 13:15).

The first recorded instance of the use of the verse "Hear, O Israel" to indicate acceptance of death and of the righteousness of God occurs in the story of the martyrdom of Rabbi Akiva. As an old man, Akiva defied the Roman decree against the public teaching of the Torah. He was imprisoned at Caesaria and taken out early one morning to be executed. Rabbi Akiva was not seeking a verse to recite but wanted to fulfill the commandment to recite the Shema in the morning:

> When they brought Rabbi Akiva to be executed, it was the time of the recitation of the Shema. Although they were raking his flesh with rakes of iron, he took upon himself the yoke of Heaven. His disciples said to him, "Our master—do you go so far?!" He said to them, "My entire life I was troubled by the verse 'with all your soul'—even if He takes your soul. I thought, If it comes to that, will I be able to fulfill it? And now that it has come about, shall I not fulfill it?" He prolonged the word "one" until his soul departed while he was saying "one."[28]

Akiva's fulfillment of the commandment was also a proclamation of defiance of the Roman authorities. They might kill him, but they could not bring him to deny that God, and no human emperor, was his king! This act was worthy of imitation and served as the classic example emulated by countless others. When reciting the Shema as part of worship, no sensitive person can help but be aware that he or she is saying words uttered by millions of Jews who were slain because of their faith. From Akiva to Auschwitz, believing Jews have proclaimed this verse as they faced the knowledge that because they were Jews they were about to be killed. It has also become the practice for any Jew to recite these words on his or her deathbed, departing this world with the words of Jewish belief on one's lips.

The Blessings of the Shema

The three biblical paragraphs that have been discussed are preceded and followed by blessings. The general outline of these blessings—the number and theme of each of them—was determined long ago, at the very latest by the time of the Mishna in the second century C.E.:

In the morning, two blessings are recited before the Shema and one after it. In the evening, there are two before it and two after it.[29]

Much freedom was given in formulating the text of the blessings of the Shema, and therefore different versions were eventually codified, probably during the period of the Geonim in the ninth or tenth century. Even today, the texts are not uniform and there are differences between the Ashkenazic and Sephardic rites, as well as among various traditions within these two major streams. For all that, the differences are not so great as to significantly alter the meaning. The intention of each blessing is clear. Although we will discuss only the standard Ashkenazic version, the ideas presented will be the same no matter what traditional prayerbook you open.

First we need to know why there are blessings surrounding the Shema at all. Why not simply recite the passages from the Torah? Surely they are the main concern. Rabbinic Judaism, however, prescribed that blessings be recited before and after the ritual recitation of any biblical passage. This is true of the reading of the Torah as part of the service, the reading from the Prophets, the reading of the Five Scrolls at various holidays— and it is true of the Shema as well. Thus the blessing immediately prior to the Shema and the blessing immediately following it really serve first to introduce it as a biblical reading and then to affirm the truth of what has been read.

The other blessings, coming before and after those that immediately surround it, seem to be only tangentially connected to the Shema. Their existence can be best understood when we recognize that originally the Shema was an independent unit, recited not as part of a longer evening or morning service, as is the case today, but simply as a reading or declaration in its own right. In order to make this independent unit more meaningful and more appropriate to the time of day when it is recited, additional blessings were added to it.

One more observation: Just as we distinguished between a prayer— a human being addressing God—and a reading such as the Shema—God addressing the human being—so we should distinguish between prayer and blessing. While both are addressed to God, they serve different purposes. In the technical sense, "prayer" in Judaism is a request; essentially it is the person asking God for something. A blessing, on the other hand, asks for nothing. It concentrates rather on praising God and describing His actions and attributes. Although over the years some brief aspects of prayer have also been incorporated, the blessings are overwhelmingly opportunities for the individual to respond to the presence of God, to become sensitive to the actions of God in the world, and to be reminded of that presence. To bless is even more than to praise. It is to bestow upon God the highest attributes we are capable of imagining and to proclaim Him before the entire world.

The pattern of the blessings of the Shema is:

morning: 1. The Blessing of Light
          2. The Blessing of Torah
             The Shema
          3. The Blessing of Redemption

evening: 1. The Blessing of Evening
          2. The Blessing of Torah
             The Shema
          3. The Blessing of Redemption
          4. The Blessing of Protection

The Call to Bless   In our texts, the first blessing of the Shema is prefaced by a call to the congregation to bless the Lord, commonly called the Barchu from its first word ("bless"). The congregation responds with the words "Blessed is the Lord who is blessed for all eternity."[30] The Barchu, however, is not a general call to prayer. It only appears prior to the recitation of the Shema. It is a call to bless God through the blessings of praise that surround the Shema.

God the Creator   The first blessing of the unit of the Shema, which is also the formal opening of today's service, be it evening or morning, reminds us that we are in the presence of God the creator. Through the experience of the wonder of the world that surrounds us, we are brought

to an appreciation of the divine. This is also an appropriate introduction
to the Shema, since the Shema proclaims the existence of the one God
who is the essence of all being. Thus the theme of creation is joined to
the Shema, so that three themes basic to Jewish belief are explicitly
discussed: creation, revelation, and redemption.[31] On the other hand,
these first blessings are also an apt beginning for worship in the evening
or the morning, a natural reaction to the approach of night or to the rising
of the sun. "In the morning I will seek You," said the eleventh-century
poet Solomon Ibn Gabirol, ". . . I will offer my morning and evening
prayers before You." The daily occurrence of the change from light to
dark or dark to light, the appearance of the sun or its setting, the rising
of the moon and the stars can arouse feelings of awe in anyone. Pagans
worshiped these heavenly bodies as deities in themselves. Israelites saw
them as manifestations of the creation of God. Repeated throughout the
biblical story of creation is the verse "And there was evening and there
was morning." The majestic account of creation begins with "Let there
be light" (Gen. 1:3) and with the account of the separation of "the light
from the darkness. God called the light Day, and the darkness He called
Night. And there was evening and there was morning, a first day" (Gen.
1:4–5). The first blessings of the Shema are poetic elaborations on the
creation of light and the theme of the separation of light and darkness.

In the evening the text is:

Blessed are You, O Lord our God, king of the universe,
Who brings on the evening by His word,
Opens the gates with wisdom,
Changes the times with understanding,
Rotates the seasons,
And sets the stars in the sky in their watches
According to His will.
He creates day and night,
Rolling away the light before the darkness
And the darkness before the light,
Causing the day to pass and bringing on the night,
Separating day from night—
The Lord of hosts is His name.
God who lives and exists forever,

May He reign over us for all time.
Blessed are You, O Lord, who brings on the evening.

The allusion to God's reign echoes the Shema's idea of the acceptance
of God's kingship. The rest of the blessing discusses creation and affords
us an opportunity to bless God upon contemplating the spectacle of the
evening sky.

The parallel Blessing of the Morning has acquired many poetical
enlargements on the theme of light, which appear in different variations
on weekdays and on the Sabbath. Most of these were written to enlarge
upon the idea of light, the theme of the blessing which is clearly enunciated in the opening line, the *peticha:*

Blessed are You, O Lord our God, king of the universe,
Who forms light and creates darkness,
Makes peace and creates everything!

The language of this blessing is taken directly from a magnificent passage
in Isaiah 45:7 in which God asserts His sole authority over everything,
denies the existence of any other gods, and claims credit for all of
creation:

I form light and create darkness,
I make peace and create woe.

Eager to avoid any misunderstanding about this last phrase, which was
intended as a polemic against the dualistic concept of one god who creates
peace and goodness and another who creates woe and evil, the Sages
changed the language, eliminating "woe" and substituting "everything."
They deemed this "more appropriate language."[32] Bezalel Porton has
suggested that there was a more positive reason for the change: the Sages
were not only trying to avoid a theological problem, they were attempting
to make a theological statement and emphasize the totality of God's
creation. He is the source of everything; everything belongs to Him and
Him alone.[33] The connection with the assertion of the Shema that only
one God exists is obvious. The emphasis, however, is on the light of the
morning, which is evidence of the wonders of creation.

The expression *ha-meir la-aretz* ("Who gives light to the earth") in
the succeeding paragraph expands on the theme of creation and emphasizes the rabbinic concept of God's quality of mercy:

Who mercifully gives light to the earth and to those who dwell
   upon it,
And in His goodness daily renews the act of creation.
How numerous are Your works, O Lord.
All of them did You make with wisdom.
The earth is filled with Your creations.

At this juncture, various liturgical poems are inserted into the blessing.
On weekdays we find a poem in which each word begins with successive
letters of the Hebrew alphabet: *el, baruch, gadol deah*—"Blessed, great,
and understanding God."

On the Sabbath, when time is of no consequence, several *piyyutim*
are added, most of which are not specifically connected to the Sabbath
as such. Ha-Kol Yoducha ("Everyone acknowledges You"), for example,
dwells on the idea of creation. The word *ha-kol,* meaning "everyone" or
"everything," serves as a refrain, the *piyyut* concluding with *yotzer ha-kol*
("Creator of everything"). Ein Ke-Erkecha ("none is like You") enlarges
on the theme of God's uniqueness. El Adon ("God, master of all creations") is an acrostic poem that dwells on creation and on "the good
lights our God created."

The hymn L'El Asher Shavat ("To the God who rested from creation") is unusual in having been composed especially for the Sabbath.
Describing God's resting on the seventh day, it interprets the special
psalm of the Sabbath, Psalm 92, not as a poem written to be recited on
the Sabbath but as one sung unto the Lord by the Sabbath itself.

Yet another insertion into the first blessing of the Shema is a section
known as the Kedusha ("holiness"), which appears both on Sabbath and
weekdays. The theme of this section is the daily proclamation by the
angels of God's holiness and kingship. There are three times during the
morning service when a Kedusha is recited. This is the first. The second
is in the repetition of the Amida, and the third is toward the end of the
service. All are based on the same verses from the Prophets. The first—
"And one would call to the other, 'Holy, holy holy! The Lord of Hosts!
His presence fills all the earth!' " (Isa. 6:3)—describes the angels' praise
of God. The second is Ezekiel's vision of the divine chariot, when he
hears the words "Blessed is the Presence of the Lord, in His place"
(Ezek. 3:12). The Sages connected these celestial ceremonies of praise

with the proclamation of God's sovereignty made by Israel on earth. They taught: "The ministering angels do not mention the name of the Holy One on high until Israel mention it below."[34] Thus Israel's praise of God has a cosmic significance. It is an imitation of the angels' proclamation, yet more important than theirs since, to the Sages, Israel praises God more than the angels and has priority over them.[35]

The Kedusha begins with an alphabetical introduction, Kulam Ahuvim ("They are all beloved") describing the angels:

> They are all beloved, they are all chosen, they are all
>   mighty—
> They all do the will of their maker in awe and fear—
> They all open their mouths in holiness, purity, song, and
>   melody,
> Blessing, praising, exalting, lauding, sanctifying, and proclaim-
>   ing the sovereignty
> Of the name of God, the great, mighty, and awesome king.
>   Holy is He!
> They all accept upon themselves the yoke of the kingship of
>   Heaven from one another,
> Giving permission to one another to sanctify their creator
> With pleasure, in clear and pleasant language together they all
>   proclaim "Holy" in reverence—
> Holy, holy, holy! The Lord of Hosts!
> His presence fills all the earth!
> The *ofanim* and holy creatures are borne alongside the *seraphim*
>   with a great sound and praise and proclaim with them:
> Blessed is the presence of the Lord, in His place!

This mystic poem, with its depiction of heavenly creatures celebrating their acceptance of the yoke of God's kingship, adds to the sense of the wonder of creation and provides an introduction to the Shema, which follows shortly. Our recitation of the Shema is the acceptance of God's kingship, just as is the heavenly ceremony conducted by the angels.

A belief in angels is rarely taken seriously today. Yet the poetic imagination can make use of such images without expecting us to accept them literally. How often do we speak of things we know to be factually untrue? The sun does not rise or set, breezes do not murmur or caress, yet these expressions capture the imagination.

Returning to the main theme, this blessing of creation comes to a climax with a series of God's wondrous deeds:

> He alone does wonders and creates new things.
> He is master of battles, sowing victory, causing salvation to
>   sprout up,
> He is creator of healing, awesome in praises, Lord of wonders—
> Who daily renews the act of creation, as it is said:
> "He forms the great lights,
> for His loving-kindness endures forever" [Ps. 136:7].

Piling praise upon praise, description upon description, this becomes a powerful coda to the theme of God as creator. The idea of God's daily renewal of creation is anchored in an interpretation of a biblical verse, "He forms the great lights, for His loving-kindness endures forever." Since the Hebrew verb is in the present tense ("He forms"), this is understood to mean that the act of creation is not something that was done once and for all time. Rather, creation is an ongoing process in which the exuberance of God's power can be seen and felt anew each day.

Since this blessing is a hymn of praise and not a prayer of petition, the next line comes as a surprise.

> Let a new light shine upon Zion, and may all of us be worthy to
> bask speedily in its light.

This is obviously a messianic reference and a petition for God to bring salvation. Saadia Gaon considered it inappropriate. His opposition was not to the idea of salvation; rather he felt that the sentence distracted the worshiper from the basic theme of the blessing—creation—by bringing in a messianic, eschatological thought unrelated to the subject of the paragraph. His qualms, however, had little effect on others. The longing for salvation and redemption among the Jewish people was so strong that these words became a permanent part of the blessing.

The blessing concludes: "Blessed are You, O Lord, creator of the lights."

The Blessing of Torah   The second blessing is known as the Blessing of Torah. It is the blessing recited prior to saying the words of Torah known as the Shema. The Talmud mentions two versions of this blessing; Ahava Rabba ("Great love") and Ahavat Olam ("Everlasting love").[36] These are not really titles, but merely the opening words, which are used to identify the blessing. The two versions were not composed specifically in order to have one appropriate for the morning and another for the evening, which is how they were eventually utilized, but were variations on a particular theme: an introduction to the Shema.

How should we construct a blessing of Torah? The fact that the Talmud terms it "the Blessing of Torah"[37] indicates that the Sages considered the Shema to be essentially a reading from the Torah, a reflection of its origins. Eventually the Ashkenazic tradition chose to use both of these blessings, placing Ahava Rabba in the morning and Ahavat Olam in the evening. Perhaps the fact that the latter is shorter played a role in their choice, since there is a general tendency to lengthen the morning service and shorten the evening one. Evening was not a time to be out late—darkness has always been dangerous. This is the text of the evening blessing:

> With everlasting love have You loved the House of Israel, Your
>   people.
> Torah and commandments, laws and statutes have You taught
>   us.
> Therefore, O Lord our God, when we lie down and when we
>   rise up we will meditate on Your laws.
> We will rejoice in the words of Your Torah and in Your com-
>   mandments from everlasting to everlasting.
> For they are our life and the length of our days;
> We shall think about them day and night.
> Do not ever remove Your love from us.
> Blessed are You, O Lord, who loves His people Israel.

The text is simple and direct. It is almost totally devoid of petition or request—a pure blessing, proclaiming God, His nature, and His deeds. The word that is repeated over and over—the leitmotif of the blessing—is "love." It appears twice in the opening and twice in the conclusion. The word *olam* ("everlasting") appears three times, the last in the form

olamim, meaning "ever" or "forever." God's love is everlasting; our joy
in His gift to us of Torah and commandments is everlasting. Our only
request is that this love indeed be with us everlastingly. Other key words
that are repeated are: Torah, laws, commandments, and the people Israel.

The Lord is characterized by His love for His people Israel. This
love is expressed in His gifts to Israel: Torah, commandments, and laws.
These give meaning to our lives and our days. It is incumbent upon us
to study and think about them at all times. The fact that all versions of
this blessing begin with the word "love" is not accidental. In the Hebrew,
that is the first word of the second line of the Shema: "You must love
the Lord your God." A connection is being made between these two:
there is reciprocal love. God shows His love for us by giving us Torah
and commandments, and we must therefore return this love through all
of our deeds.[38]

The Blessing of Torah used in the morning is much longer and
includes many requests. Nevertheless, the themes we found in the evening blessing are also the basis for this text.

> With great love have You loved us, O Lord our God.
> With overwhelming compassion have You shown compassion to
>   us.
> Our father, our king—
> For the sake of our fathers who put their trust in You and
>   whom You taught the laws of life—
> Be gracious to us and teach us.
> Our father, merciful father—
> The Merciful One!
> Have mercy upon us and permit us to understand, to discern,
>   to heed, to learn and teach, to observe, perform, and ful-
>   fill all the words of instruction of Your Torah in love.
> Enlighten our eyes in Your Torah;
> Let our hearts cling to Your commandments;
> Unite our hearts to love and revere Your name so that we shall
>   never be put to shame.
> For we have trusted in Your holy, great, and revered name.
> Let us rejoice and be happy in Your salvation.
> Bring us in peace from the four corners of the world,

Lead us uprightly to our land,

For You are a God who works salvation.

You have chosen us from all the peoples and tongues and
    brought us near to Your great name in truth

So that we might acknowledge You and proclaim Your unity in
    love.

Blessed are You, O Lord, who chooses His people Israel in
    love.

The frequency of words in a particular paragraph often serves as an indication of the major concerns of those who formulated it. In this version the word "love" appears six times: three of these are in reference to God's love for His people Israel, and three in reference to Israel's love for God. The word "mercy" appears three times, and "compassion" twice. Both of these are cognates of "love." Torah is mentioned twice. Commandments and laws are referred to, and there are four usages of the word "teach" as well as eight other words that refer to understanding and observing Torah and commandments: understand, discern, heed, observe, perform, fulfill, enlighten, and cling. The message is the same as that of the evening blessing: God's love for Israel is expressed through the Torah and commandments He has given us. Our duty is to study them well and observe them. We request God to help us understand the Torah and love Him as we should.

Toward the end, a new theme appears, which was not mentioned in the evening blessing: the request for salvation through bringing Israel back to its land. Petitions for redemption were added to these prayers of praise as the desire for redemption grew in the exiled people. Mentioning the four corners of the world has led to the custom of gathering the four fringes of the tallit together when the words asking for salvation are recited:

Bring us in peace from the four corners of the world.

The four corners of the tallit become symbols of the four corners of the world. We bring them together as God brings His people together. We continue to hold them throughout the recitation, kissing them each time the word "fringes" is mentioned in the third paragraph of the Shema.

If we try to relate the themes in these blessings to the themes in the

Torah passages that make up the Shema, we find that the theme of salvation is connected to the third paragraph, which concludes with the description of the redemption from Egypt. In the rabbinic mind, the redemption from Egypt was not merely an event that took place more than a thousand years ago, but a paradigm of an event that will take place in the future. The ancient redemption was a foreshadowing of the future redemption, when Israel will be released from exile and gathered together once again in its own land. That redemption has been at least partially realized in the creation of the Jewish homeland, the State of Israel.

Many other themes of the Shema are repeated in these blessings. The proclamation of God as one is echoed in the phrase "proclaim your unity." The word "Israel" is reflected in "the House of Israel, Your People," "His people Israel," "You have chosen us from all peoples and tongues," and "who chooses His people Israel." The command to love the Lord is mirrored in "with everlasting love," "with great love," and the many other uses of the word "love" in which the command to love God is also turned the other way—our love of God is a response to His love of Israel. The identification of the LORD (the divine name) as our God is mentioned in the phrases "Your great name," "Your holy, great, and revered name"; the words "your heart" are echoed in "let our hearts cling" and "unite our hearts." The command to think of, recite, and impart these words is found in the phrases "to understand, to discern, to heed, to learn and teach," "teach us," "have You taught us," "we will meditate on Your laws," and "we shall think about them." "When you lie down and when you get up" is repeated in the phrases "when we lie down and when we rise up" and "day and night." The interpretation of the Shema as a reading from the Torah is mentioned in "Torah and commandments, laws and statutes have You taught us," "we will rejoice in the words of Your Torah," "whom You taught the laws of life," "teach us," "all the words of instruction of Your Torah," and "enlighten our eyes in Your Torah." The idea of accepting the yoke of God's kingship and of the commandments is found in the words "our God," "that we might acknowledge You and proclaim Your unity," "we will rejoice . . . in Your commandments," "to observe, perform, and fulfill," and "let our hearts cling to Your commandments."

It is obvious, then, that the formulators of these blessings intended to use them to stress the basic ideas of the paragraphs of the Shema and the purpose of reciting it as they understood it. Thus the blessing prepares us for the recitation, directs our minds to the meaning of what we are doing, and expresses our gratitude to and acknowledgment of God, the source of Torah and commandments which enrich our lives and give them meaning. The blessing prepares us for the act of accepting the kingship of God and obedience to His commandments.

The Blessing Following the Shema   The blessing following the Shema is also found in two interchangeable versions: Emet Ve-Emuna ("In truth and faith") and Emet Ve-Yatziv ("True and steadfast"). Originally the Sages merely determined the themes that should be dealt with in this blessing:

> One who recites the Shema in the morning must make mention of the Exodus from Egypt in the blessing "True and steadfast."
> Rabbi Judah the Prince says: One must make mention of God's kingship.
> Others say: One must make mention of the parting of the sea and the smiting of the firstborn.
> Rabbi Joshua ben Levi says: One must make mention of all of them and conclude with "Rock of Israel and its redeemer."[39]

Taking these requirements into account, individuals would make their own formulations. Eventually different versions emerged and various traditions arose as to which was to be said when. In the Ashkenazic Siddur, once again the shorter one has been placed in the evening service.

> In truth and faith, God has fulfilled all this for us.[40]
> He is the Lord our God,
> There is none beside Him and we, Israel, are His people.
> He rescues us from kings,
> He is our king who redeems us from the grasp of tyrants.
> The God who requites our oppressors and exacts vengeance
>   upon our mortal enemies,
> Who performs great deeds beyond understanding
> And wonders beyond counting.

He keeps us in life
And prevents us from collapsing,
He guides us to rise above our enemies
And exalts us above those who hate us;
He performs miracles for us and vengeance upon Pharaoh,
Signs and wonders in the land of the children of Ham,
He smites with His wrath all the firstborn of Egypt
And takes out His people Israel to eternal freedom;
He causes His children to pass through the divided Sea of
    Reeds;
He drowns in the depths those who pursue them and hate
    them.
His children saw His might,
Praised and acknowledged His name, and willingly accepted
    His kingship upon themselves.
Moses and the children of Israel declaimed the Song [of the
    Sea] with great joy.
They all said, "Who is like You among the gods, O Lord; who
    is like You, glorious is holiness, awesome in splendor,
    working wonders!" [Exod. 15:11].
Your children beheld Your Majesty splitting the sea before
    Moses.
"This is My God" [Exod. 15:2], they declaimed, and said,
    "The Lord will reign forever and ever!" [Exod. 15:18].
And it is said, "The Lord has rescued Jacob and redeemed
    him from the power of one stronger than he" [Jer. 31:11].
Blessed are You, O Lord, who redeemed Israel.

Two major themes are evident here. The first is an affirmation of the truth of what was read from the Torah. This is a dramatic, poetic way of saying "Amen!" The Hebrew word "amen" comes from the root meaning "faith," "belief," or "reliability." In order to identify ourselves with something we have heard, we need not repeat it but merely affirm it by saying "Amen"—I believe it. This blessing begins with the word "true"—we affirm the truth of the three biblical paragraphs we have just recited—and then adds a synonym from the same Hebrew root as "amen," *emuna*, meaning "faithful," "believable," "dependable." The blessing then mentions specifically the major themes of the Shema, which it affirms: that there is no God but the Lord, that we are His people, and that He has rescued and redeemed us from our enemies. These words are reliable and we have seen them come true.

The second theme follows directly from the idea of redemption. It consists of a detailed description of the redemption from Egypt, which, although only briefly mentioned in the third paragraph of the Shema, is one of the major dogmas affirmed by the Shema. We saw that this was also mentioned briefly in one of the blessings before the Shema. Here it becomes the major subject of the blessing. Its emphasis derives from the fact that this blessing immediately follows the recitation of the verse in the Shema mentioning redemption and so is in greater proximity to it. Eventually this blessing also connected the Shema with the prayer that follows it, the Amida, whose major theme is redemption.

Since the ancient practice in the Land of Israel was not to recite the third paragraph of the Shema in the evening because it dealt with the tzitzit (fringes), which are worn only during the day and not at night, there was a debate as to whether or not the theme of redemption should appear in the evening blessing. The decision to do so was based on the Sages' interpretation of the verse "So that you may remember the day of your departure from the land of Egypt all the days of your life" (Deut. 16:3). The phrase "the days," they said, indicates that we are to mention the Exodus during the daytime. The word "all" means that it is to be mentioned at night as well.[41] This is the technical justification for including it. More important is the belief that the redemption of old is too enormous an event not to be mentioned and acknowledged as God's great deed for us, which promises redemption in the future as well.

In order to articulate this second theme, the blessing not only retells the story of the Exodus and the events at the sea, but also quotes three verses from the Song of the Sea:

Who is like You among the gods;
This is my God;
The Lord shall reign forever and ever.

To understand why these particular verses appear here, and why so much emphasis is placed on the events at the sea and the magnificent song of redemption which the children of Israel sang there, we must consider the place of the song in the thinking of the Sages who formulated this blessing.

> When the Holy One, blessed is He, revealed Himself at the sea, no one needed to ask, "Which one is the king?" As soon as they saw Him, they recognized Him and they all proclaimed, "This is my God." Even the humblest maidservant beheld at the sea that which Isaiah, Ezekiel, and all the other prophets had never seen.[42]

The rabbis viewed the salvation at the Sea of Reeds as the supreme experience of God's redemption of Israel. Every Israelite, they taught, actually saw God and could point to Him. Prophets experienced Him in visions, but here even the most humble Israelite beheld God. Not only that, but the experience resulted in the highest point of acceptance of God's kingship ever known. Both the people of Israel and the nations of the world proclaimed the words of this song in order to demonstrate their recognition of the might and power of the Lord, to the exclusion and negation of all who had been worshiped as gods:

> When Israel saw that Pharaoh and his army had perished in the Sea of Reeds, that the kingdom of Egypt was extinct, and that judgments had been rendered against their idols, they proclaimed, "Who is like You among the gods, O Lord." Not only did Israel recite the song, but once the nations of the world heard that Pharaoh and his army had perished in the sea, that the kingdom of Egypt was no more, and that judgment had been rendered against their idols, they all rejected their idols and began to acknowledge God, saying, "Who is like You among the gods!" We also find that the same thing will happen in the future, when the nations of the world will reject their idols.[43]

This verse, "Who is like You among the gods, O Lord," is quoted in the blessing after the Shema and came to represent the acceptance of God's kingship and the total rejection of idolatry. It was this verse above all others that symbolized the acceptance of God by Israel and by all mankind, both in the past, at the sea, and in the future, at the end of days.

It is clear that these rabbinic concepts and legends are incorporated as a hidden subtext beneath the words of the blessing, so that the events at the sea are described not merely in biblical terms but as the Sages understood them: the time of complete revelation of God and His acceptance by all. Thus we conclude the unit of the Shema by emphasizing the last line of the third paragraph: "I the Lord am your God, who brought you out of the land of Egypt to be your God; I, the Lord your God" (Num. 15:41). This classic, archetypical redemption also set the stage for the redemption that is to come. It has always been the hope of Israel that its subjugation to the nations of the world would end, that Jewish independence would be restored, and that this would lead to a time of universal peace and recognition of the one true God. If this redemption has been realized in part in our days, there is much more that awaits us in the future.

The Song of the Sea, quoted so extensively, serves three purposes. It is the principal example of redemption, for which we thank and praise God, connecting it with the end of the third paragraph of the Shema. It is the text that first served as Israel's acceptance of the kingship of God, thus tying it to the first paragraph of the Shema. And it is the paradigm of the future redemption for which we pray, the time when once again we will sing a song of triumph.

The morning version of this blessing begins with similar terms:

> True and steadfast, firm, enduring, right, faithful, beloved, precious, wonderful, pleasant, awesome, mighty, correct, acceptable, good, and lovely is this for us forever.

This great "amen," much expanded from the evening version, continues, repeating and emphasizing the word "true":

> True—You are the everlasting God, our king, the Rock of
>   Jacob, the shield of our salvation.
> He exists and His name exists through all generations;
> His throne is firm and His kingship and faithfulness exist
>   forever.
> His words live and exist, are faithful and precious throughout
>   all eternity.
> For our ancestors and for us,

For our children and all our generations and all the generations
    of the seed of Israel Your servant,
For the first generations and the last,
Good and everlasting is this word.

True and faithful is it, a law that will never pass away.
Our king, the king of our ancestors,
Our redeemer, the redeemer of our ancestors,
Our creator, the Rock of our salvation,
Our rescuer and savior—this is Your name from everlasting.
There is no God except for You.

You have ever been the help of our ancestors,
The shield of salvation for their children after them in every
    generation.
Your dwelling is in the heights of the world,
Your judgments and righteousness are to the ends of the earth.
Happy is the person who listens to Your commandments,
Who places Your Torah and Your words upon his heart.

Note how key words from the Shema—listen ("hear") and "heart"—
are echoed here.

Having affirmed the kingship of God and the truth of His Torah, the
blessing continues, emphasizing God's role in the salvation of Israel
throughout its history. This provides another setting for a reenactment
of the salvation at the Sea of Reeds.

True—You are the master of Your people
The heroic king who fights their battles.
True, You are the first and You are the last.
Besides You, we have no king, redeemer, or savior.

From Egypt You redeemed us, O Lord our God,
From the house of slavery You saved us.
All their firstborn You killed, but Your firstborn You redeemed.
You split the Sea of Reeds,
You drowned the haughty,
You caused Your precious ones to pass through,
You made the waters cover their enemies,

Not one of them remained!

For this Your beloved praised and exalted God,
Your dear ones sang melodies, songs, praise, blessings, and ac-
    knowledgments of the king, the God who lives and exists.
High and exalted, great and awesome,
Bringing down the haughty and raising up the lowly,
Freeing the imprisoned and rescuing the humble,
Helping the poor and answering His people when they cry out
    to Him.

Praises unto the Most High God!
Blessed is He and the source of blessing.
Moses and the children of Israel declaimed the song unto You
    with great joy. They all exclaimed—
"Who is like You among the gods, O Lord,
Who is like You, glorious in holiness, awesome in splendor,
    working wonders."
Those who were rescued praised Your name with a new song
    at the shore of the sea,
Together they all acknowledged You and proclaimed You king,
    saying, "The Lord shall reign forever and ever!"

Once again the verses from the Song of the Sea that proclaim the acceptance of God and His kingship are invoked, and following this description of the first redemption, the blessing concludes by urgently
petitioning God to repeat His act of redemption. Once again the exile's
desperate need for rescue intrudes upon a blessing of praise and turns it
into a petition for salvation:

Rock of Israel!
Arise and help Israel!
Rescue—as You promised—Judah and Israel!
Our redeemer—the Lord of Hosts is His name—the Holy
    One of Israel!
Blessed are You, O Lord, who redeemed Israel.

The word "Israel," the second Hebrew word in the Shema, becomes
the last word of the blessing following the Shema, repeated five times,

at the conclusion of each phrase of this poetic creation. At the beginning of the Shema, Israel is addressed and bidden to listen and be faithful to God. At the end, God is addressed and bidden to be faithful to His word that He will come to the rescue of Israel.

The very last words, "who redeemed Israel," are in the past tense. This is appropriate for the references to the sea, a redemption that took place in the past and for which we thank the Lord. It is not appropriate when we consider that the end of the blessing has become a petition for immediate redemption. God should be called "redeemer of Israel," one who acts now and in the future, not described according to His past actions. The ancient version used in the Land of Israel concluded with "Rock of Israel and its redeemer," which is more in keeping with the spirit of the text.[44]

Prayer for Protection   In the evening service, one more paragraph follows this Blessing of Redemption. Known as the Hashkivenu ("Let us lie down"), it differs significantly from the other blessings of the Shema. Although a connection is established through the opening word, which is taken from the verse "when you lie down and when you get up" (Deut. 6:7) in the first paragraph of the Shema, the rest of the paragraph is a petition for safety through the perils of the night. The weekday version reads in part:

> Let us lie down in peace, O Lord our God,
> And let us arise unto life, O our king.
> Spread over us the tabernacle of Your peace. . . .
> Protect us and remove all enemies from us. . . .
> Blessed are You, O Lord, who guards His people Israel
>   forever.

While the other paragraphs surrounding the Shema are blessings of praise closely connected to the paragraphs from the Torah, in this petition we ask God's protection against the darkness and the forces of darkness. When we remember that the Shema and its blessings were originally a unit recited by themselves, it is understandable that in the evening one would have wanted to add a request for God's assistance and protection through the night. In the morning there is no similar fear and therefore no parallel prayer.

The Significance of the Shema Today

The daily recitation of the Shema provides us with an opportunity to reacquaint ourselves with the basic doctrines upon which the faith of Israel was built when first proclaimed by Moses and which remain the foundations of Jewish faith today. Throughout the centuries sages and philosophers have expounded these concepts and reinterpreted them in light of new currents of thought and conditions of life: the existence of one God whose unity signifies a universe of order and not chaos; a God of moral and ethical concern giving existence meaning and hope; a God whose acts of redemption are an assurance for a better future. The Shema is an assertion of faith and certainty against currents of nihilism, meaninglessness, chaos, and amorality. One who recites the Shema resembles the children of Jacob who respond to the question: Is there doubt in your heart regarding the existence of Him who spoke and the world came into being? "We have no doubts in our hearts."

This testimony is especially important today, when belief and identification with the Jewish tradition and the Jewish people cannot be taken for granted. Living in a modern, postemancipation world, in secular, democratic societies, we welcome periodic opportunities to remind ourselves of our belief and to reaffirm our identity.

The formulation "Hear, O Israel, the Lord is our God, the Lord is one!" remains the definitive declaration of Jewish belief. It is as close as we can come to providing a description of a divine reality, which is by definition indescribable. We emphasize the name of God—the very unutterability of which expresses the inability of the human mind to fathom the divine. We do not even pretend to be able to describe the Lord whose name represents existence and being. We say of Him the least and the most we can say—that of all that exists, of all we know and do not know, of all we experience, we make Him alone our God. Whatever else humans may worship—other deities, human beings, nations, flags, ideologies, wealth, or power—we worship only Him. His oneness means that the world in which we live is a harmony; it is a universe and not a battlefield of warring forces. Beyond it and beneath it there is unity of will and purpose.

Understanding the Shema as a pledge of loyalty to that One, there is need to recite it and thereby to reject the false ideologies and lesser loyalties that compete for our minds and souls. As the story of Akiva's martyrdom indicates, there is great freedom in knowing that ultimate loyalty belongs only to the Ultimate Reality, who alone can command our love and our obedience.

One need not believe literally in physical reward and punishment to accept the doctrine of the second paragraph of the Shema. Its importance is not in the specific way in which it was formulated and concretized, but in the very assertion that there is meaning in our actions, that there is responsibility for what we do. The human echo of the existence of that Ultimate Reality is that there also exists ultimate responsibility. If man is not the master of the world but is accountable to a greater power, our actions take on grave importance and must be carefully measured.

The Shema is a declaration of the continuity of the Jewish people in which we affirm to our ancestors that we remain loyal. We reenact the theophany at Sinai, repeating the words of Israel "We will heed and obey," taking upon ourselves the yoke of God's kingship and the responsibility to seek out His ways in the world and live by them. We also affirm the unity of the world and of mankind, for all that exists is the work of one God. We reject the power of false gods and the validity of false ideologies, and open our hearts to that which is true and eternally enduring.

9

The Amida

AN OPPORTUNITY TO SPEAK

*I*n traditional Jewish usage, "prayer" and the Amida are synonymous. When we use the word "prayer," we usually mean any attempt on our part to express ourselves to God, be it in thankfulness, in praise, or in an attempt to solicit God's help. Within the structure of formal Jewish worship, however, "prayer"—*tefilla*—always refers to one specific prayer, the Amida. The Sages called it *ha-tefilla*—the Prayer—almost as if there were no other. Today it is usually referred to as the Amida, the prayer said while standing, or the Shemoneh Esrei ("The Eighteen") because of the number of separate paragraphs (usually called *berachot*—blessings) it originally contained. The common rabbinic phrase "to stand to pray" always refers to this prayer.[1] The requirement to stand also distinguished it from the Shema, which could be recited in any position: standing, sitting, lying down, or walking.[2] This is understandable when we remember that the Shema is considered to be a recitation of Torah, while the Amida is a prayer addressed directly to God. One does not come before God in less formal style than one would come before a human ruler. This also explains why there are actions, such as bowing and moving forward and backward, during parts of the Amida that imitate the choreography of court etiquette. Bowing—bending first the knees and then the upper body—is performed the first two times the words "Blessed are You, O Lord" are recited and then again toward the conclusion, at the beginning and end of the paragraph of thanksgiving ("We thankfully acknowledge"). Before beginning the recitation of the Amida, one is to move backward and then forward three steps, and, at the conclusion of the Amida, to step back three steps and bow in each direction.[3] All of this helps to concretize the prayer and make one conscious that one is not merely uttering words, but is standing in the presence of God and addressing Him. Such considerations explain the insistence on having the worshiper face toward the Temple in Jerusalem when reciting the Amida, since the Holy of Holies in the Temple was thought of as the symbolic dwelling place of God's Presence, the *Shechina*.[4] Thus all the prayers of Israel are directed toward one place, toward the God who, as it were, "dwells in Jerusalem."[5]

The Amida is so important that it is recited at every service. It is composed of the requests *(bakashot)* that the Sages decided should be recited by everyone. The emphasis is on petitions. Where other parts of the service may stress the praise of God, the Amida's purpose is to ask that God grant our needs, both personal and communal.

Originally, the rabbis viewed this prayer as an independent unit, with its own regulations. It was separate from the recitation of the Shema and was not a part of a larger order of service, as it is today. The Shema and the Amida developed independently, with different purposes and different origins.

The rabbis considered the Shema to be biblically prescribed. The verse "Recite them . . . when you lie down and when you get up" (Deut. 6:7) was understood as a command of the Torah requiring us to recite these passages twice daily, once in the evening and again in the morning. The Amida, on the other hand, was the creation of human beings, and the decision as to when to recite it was made by the rabbis themselves:

> One hundred and twenty elders, among whom were several prophets, ordained eighteen blessings according to a specific order.[6]

> Just as the Torah fixed the times of the Shema, so the Sages fixed the times of the Prayer.[7]

Although Maimonides and others authorities believed that the Torah commands us to pray, the specifics of what must be said and the requirement to recite certain prayers at certain times were a rabbinic enactment.[8]

The times of recitation of the Amida—evening, morning, and afternoon, with an additional time on Sabbath and holy days—were associated with the times when sacrifices were offered in the Temple: "The Prayer is recited at the times when the Tamid sacrifice would be offered."[9] Although this correspondence to the offering of the Tamid sacrifice was correct concerning the morning and the afternoon, there was no evening offering in the Temple. Therefore the Sages had to resort to a rather farfetched connection between the evening service and the sacrifices: they said that the evening Amida was recited because the limbs and other parts of the sacrificed animals continued to burn on the altar all through the night.[10]

It is much more likely that the set times were really a reflection of the natural division of the day into three parts and the desire to pray to God during each of those times. This is the concept underlying the midrash that indicated that the fathers ordained the three daily prayers, each at a different time of the day:

> Abraham ordained the morning prayer, as it is said, "Next morning, Abraham hurried to the place where he had stood before the Lord" (Gen. 19:27), and "standing" always means "praying."
>
> Isaac ordained the afternoon prayer, as it is said, "And Isaac went out to meditate in the field toward evening" (Gen. 24:63).
>
> Jacob ordained the evening prayer, as it is said, "He entreated the Lord there at night." (Gen. 28:11).[11]

The day has a natural rhythm. The same impulse that led to the institution of sacrifices at different times of the day also led to the determination that one should address oneself to God three times a day. The attainment of the feeling of being in the presence of God requires continual effort and must be renewed not only daily, but at regular times within the day.

In the words of Rabbi Samuel bar Nachman:

> [The three prayers were instituted] to parallel the three different periods of the day. In the evening one should say: May it be Your will, O Lord my God, to take me out of darkness into light. In the morning one should say: I give thanks unto You, O Lord my God, for taking me out of darkness into light. In the afternoon one should say: May it be Your will, O Lord my God, that as You have allowed me to witness the rising of the sun, so You will allow me to witness its setting.[12]

The Structure of the Amida

The Amida is divided into three sections, each with a character of its own:

The first three—one resembles a slave praising his master.

The middle ones—one resembles a slave who asks his master for a favor.

The last three—one resembles a slave who has received a favor from his master and departs, going on his way.[13]

The pattern is to begin with praise, then to present one's requests, and to conclude with praise and thanksgiving.

The central section is crucial: the Amida is a prayer in which we petition God for our needs. The introductory blessings merely create the appropriate setting for the requests that follow, since it would not be proper to make a request before praising God.

This may be compared to an advocate, standing on the podium, who opens not with the needs of his client but with the praise of the king. "Happy is the world because he is its king! Happy is the world because he is its judge! The sun shines on us for his sake. The moon shines on us for his sake." The audience joins him in praising the king. . . . So too the Eighteen Blessings, which the early prophets ordained that Israel should recite daily, commence not with the needs of Israel but with the praise of God: "The great, mighty, and awesome God. You are holy and Your name is awesome." Followed by "Who releases the captives" and concluding with "Who heals the sick" and "We thankfully acknowledge You."[14]

Praise is not seen as unimportant, but it is not the ultimate purpose of the Amida. The blessings recited before and after the Shema are pure praise—that is the very definition of a blessing. On the other hand, a prayer in the technical sense is a request, a petition. Thus, no matter what the occasion, the central part of the Amida always contains some sort of petition.

The tripartite structure of the Amida also reflects the fact that the middle part is flexible and changes to fit the occasion, while the first and third parts always remain the same. Thus the complete structure of the weekday Amida—from which the name Eighteen was derived—consisted of three opening paragraphs praising and describing the nature of God to whom the prayers are to be addressed, followed by twelve petitions, and concluding with three final blessings which the rabbis described as thanksgiving or praise.

On the Sabbath and holy days, those middle twelve petitions are omitted and paragraphs appropriate for the specific day are substituted. The Sabbath is not a time to direct one's thoughts toward one's needs but to rejoice and enjoy the world God has made. As the rabbis astutely understood, even mentioning such matters as illness or the need for good crops will sadden us and detract from the joy of the Sabbath, which is intended to be a time at least a little like the world-to-come, free of trouble and need. The twelve petitions were eventually enlarged to thirteen, but the ancient name Eighteen was always retained.

Introductory Blessings   The first three blessings have been called blessings of praise. That simple designation, however, does not do justice to these sections and their complex meaning. When taken as one large unit, these first three paragraphs, known respectively as Patriarchs, Wonders, and Holiness, are actually an attempt at a description and definition of God. In this way they differ from all other sections of the Amida. They are not only praise, but an affirmation of Jewish belief concerning the nature and actions of God. Praise may be important in sensitizing us to God's presence in the world and a necessary part of human attempts to refine our nature, but it is certainly not needed by God. If anything, He tolerates it for our sake. Thus Rabbi Hanina sarcastically reprimanded one who changed the wording, adding words of praise which had not been included in the official formula:

A certain person once led the prayers in the presence of Rabbi Hanina thus: The great, mighty, awesome, powerful, strong, and brave God.

Rabbi Hanina explained that we would not dare use the words

"great, mighty, and awesome" had they not been written by Moses in the Torah and decreed by the men of the Great Assembly.[15]

More crucial than praise is our need to be aware of and consider the nature of the one to whom we wish to turn in petition. There is a custom of inscribing the phrase "Know before whom you stand" at the front of the synagogue. It is not coincidental that the name of the central prayer is derived from the same word, "standing." Thus we are advised to be aware of God when we stand in prayer. This awareness can be attained through a careful consideration of the introductory paragraphs. Addressed directly to God—as are all blessings—they are also addressed to us. They help us understand before whom we pray and serve as a confession of belief. They come as close to being an official creed of Jewish belief as we have. Consider the first paragraph, the Patriarchs:

> Blessed are You, O Lord our God and God of our fathers,
> God of Abraham, God of Isaac, and God of Jacob.
> The great, mighty, and awesome God;
> Supreme God,
> Who performs acts of loving-kindness,
> Creator of all,
> Remembering the faithfulness of the fathers
> And lovingly bringing the redeemer to their descendants
> For His own sake.
> Helping, saving, and protecting king!
> Blessed are You, O Lord, protector of Abraham.

It is immediately obvious why this paragraph acquired the name Patriarchs *(avot)*. Some versions conclude with the phrase "protector of the Patriarchs" rather than merely "protector of Abraham." We are in the presence of the God of history, embarking on a journey back to the beginnings of the people of Israel, returning to the earliest times of the Patriarchs, when the relationship between God and their descendants was established. God was not then referred to in abstract terms, as He was later by Moses, but as one who had a direct and personal relationship with these individuals. He is called the "protector" (or "shield") of Abraham (Gen. 15:1), "the Fear of Isaac" (Gen. 31:42), "the Mighty One of Jacob"

(Gen. 49:24). It was this relationship, in which God personally chose and blessed each of these fathers, that was carried with the people of Israel into their Egyptian bondage. When God speaks first to Moses at the burning bush, that is how He identifies Himself:

> He said, "I am the God of your fathers, the God of Abraham, the God of Isaac, and the God of Jacob." (Exod. 3:6)

This is repeated when Moses is told to tell the Israelites:

> The Lord, the God of your fathers, the God of Abraham, the God of Isaac, and the God of Jacob, has sent me to you. (Exod. 3:15)

This phrase is repeated again in the very next verse. Small wonder that the rabbis chose to construct the opening of the Amida from these verses. The term "supreme God" is also a reference to this early period, coming from the blessing with which Melchizedek, king of Salem, blessed Abraham:

> Blessed be Abraham of the Supreme God [or: God Most High],
> Creator of heaven and earth.
> And blessed be the Supreme God,
> Who has delivered your foes into your hand.
> (Gen. 15:19–20)

Thus it is the God of history, the creator of heaven and earth, the God who chose Abraham whom we address. It is equally obvious that the true subject of the blessing is not the Patriarchs but God and His relationship to them. What did He do? What does He do? He creates all, He is faithful to all, He rewards all, and—in the future—He will bring redemption to the descendants of those fathers with whom He established His covenant. He can be depended upon. The use of the present tense throughout the blessing is an indication that the power of God is continuously at work and that the act or process of redemption is actually going on at every moment.

The reference to the fathers also serves to remind us of who we are. When we stand before God in petition, we stand there not only as individuals living in the present day but as descendants of these great people with whom God had a special relationship. We are not alone, but part of a long and great tradition.

Many prayers contain phrases taken from the Bible. The first paragraph of the Amida is almost a pastiche of biblical phrases. Besides those already cited, it contains a quotation from the Book of Deuteronomy: "the great, mighty, and awesome God" (Deut. 10:17). This threefold description of the indescribable God was viewed by the Sages as a classic definition of God. It is quoted in other parts of the Siddur as well.[16] It is even possible that the three opening paragraphs of the Amida are based on it, inasmuch as the first paragraph describes the greatness of God (supreme God, creator of all); the second, the might of God; and the third, His quality of awe—another term for holiness. The importance of the phrase is emphasized by the fact that it is quoted in Nehemiah, as was noted by the Sages:

> Moses established the appropriate form of prayer, "The great, mighty, and awesome God" (Deut. 10:17).
>
> Jeremiah said, "The great and mighty God" (Jer. 32:18)—eliminating "awesome." Why did he say "mighty"? One who can watch the destruction of his house and say nothing may be called "mighty." Why did he not say "awesome"? "Awesome" refers to the Temple [which was to be destroyed].
>
> Daniel said, "The great and awesome God" (Dan. 9:4)—eliminating "mighty." His sons have been captured and imprisoned, so where is His might? Why did he say "awesome"? It is appropriate to call Him awesome in view of the awesome things He did regarding the fiery furnace.
>
> The Men of the Great Assembly restored greatness to the one to whom it is due, as it is said, "The great, mighty, and awesome God" (Neh. 9:32).[17]

According to the tradition, these same Men of the Great Assembly were the ones who instituted this very prayer.[18]

If the first paragraph stresses the greatness of God, the God who has revealed Himself in our history, the second (Wonders) concentrates on the revelation of the miraculous powers of God through nature, those "miracles which are daily with us," to quote a phrase that appears else-where in the Amida, as well as the miracle of resurrection expected in the future.

> You are mighty forever, O Lord.
> Reviver of the dead are You,
> Powerful to save.
> Causing the wind to blow and the rain to fall.
> Sustaining the living with steadfast kindness,
> Reviving the dead with great mercy.
> Upholding the fallen,
> Healing the sick,
> Freeing the fettered,
> And keeping faith with those who sleep in dust.
> Who is like You, master of might.
> Who is similar to You,
> King who brings death and revives and causes salvation to
>   spring forth.
> Faithful are You to revive the dead.
> Blessed are You, O Lord, reviver of the dead.

The opening paragraph mentioned that God "performs acts of loving-kindness." Here these acts are enumerated. Anything done to help others is considered an act of loving-kindness. It is so important that the rabbis counted it as one of the pillars upon which the world stands.[19] Human beings imitate God when they perform such deeds, which are here as-cribed to God—helping the sick, freeing those imprisoned, and feeding the hungry. God's actions, however, are on a much larger scale and are a sign of His great powers.

In the version of the blessing that has come down to us, the subject of the resurrection of the dead forms the framework of this paragraph, although it is actually only one example of the powers of the Almighty. This idea appears at the beginning, the middle, and the end. All else is woven around it. The emphasis is understandable when we realize that the doctrine of the resurrection was an innovation in Judaism which came into existence during the period of the Second Temple and was not universally accepted. As a matter of fact, it was one of the main disputes between the two major groups within Judaism at that time—the Pharisees who advocated it and the Sadducees who denied it. So fierce was this dispute that the Sages placed "those who deny that the resurrection of the dead is taught by the Torah" first on a list of people "who have no share in the world-to-come."[20] It was for this reason that the Pharisees placed so much emphasis on it and featured it so prominently in their official prayer. Thus it would be impossible for any Sadducee to lead such a public prayer. Very near the beginning of the recitation, he would confront words he could not possibly utter. When we remember that these opening paragraphs are not only praise for what God does, but also credal recitations, this repetition of the idea that God gives life to those who lie in dust falls into place.

Biblical religion separates the realm of the dead from the realm of God. Although some shadowy existence after death is posited, as can be seen from the story of the witch of Endor, in which Saul has the spirit of Samuel conjured up for consultation (1 Sam. 28:8–19), the psalm puts it neatly: "The dead cannot praise the Lord, nor any who go down in silence" (Ps. 115:17). Death means "being gathered to [your] fathers" (Gen. 25:8), but for all the later attempts to read it in, the Torah makes no mention of any life or resurrection thereafter.[21] Since concepts of immortality did exist in the ancient world in abundance, it seems strange that the religion of Israel studiously avoided them. Perhaps this was a reaction to the overemphasis on the afterlife found in Egyptian religion, with its cult of the dead, or it may reflect a fear of establishing an ancestor worship which would damage the purity of the monotheistic belief. The Torah warns against such worship of the dead. When setting aside a tithe, one has to declare, "I have not deposited any of it with the dead" (Deut. 26:14). The realm of the dead was the realm of the impure. It could not, however, remain that way forever. Human beings find it difficult to contemplate their complete obliteration. Having life and consciousness, it seems impossible to believe that these may be taken from us permanently. Certainly we do not want this to happen. Nature-based religions have seen in the very cycles of the earth's seasons and the renewal of crops proof that death is not final. Judaism found it in the unlimited powers of God, who can revive the earth through rain and similarly revive human life. It became inconceivable to Jews that there could be a realm beyond the power of God, and eventually the religion, which had put aside consideration of human immortality—if not actually denying it—found a way to include the dark realm of death within the kingdom of God as well.

The immediate cause of this reconsideration was the martyrdom of the Maccabean period, the second century B.C.E. The deaths both of civilians who were killed because they refused to disobey the Torah and of soldiers who died in a holy cause brought people to seek the reassurance that such deaths were not in vain, that God would not permit such a thing as the total extinction of a righteous person to happen. The idea of a resurrection is found first in the Book of Second Maccabees. It is mentioned in the well-known story of the martyrdom of seven brothers:

> You—the wicked one—remove us from this world, but the everlasting king will wake us—the dead—for the sake of His Torah—to return to everlasting life![22]

The Pharisees taught that not only the soul but also the body survived. The revival of the dead meant the resurrection of the body along with the soul. This belief too must be seen in the light of the Jewish concept of the body. In Greek thought, although the cult of the body was taken to the extreme, it was, as Plato made clear, the soul and not the body that was immortal and divine.[23] Jewish doctrine, while dividing the human being into body and soul, and even considering the body as that which is created from the earth and the soul as that which is created from heaven, nevertheless held the body in great respect. It was not only the creation of God but even the image of God. No less a Sage than Hillel could say that when he went to bathe, he was doing a great thing because he was cleaning the very image of God!

> If the images of kings which are placed in theaters and circuses are cleaned and polished by those in charge of them—and such people are even given great honors—how much more must this be so for us who have been created in God's image and likeness?[24]

Thus Pharisaic Judaism created a doctrine of immortality that reflected its positive attitude toward the body as a divinely created entity, sharing with the soul credit and responsibility.

In explaining the concept of the judgment of body and soul, Rabbi Judah the Prince told this parable:

It may be likened to a human king who had a beautiful orchard. The king placed two guards within it, one of whom was lame and the other blind. The lame guard said to the blind one, "I see beautiful, choice figs in the orchard. Come and carry me on your shoulders so that we can take them and eat them!" The lame guard rode upon the shoulders of the blind one and they took the figs and ate them. After a few days the owner of the orchard came and said to them, "My beautiful, choice figs—where are they?" The lame guard said, "Do I have legs that would enable me to reach them?" The blind guard said, "Do I have eyes that would enable me to see them?" What did the owner do? He placed the lame guard on the blind one and judged them as one. So the Holy One brings the soul and implants it in the body and judges them as one.[25]

In the Middle Ages, Maimonides, who was greatly influenced by Greek philosophy, found the doctrine difficult and stated that bodily resurrection was only a stage, after which the body would die once more and the soul would continue to all eternity.[26]

Today there are many who question this doctrine. Reform prayer-books have changed the wording from "reviver of the dead" (literally: "You give life to the dead") to "You give life to all." Some have suggested that the phrase be understood as referring to the ability of God to give life to inert matter, the very origin of life itself. Obviously that was not the intent of the authors of this prayer, but the power of interpretation of texts is great. Others see immortality expressed either physically in the birth of children, so that the dead live on in their progeny, or spiritually through accomplishments, so that the good we have done—the creations of our mind and spirit—gain eternity for us. Perhaps this is the minimum that this prayer can be taken to imply.

The rise of scientific knowledge and the reign of rationalism over the modern mind have caused many—including those who believe in the existence of a supreme power—to question the idea not only of resurrection but of immortality. Certainly the arguments that can be raised against it are many and powerful. On the other hand, in view of the inability of the human mind to grasp the very nature of life and its origins, the concepts of space and time, of infinity and the composition of matter, how can one speak with certainty of the impossibility of such a thing? Better—and wiser—to speak of our inability to grasp the real meaning of such a concept and to acknowledge that in this, as in so many other things, we speak in symbols, in words that indicate a direction and not a definition. When we praise God for "reviving the dead," we are indicating that the power of God extends beyond that which we know as life and that the meaning and significance of human life extends beyond the realm of this earth and this universe. To be more precise would be presumptuous. The rabbis were fond of the phrase "The eye has not seen and the ear has not heard." There are some things that we are simply not capable of even imagining. Nor should we forget that the phrase is in the present tense. The force of life that renews itself daily within living things, thus transforming otherwise inert matter into life, is an indication of the vivifying powers of God.

Furthermore, it is important to remember that the resurrection of the dead does not exhaust the meaning of this paragraph and is actually not its basic subject. It is a part of it, but not all. Although it does appear often in the version we use, a Geniza text mentions it less and includes a description of God as He who "brings low the haughty; mighty one who executes judgment upon tyrants, living for all eternity," and only afterward does it mention "causing the dead to rise."[27] Actually, the core of this blessing is a paraphrase of Psalm 146:7–8:

> Who keeps faith forever,
> who secures justice for those who are wronged,
> gives food to the hungry.
> The Lord sets prisoners free,
> the Lord restores sight to the blind.
> the Lord makes those who are bent stand straight.

The mention of rain, which is inserted during the winter season of the Land of Israel (from the end of Sukkot until the beginning of Passover), further indicates that the subject is not solely the resurrection but the miraculous actions of the Lord in sustaining life in this world. The climate and topography of Israel are such that rainfall is critical to the ability to raise crops and thereby sustain life. We have seen how the Bible used it as the symbol of God's rewards and punishments in the second paragraph of the Shema. Here it becomes the embodiment of

His power. The rabbis said that God had three keys in His possession: rain, prosperity, and the resurrection.[28] All three are the subject of this prayer.

The third of these opening paragraphs concerns the holiness of God, the last quality listed in the verse from Deuteronomy: "awesome." Awesomeness is a description of the transcendent nature of God. It is the sense of His mysterious presence, which permeates a story such as that of Jacob and his dream. Jacob has a vision of God standing at the top of the stairway leading to heaven and when he awakes he says, "How awesome is this place! This is none other than the abode of God, and that is the gateway to heaven" (Gen. 28:17). This feeling of wonder and awe in the presence of God lies at the root of all mysticism. It is different from the experience of God working through man, history, or nature; this is God in His very essence, ultimately incomprehensible to human beings but nevertheless experienced by them. The blessing as it appears in Ashkenazic prayerbooks is very brief:

> You are holy,
> Your name is holy,
> Holy beings praise You every day, *Sela.*
> Blessed are You, O Lord, the holy God.

The very brevity indicates the profound mystery that underlies this prayer. It is not difficult to expound at length on God's role in history or on His powers as evidenced in nature, but to speak of His holiness— His essence—is beyond our capabilities. This same brevity characterizes another version of this prayer found in the Geniza, which was used daily in the Land of Israel and is recited today only on the High Holy Days:

> Holy are You;
> Your name is awesome!
> Aside from You we have no God.[29]

The explicit use of the word "awesome," the same word that appears in the story of Jacob, emphasizes the point. In all cases, the central word "holy" (*kadosh*) remains the focus. The prayer calls our attention to the fact that the being we are about to address is of supreme greatness and far above human understanding. Holiness is His essence, and holiness is an undefinable quality. It is whatever God is. When Israel is commanded to "be holy, for I . . . am holy" (Lev. 19:2), it is being told to attempt to follow in the ways of God, to feel close to God, to know that Israel belongs to God. True holiness is God's alone. When the prophet Isaiah experiences the presence of God, beholding the "Lord seated on a high and lofty throne" (Isa. 6:1)—thus echoing Jacob's vision—Isaiah also sees angels attending Him and hears their words:

> And one would call to the other,
> "Holy, holy, holy!
> The Lord of Hosts!
> His presence fills all the earth!" (Isa. 6:3)

In the version of this prayer we use today, this triple repetition of "holy" is utilized by giving three descriptions of God's holiness: You are holy; Your name is holy; the holy God. When it speaks of "holy beings" who praise God daily, it is probably referring to the angels seen and heard by Isaiah. We human beings imitate them and praise God, the Holy One, using their words. The connection between the angels and Israel is stressed, for example, in a midrash to Job 38:7, "When the morning stars sang together and all the divine beings shouted for joy." Interpreting the morning stars to refer to Israel and the divine beings as the ministering angels, the midrash says that "the ministering angels do not mention the name of the Holy One, blessed be He, on high until Israel mentions it below."[30]

This mystical concept is enlarged upon in a *piyyut*, a liturgical poem, which is substituted for the third blessing during the reader's repetition of the Amida. This *piyyut*, known as the Kedusha (the prayer of holiness), is recited antiphonally by the leader and the congregation. There are many different versions of it. Lengthier and more elaborate ones are recited on the Sabbath and holidays, shorter ones on weekdays. There are also differences between the versions used by Jews from different parts of the world. It would be impossible to reproduce all of them here. Examining the text for weekdays will suffice, since it contains all the essential elements.

We will hallow Your name in this world
As they hallow it in the heavens above,
As it is written by Your prophet:
And one would call to the other—

"Holy, holy, holy!
The Lord of Hosts!
His presence fills all the earth!" (Isa. 6:3)

Others would respond, "Blessed———"

"Blessed is the Presence of the Lord, in His place." (Ezek. 3:12)

And in Your holy words it is written:

The Lord shall reign forever,
your God, O Zion, for all generations.
Hallelujah. (Ps. 146:10)

Throughout all generations we will recount Your greatness,
And forever and ever we will proclaim Your holiness.
Your praise will never depart from our lips
For You are the great and holy God and king.

Blessed are You, O Lord, the holy God.

Since every version of this *piyyut* features the three verses from Isaiah, Ezekiel, and Psalms, it is clear that the Kedusha is basically a poetic setting for recitation of those verses. The Ezekiel passage is reminiscent of the one from Isaiah, in that here too a prophet has a vision of the Presence of God. This "vision of the chariot" depicts God enthroned in a great chariot-throne surrounded by winged creatures. The prophet also hears the words of the angels. An entire school of mystical speculation grew up in early Judaism, based on this vision of Ezekiel. Using these mystical verses and the verse from Psalms proclaiming God's eternal kingship, the poets formulated recitations in which Israel imitates the heavenly praise of God and proclaims His holiness.

The ties between this third blessing of the Amida, especially in its poetical form, and mystical practices are obvious. Thanks to the pioneering work of Gershom Scholem,[31] we now know that during the early rabbinic period, mystical prayers and practices existed in which individuals would attempt to ascend to heaven and come into the presence of God. Special formulas were to be recited that would help the person progress and ward off the dangers to be met on the path. In texts Scholem printed, the two verses from Isaiah and Ezekiel play a major role. The words that come from heavenly beings were considered effective in helping one in the mystical ascent.

These mystical prayers and practices did not become an integral part of the Siddur and the order of prayer that the Sages decreed for common use. Mysticism had—and has—its dangers. Therefore such practices were considered inappropriate for general use. The Kedusha is the prayer that comes closest to them.[32] There was even some hesitation about the Kedusha, and at first it was recited only on the Sabbath.[33] Gradually it was included as a daily recitation, its mystic origins virtually forgotten. The practice of raising oneself onto one's toes each time the word "holy" is recited is a remembrance of the mystic quest.

Holiness is not exclusively a mystical concept in Judaism. It is also attainable in ways that are not mystical. The human being may attain holiness by following the ways of God. Thus Leviticus 19 tells us to be holy and sets out a series of regulations that includes both ethics and ritual. Every commandment we fulfill is intended to make the individual holy. Therefore this blessing can also be seen as a reminder that God is the source of all holiness. He reveals Himself to us not only in history and nature, but also in His demands on us to be like Him and to attain to His ethical and moral qualities. Humans cannot become God and cannot really cling to Him, but they can imitate His qualities:

> As God is called "merciful," so should you be merciful,
> As the Holy One is called "gracious," so should you be
>   gracious,
> As God is called "righteous" . . . so you too should be
>   righteous.
> As God is called "loving" . . . so too should you be loving.[34]

Holiness also means causing others to recognize God and proclaim His holiness. To publicly proclaim His qualities is considered an act of *kiddush ha-shem*. Since such acts can only be done in public, the Kedusha, along with various versions of the Kaddish, can only be recited when there is a minyan present, the minimum quorum representing a public assembly.

. . .

According to *Sefer Ha-Eshkol* and *Shibolei Ha-Leket,* thirteenth-century works reflecting earlier midrashim, these three paragraphs which emphasize three aspects of God may also be connected to the three Patriarchs. Thus they taught that the first paragraph—God's greatness—is clearly connected to Abraham, the first to recognize this greatness. The second, God's miraculous powers in sustaining life and restoring the dead, was first recited by Isaac and the angels at the time of the binding of Isaac. As Shalom Spiegel demonstrated in his superb book *The Last Trial,*[35] legends existed that claimed that Isaac was actually slain and then came back from the dead! He was the Patriarch who experienced in his flesh the meaning of death and resurrection, and so blessed God who gives and restores life. The third, God's awesome holiness, was the creation of Jacob and the angels when he experienced this transcendent aspect of God in his dream of the stairway to heaven (Gen. 28:12–17).

It is clear that the opening section of the Amida serves not only to praise God, since one does not present requests and petitions before uttering praise, but also prepares the human being for this encounter by clearly delineating the nature of God as Judaism understands Him, through the ways in which He interacts and functions with us. In order to better know "before Whom we stand"—not merely intellectually but also emotionally and experientially—we attempt to replicate the experience of our ancestors and of the generations. In brief, succinct language, we reiterate traditional beliefs and, passing them through our mind and soul, make them our own.

We remember that God may be experienced in His imminent closeness, as He was by Abraham, who established a relationship with Him as the one upon whom man can rely, as He who guarantees the order, justice, and meaningfulness of life: the God of creation and of history.

We affirm that He may be experienced, as He was by Isaac, in the miraculous events of life, the feeling of sudden reprieve that comes when we are snatched from danger or the simple wonder of reawakening to life day after day. God is found in our experience of the world in which we live and which provides the possibility of life and its sustenance. Thus it is God who restores life to the dead—the inert.

We recall that God may be experienced in His transcendency—in the mystical feeling of the otherness of His presence—as He was by Jacob, as a being beyond our comprehension, "the Holy One," the wholly other.

The Weekday Petitions   The three opening paragraphs are followed by thirteen paragraphs[36] which form the central part of the weekday Amida: (4) Knowledge; (5) Repentance; (6) Forgiveness; (7) Redemption; (8) Healing; (9) the Blessing of the Years; (10) Ingathering of the Exiles; (11) Judges; (12) the "Blessing" of the Heretics; (13) Converts; (14) Rebuilding Jerusalem; (15) Restoring the Line of David; (16) Hearing Petition. These are all requests and petitions. There are two ways of looking at these thirteen blessings. One can understand them either as discrete requests pertaining to the good of the individual and of all Israel or as a progression of requests for the steps that lead to redemption. Although many of the individual blessings may have originated as personal requests, I believe that the final edited version established after the destruction of the Temple was intended to be read as one interconnected prayer for redemption, each paragraph discussing one step in that process. Let us consider it first in that light.

The theme of redemption was already mentioned in the opening paragraph:

> Supreme God,
> Who performs acts of loving-kindness,
> Creator of all,
> Remembering the faithfulness of the fathers
> And lovingly bringing the redeemer to their descendants.

It is to God the redeemer that we appeal in these middle blessings.

What is meant by redemption, and who is the redeemer? When the Second Temple lay in ruins; when Jerusalem had been destroyed and Jews forbidden to live there; when thousands had been sent into exile, enslaved, and degraded; when even limited Jewish self-government ceased to exist—the most fervent hope Jews entertained was the reversal of the disaster. Even before the destruction, Jews had yearned for liberation from the yoke of foreign rule, and many had dreamed of supernatural events that would bring this world to an end, witness the resurrection of the dead and the judgment of all mankind, and usher in a new era: the world-to-come.[37] The prayer that the Sages decreed after the destruction makes no specific mention of apocalyptic events. It even avoids direct reference to a messiah. It voices, rather, the hope that God will reverse the calamity that has befallen the Jewish people and restore the ideal situation that existed—in their view if not in reality—during the days of the First Temple, when a true king ruled and God's Presence dwelt in Zion. At the very least, then, redemption implied the ingathering of Israel in its own land, ruled by a king of the Davidic dynasty; and the Temple rebuilt with the Presence of God (the *Shechina*) dwelling within it. In the words of the Babylonian Amora Shmuel, "The only difference between this world and the messianic times is that the yoke of the nations will be removed."[38]

As for the identity of the redeemer, although it could be the Messiah, we must note that the title "messiah" itself appears nowhere in the prayer (except once where it refers to David himself and is used in its original meaning of "anointed one"). The subject of the phrase "redeemer of Israel" in one of the blessings is clearly God Himself. It may well be that because of the perceived dangers in messianic belief and the disastrous consequences of two messianic movements—first Christianity and later the Bar Kochba revolt—there was hesitancy about including messianic references in the daily liturgy. It is God Himself who will come and redeem Israel.[39]

The process of redemption is outlined in the list of requests (*bakashot*) of the Amida. That list begins with the prayer for understanding and knowledge (4). Knowledge is the prerequisite for repentance. This is made clear by verses from the Prophets. Jeremiah, for example, states:

Return, O Rebel Israel. . . .
Only know your sin: for you have transgressed against the
Lord. (Jer. 3:12–13)

In order to return to God, one must recognize one's sins. Only from such understanding can one arrive at the possibility of repentance. The cause of the catastrophic condition was the sins of the people of Israel. In order to mend this situation, Israel must understand what it has done and turn in repentance.

The Blessing of Repentance (5) follows, a request that God help us to repent, to regret our actions and change our ways, and that He accept our repentance.

The next blessing, Forgiveness (6), asks God to forgive our sins. It emphasizes one of rabbinic Judaism's cardinal concepts: that God is gracious, abundantly forgiving. Of the two qualities ascribed to God— mercy and justice—that of mercy predominates. Moses' dialogue with the Lord after the incident of the golden calf concludes with a proclamation that made that clear for all time:

> The Lord! the Lord! a God compassionate and gracious, slow
> to anger, rich in steadfast kindness, extending kindness to the
> thousandth generation, forgiving iniquity, transgression, and sin.
> (Exod. 34:6)

Now that Israel has recognized its errors and repented, it can rely upon God to accept this and to forgive and erase our wrongdoings.

This trinity of requests describes the beginning of the redemptive process. Understanding leads to a return to God; God accepts our repentance; God forgives our sins. The way is now open for redemption, which the next petition (7) specifically requests:

> Behold our affliction,
> fight our battle,
> redeem us speedily for Your name's sake,
> for You are a mighty redeemer.
> Blessed are You, O Lord, redeemer of Israel.

Where the blessings following the Shema described God's actions in the past and therefore concluded with the words "who redeemed Israel," here the noun "redeemer" is used, indicating that this is the way in which God acts now and will act in the future. This too shows the major difference between those blessings, which praise God for what He has done, and this prayer, which requests God to act now. In praising God, we describe what He has done; in petitioning Him, we speak of what He is and what He can do in the future.

Proceeding with the stages of redemption, which are now in an active phase, we come to the prayer for healing (8). The healing referred to is not the sickness of the individual but the unhealthy state of the people.

It is national recovery for which we are praying. A verse from Jeremiah is reworked in the plural form and becomes the text of this prayer:

Heal me, O lord, and let me be healed.
Save me, and let me be saved;
For You are my glory. (Jer. 17:14)

Just as Jeremiah was referring to spiritual health, so this blessing asking that God "heal us completely from all our wounds" is referring to the wounds with which the nation has been afflicted. It concludes by borrowing another phrase from Jeremiah:

Those who despoiled you will be despoiled,
And all who pillaged you will I give up to pillage.
But I will bring healing to you
And cure you of your wounds. (Jer. 30:16–17).

Part of this healing process is the request found in the blessing of prosperity of the land, the prayer for a good year (9). The text used in the Land of Israel, discovered a hundred years ago by Solomon Schechter in the storeroom (the Geniza) of a Cairo synagogue, makes this abundantly clear:

Bless this year for us, O Lord our God, for good,
Through all manner of produce,
And speedily bring the climatic year of our redemption.[40]

This year of redemption will bring with it the ingathering of the exiles, the subject of the next blessing (10), which begins with a majestic call to freedom:

Sound the great ram's horn for our freedom,
Raise the banner to gather our exiles
And gather us together from the four corners of the earth.

The opening phrase is taken from Isaiah 27:13:

And in that day, a great ram's horn shall be sounded; and the strayed who are in the land of Assyria and the expelled who are in the land of Egypt shall come and worship the Lord on the holy mount, in Jerusalem.

The ingathering of the exiles into the Land of Israel will bring about the reestablishment of the just rule that existed when the judges of Israel in the Great Sanhedrin and smaller courts dispensed rulings in accord with God's will. Thus the next blessing (11) prays that God "return our judges as before."

With the reestablishment of the people of Israel in the Land of Israel under the rule of Torah, there will be no place for heretics. The following paragraph (12) calls for the extinction of heretics. It is frequently called "the Blessing of the Heretics," a euphemism for "the curse of the heretics," for that is what it is. The ancient text Schechter found in the Cairo Geniza is much stronger than the one we use today. Formulated sometime in the second century C.E., it speaks against all those who have renounced Judaism and specifically against Jewish-Christians and other heretics.

Feelings against the early Jewish-Christians ran high. It is more difficult to tolerate those who are within the group and leave or betray it than outsiders who are far from us. Christianity began as a sect within Judaism which observed the commandments and felt itself loyal to the teachings of the Torah. The major difference was that this group believed that the predicted messiah had already come. Eventually the differences widened as belief in this messiah became the criterion for salvation, as the influence of Paul resulted in a negative attitude toward the observance of the commandments, and when the messiah was ascribed divine status. The conflict between Jews and Jewish-Christians can be felt in the statement of the second-century Sage Rabbi Tarfon that he would burn the Christian texts even if they contained the divine name. If in danger, he would seek refuge in a temple of idolatry but not in their house of worship, because "they [the Christians] know the true God and deny Him, while the others [idolaters] are ignorant of Him when they deny Him."[41] His contemporary, Rabbi Ishmael, added that it was certainly permitted to destroy God's name in Christian texts, since their purpose was to stir up jealousy and hatred between Israel and God.[42]

One can understand the enmity in those early times against Jews who left their Judaism and joined other sects, especially the Jewish-Christians, who claimed to be the true Israel and the real carriers of God's covenant and blessing. Ironically, the prayer for redemption specifically condemns that group of Jews who claimed that redemption had already taken place. This also emphasizes the difference between Judaism's concept of redemption and that of Christianity. For Judaism, redemption concerns this world and is centered upon the collective people of Israel. For Christianity, it is a question of the status of the individual in the eyes of God.

The version of this "blessing" we use today was formulated in Babylonia, where the threat of Christianity was not felt, and is much more general. It speaks against informers and against the wicked and the proud.

The opposite of heretics, who abandon Judaism, are converts who enter the ranks of Israel and come under the wings of God's Presence. The heretic weakens Judaism. The convert strengthens it. Thus the thirteenth petition prays for the welfare of the convert and the righteous. This text may also be expressing the belief that, at the time of redemption, those who had denied God would come to recognize Him.

The path of redemption comes quickly to its final steps. Petition 14 calls for the rebuilding of Jerusalem and for God to restore His Presence within it. The fifteenth prays for the restoration of the Davidic line of kings. The king of Davidic descent is the true anointed one, who will save the people from their enemies. Lest there be any doubt, however, that it is God and no one else who effects salvation, the prayer contains the words "For we continually hope for Your salvation." It is God, not the Davidic king, who is crucial to redemption. The Davidic dynasty had come to be accepted by all Jews as the only legitimate line of kings. The biblical statements that God had established an everlasting covenant with David's house were accepted and the split that took place between Israel (the northern kingdom) and Judah (the southern one) when the kingdom of Israel rejected David's dynasty and accepted rival kings was viewed as a major disaster and a revolt against God's will. Although the Davidic dynasty was not restored when Jews returned from the Babylonian exile, it was believed that eventually this would come about. Even the famous and—at first—pious Maccabeans were recognized not as legitimate kings by the Sages, but only as temporary rulers who used that title. The true king would be restored at the proper time. David's line was the symbol of piety, righteousness, and justice, an extension of God's rulership over Israel. The golden age to come could hardly be imagined without it.

In the early versions of the Amida as used in the Land of Israel, these two blessings concerning David and Jerusalem were only one. Indeed, their subject matter is closely intertwined in Jewish thought. David and Jerusalem came into Jewish history together and would be restored together as well. In Babylonia, however, they appeared as two separate blessings. We cannot be certain which version is the original, but the assumption that they were one and then split into two would explain the fact that the Shemoneh Esrei—the Eighteen Benedictions— today contains nineteen. The power of tradition is such, however, that the ancient name was retained even though the reality had changed long ago.[43]

For the moment we shall skip over the sixteenth blessing, since logically it does not belong in its present place. Redemption reaches its climax in the seventeenth petition, known as the Service, the first of the three concluding paragraphs. This calls for the restoration of the Temple service and concludes with the words:

> Let our eyes witness Your return to Zion in mercy.
> Blessed are You, O Lord, who returns His Presence to Zion.

The full impact and meaning of this prayer can be realized only when we understand that rabbinic legend posited the removal of the Presence of God (the *Shechina*) when the people went into exile. According to the midrash, wherever Israel went in exile, God's Presence went with them:

> Rabbi Akiva says . . . , "Wherever Israel went in exile, God's Presence, as it were, went with them. . . . When they went into exile in Edom [Rome], God's Presence was exiled with them . . . and when they return in the future, God's Presence, as it were, will return with them."[44]

The return of God to His dwelling in Zion is the signal that the process of redemption is complete. God has returned from exile together with His people.

Thus, these middle petitions describe the process of redemption in the following manner: the people of Israel will understand what they have done and will turn to God in penitence. He will forgive their sins and begin to redeem them. He will heal them of their suffering and bring the year that will end their exile and begin their redemption. He will sound the horn of freedom and gather the exiled people from the four corners of the earth. In the Land of Israel, He will restore the Sanhedrin, remove the heretics and the wicked, and bless the converts and the righteous. God will rebuild Jerusalem and the Temple, restore the kings of the line of David, and make His Presence dwell once more in Zion.[45]

At the conclusion of a series of requests, it is only appropriate to ask that God hear our prayer—remembering that "prayer" really means petition—and answer our requests. This is what we find in Paragraph 16:

> Hear our voice, O Lord our God.
> Pity us and have mercy upon us,
> Accept our prayer with mercy and favor.

It concludes:

> Blessed are You, O Lord, who harkens to prayer.

Logically this prayer should come at the conclusion of the entire series of petitions, following Paragraph 17, the last of the prayers for redemption. The reason that it precedes the prayer concerning the restoration of the Temple service and of God's Presence is that the latter, unlike the other petitions, is recited on the Sabbath and holy days as well. On those days, the Temple service to which it refers was not suspended. On the contrary, it was of even greater importance than on ordinary weekdays. Petitions 3 through 16, however, are considered inappropriate for the Sabbath and holy days: that is not the time to ask God for our needs, even ones as important as national redemption. Holy days are days on which we rest from all thought of our problems and our wants and simply experience that which is ours. All the prayers recited only on weekdays were placed together, and Paragraph 17 was placed at the end, along with the other concluding blessings which are recited daily.

Thus Paragraph 17 serves a double purpose. On weekdays it is the conclusion of the petitions for redemption. At other times it is a separate prayer for the acceptance of our worship and the eventual restoration of the complete worship of God as it existed in the Temple.

There are many texts that contain multiple meanings and can be understood in more than one way. Nor do multiple meanings stand in contradiction to one another. They exist side by side. Like the well-known optical illusions in which a picture can be viewed as a drawing either of an old woman or of a young girl, depending on how your eye perceives it, or the black-and-white picture in which one sees either a vase or two profiles facing one another, depending upon which you take as the figure and which as the background, the meaning of the middle blessings of the Amida, the petitions, can either be invested with the content of redemption or they can be understood as separate petitions in which we ask God's help for our individual needs and those of all Israel in our day-to-day lives. One does not have to choose between the two. The figure moves in and out of focus all the time.

This more personal and individual meaning has long been an integral part of Jewish tradition. For example, it is considered proper to add a prayer for the sick, even including the names of those who are ill, when reciting the prayer for healing (8). This indicates that this paragraph was interpreted as referring to human health and to God's powers of physical healing. The Sages also taught that "one should ask for one's personal needs in the blessing 'He hears our prayer' " (16), and the same source then continues: "If one wishes, one may ask one's personal needs at the conclusion of any paragraph," specifying things that are covered by the subject of that particular blessing.[46] Thus matters referring to prosperity would be asked in the Blessing of the Years, health in the Blessing of Healing, and so forth.

When viewed this way, the Blessing for Knowledge (4) is a prayer for intelligence and the ability to understand. The faculties of reason and wisdom make us human, and we bless God for endowing us with these precious gifts. Each of us goes astray and sins; we seek the help of God in the process of acknowledging our misdeeds and returning to Him (5). We are able to continue, knowing that we are bound to make mistakes, because we believe that God is forgiving (6). The Blessing of the Years (9) is a prayer for success in our agricultural endeavors and, in general, a prayer for prosperity. The blessing concerning exiles (10) is appropriate not only for some final redemption, but for those who live in lands of oppression, and for the realization of the Zionist ideal of settlement in the Land. The petition concerning judges (11) emphasizes the importance of justice and calls attention to the Jewish ideals of righteousness and of society under the rule of law rather than bribery and corruption.

The curse of the heretics (12) is also a general denunciation of wickedness, which is always relevant although the targets change with the times.

Since, unfortunately, wickedness seems to be ever with us, one can always find a personal application for this prayer. There are variations of the wording of this paragraph. In some versions we denounce the wicked, while in others we speak against wickedness, reminding us of the talmudic tale of Rabbi Meir. He was bothered by some wicked people who lived in his area and prayed that they should die, but his wife, the wise Beruria, pointed out to him that it is preferable to rid the world of wickedness rather than of these few particular sinners. "Pray rather that they should repent," she said to him.[47]

Similarly, the Blessing of Converts (13) is a prayer concerning all the righteous and asks God's favor upon all who are good and upon the leaders and scholars of Israel. Blessing 14 expresses the needs of the entire people for the rebuilding of Jerusalem and 15 for the restoration of David's kingdom.

Viewed in this way, the Amida can be seen as a collection of individual prayers that speak of the current needs of the individual and of the Jewish people, as well as a prayer for the complete redemption of Israel and all mankind.

The Concluding Blessings   The last three blessings of the Amida are recited whenever the Amida is said. The first of these, the prayer concerning the acceptance of our service and sacrifices (17), has been discussed above. The second, (18), is the actual conclusion of the Amida. It is the prayer of thanksgiving and acknowledgment.

> We thank You, acknowledging that You are the Lord our God
> and the God of our fathers—forever.
> The Rock of our life,
> The shield of our salvation
> Are You throughout all the generations.
> We thank You and recount Your praise
> for our lives which are given into Your hand—
> and for our souls which are in Your keeping—
> and for Your miracles which are with us daily,
> and for Your wonders and favors which are there at all times,
> evening, morning, and afternoon.

The Good One—for Your mercies never cease,
The Merciful One—for Your steadfast kindness never ends.
We have always hoped in You.
For all of this may Your name be blessed and exalted, O our
     king, always and forever.
All living beings will thank You and praise Your name in truth,
The God who is our salvation and our help.
Blessed are You, O Lord, whose name is the Good One and to
     whom it is proper to give thanks.

After presenting our petitions, and with confidence that our prayers have
been heard, we utter thanksgiving to God and affirm that we worship
Him alone. The Hebrew word with which this blessing begins, *modim*,
is a form of the same word [*hodu*] that is used often in the Psalms
whenever there is a ceremony of thanksgiving for some triumph or an
acknowledgment of God's help and mercies to Israel and mankind. Many
of the phrases in this prayer appeared in the two opening paragraphs of
the Amida.[48] Thus it seems quite clear that this paragraph consciously
echoes them in order to indicate that we are now closing a circle, bringing
the prayer to an end. Having praised and petitioned, we conclude by
giving thanks.[49]

Another version of the Modim blessing exists which the congregation
recites quietly during the reader's repetition of the Amida. The usual
practice today is for the entire Amida to be recited silently by each
individual at his or her own pace. Although our discussion of the Amida
may give the impression that it is a lengthy prayer, it takes only a few
minutes to read. The leader of the congregation then repeats it out loud,
permitting even those who might be unable to recite it to be included.
When the leader does so, the third blessing, the Kedusha, is elaborated
into a responsive recitation. When he comes to the Modim prayer, the
congregants say a variant on it while the leader recites aloud the version
they used during their original recitation. This congregational alternative
is based upon prayers used by various Sages and recorded in the Talmud.[50]
This may have come about in response to the fact that the prayer calls
upon us to give thanks to God and individuals would do so in their own
words. Eventually the words of famous Sages were codified into a fixed
response.

Although we seem to have reached the end of the Amida, one more paragraph remains, the blessing of peace (19). As Rabbi Eleazar Ha-Kappar said, "Great is peace, for all blessings conclude with it."[51] At the conclusion of the service in the Temple, after the sacrifice had been offered, the priests blessed the people before they left, pronouncing the blessing found in the Book of Numbers:

> The Lord bless you and keep you!
> The Lord make His face to shine upon you and be gracious
> unto you!
> The Lord lift up His countenance to you and grant you peace!
> (Num. 6:24–26)

This blessing is Israel's most ancient liturgical formulation. Built on a pattern of three increasing steps—three Hebrew words in the first blessing, five in the second, and the sacred number seven in the third—it concludes with the blessing of *shalom*, peace. When the Amida was concluded (and originally the Amida stood by itself, not surrounded by other prayers as it is today), it was appropriate to dismiss the congregation with this blessing.

Both the reader's repetition of the Amida and the silent reading of it conclude with a prayer based on the Priestly Blessing. This is similar to the prayer with which the oldest service, the one mentioned in Mishna Tamid, discussed above, concluded. Among the writings of the Dead Sea sect are prayers based on this blessing, quoting it and expanding upon it.[52] Rabbinic Judaism did the same thing. Two different versions of that prayer were recorded, Sim Shalom ("Grant peace") and Shalom Rav ("Great peace"). When the prayers were finally codified, rather than one version being chosen, both were retained and each was given a place at a different service. Practice differs among various groups. In most Ashkenazic synagogues today, the first is recited in the morning while the second is said in the afternoon and evening. The basic ideational content of the two is similar. Here is a translation of Sim Shalom, the longer of the two:

> Grant peace, goodness, and blessing,
> favor, loving-kindness, and mercy
> to us and to all Israel, Your people.

Bless us, our father, all of us together,
With the light of Your countenance.
For through the light of Your countenance
You have given us—O Lord our God—
The Torah of life, the love of loving-kindness, righteousness,
    blessing, mercy, life, and peace.
May it be good in Your sight to bless Your people Israel
At all times and at every hour with Your peace.
Blessed are You, O Lord, who blesses His people Israel with
    peace.

Words and phrases from the Priestly Blessing, such as "peace,"
"blessing," and "the light of Your countenance," are incorporated in it.

In addition, the practice has been for those men who can trace their
patrilineal lineage to the priestly tribe to recite the biblical blessing in
the synagogue in a ceremonial way whenever the Amida is repeated by
the leader of the service. This was done in synagogues even in the days
when the Temple still stood,[53] in fulfillment of the Torah's command:

The Lord spoke to Moses: Speak to Aaron and his sons:
Thus shall you bless the people of Israel. (Num. 6:22)

The priests (*kohanim*) stand before the congregation, their heads covered
by their tallit, their arms extended with their fingers held in such a way
as to form the Hebrew letter *shin*, the first letter in the name of God
"*Shaddai*." Before reciting the Priestly Blessing, they say the following
blessing:

Blessed are You, O Lord our God, king of the universe, who has
sanctified us with the sanctity of Aaron and commanded us to
lovingly bless His people Israel.

As Yochanan Muffs has pointed out, the word "lovingly" (literally, "with
love") has the meaning of "to bless His people Israel freely, without
reservation."[54] Even in this instance, where the priest is merely a conduit
for conveying God's blessing, as it says, "Thus they shall link My name
with the people of Israel, and I will bless them" (Num. 6:27), it is
important that the priest impart the blessing freely, without reservation.

If no priests are present, the leader of the service quotes the blessing.

In European countries and America, priests do not perform this ceremony except at the Musaf service on holidays. In Israel and among Sephardim, the older practice has been preserved, and priests bless the people at this point at every morning service. Reform congregations and many Conservative congregations have eliminated the recitation by the priests altogether, so that it is always the leader of the service who recites the blessing when the Amida is repeated. Many reasons have been offered for this change in traditional practice. Among them is the fact that not all priests today are observant and "worthy" of participating in the service. Another is that the priesthood is inherently undemocratic, and priestly prerogatives should not be preserved. The counterargument is that the priest as an individual is not important here. His personality is submerged, since all he does is convey the words of the blessing. The blessing itself comes from God. As the verse clearly states, "Thus they shall link My name with the people of Israel, and *I will bless them*." This is effectively acted out by having the priest cover his face with the tallit when blessing the people: the people do not look at him. Mystically, this has been connected with the thought that the Presence of God shines between the priest's fingers. Practically, it removes the person of the priest from our consciousness, so that we think only of the words he utters. The democratic revolution in Judaism took place long ago when the Sages—later the rabbis—replaced the priests as the teachers of Judaism and authorities on Jewish law. One must be born a priest, but anyone can attain the status of rabbi through study. The priests retain certain ceremonial prerogatives, which serve primarily as a reminder of the past, and they can hardly be said to constitute a privileged hierarchy in Judaism. This ceremony is a way of recalling the past, the Temple and its service, and, if properly performed, adds beauty and poetry to a service that should appeal to the emotions and not only to the mind.

Thus the three sections of the Amida—praise, petition, and thankful acknowledgment—are followed by one additional coda, a petition that is different from all the requests made before, applying to the entire people and to each person individually, a petition for the greatest of all gifts—peace. When we leave the presence of God, before whom we have been standing in prayer, it is that profound word *shalom* which echoes within us. It is both a fervent plea that we attain the inner wholeness that "peace" implies (the Hebrew word is the same as the root meaning

"whole" or "complete") and that the world attain the peace of which
the prophets spoke, when swords will be beaten into plowshares and the
earth with be filled with the knowledge of the Lord. Perhaps it also
indicates the sense of peace that we have achieved through addressing
God in prayer. The effect is similar to the conclusion of Beethoven's
magnificent setting of the *Missa Solemnis*. The words *"dona nobis pacem"*
("grant us peace") are repeated over and over, at one point interrupted
by the ominous sounds of the drums of war, but overcoming them.
Beethoven labeled this "a prayer for inward and outward peace," an
appropriate description of the words of the Jewish service as well.

Personal Prayers

The Amida is a collective prayer, referring in essence to the people of
Israel. When the individual recites it, he or she does so as a representative
of the group. It is also a fixed prayer, with a text or at least a pattern that
cannot be changed. In response to a felt need, the ancient custom was
for a person to follow the recitation of the Amida, the prescribed prayer,
with a personal prayer in which he was free to express his own feelings.
While the Amida is entirely in the plural, any personal prayer was in the
singular. The Talmud records the individual prayers of many rabbinic
authorities.[55] Some of these meditations eventually found their way into
the Siddur in various parts of the service. By the time of the Geonim,
one of them, that of Mar son of Rabina, was put in the Siddur for all
to use:

> My God—restrain my tongue from evil
> And my lips from speaking falsehood.
> Let my soul be silent against those who curse me,
> Let my soul be as dust before all.
> Break the council of those who think to do evil to me
> And frustrate their plans.
> May the words of my mouth and the meditations of my heart
> Be acceptable before You,
> O Lord, my Rock and my redeemer.

The beauty of this prayer and its appropriateness are evident. It does seem a pity, however, that the opportunity for individual expression has been closed by having people recite yet another prayer already written and formulated. It would seem to be a good idea for us, beginners and veterans alike, to pause after reciting the Amida, concentrate on our own feelings, and express them to God in whatever way we can. A hassidic story has it that a child once recited the letters of the alef-bet and asked God to arrange them as He thought appropriate, since He could do it so much better. Surely, then, we should not hesitate to give vent to our own words and thoughts, thus making the occasion of standing before God in prayer more than a recitation of the words of the tradition. It becomes a time to say both ancient words, which help us feel a part of the entire Jewish past, and new words of our own making, which express our own ever-changing personal thoughts.

Sabbath and Holy Day Variations

While the first three blessings (praise) and the last three (thankful acknowledgment) are always recited, the petitions of the Amida change according to the occasion. Those described above are recited on weekdays. They are not recited on the Sabbath since they are requests for mercy, and any such requests are considered inappropriate for the Sabbath, when our mood should be one of contentment, appreciating what we have and the world God has created rather than seeking ways to change it. This is the reason that the rabbis spoke of the Sabbath as "a sixtieth part of the world-to-come."[56] In place of these requests, on the Sabbath one blessing is inserted, which concerns itself with the Sabbath itself. Since the pattern of the Amida is that the middle section is always made up of requests, the middle blessing on the Sabbath is also a request, albeit of an entirely different nature. In it we ask God to accept with favor our observance of the Sabbath. It describes the nature of the day and its importance, demonstrating its great sanctity.

On weekdays, the middle blessings are identical for all three daily services. On the Sabbath there is a different blessing for each service. The Sabbath Amida is called the Prayer of Seven because it consists of seven paragraphs; the usual first three, one blessing concerning the Sabbath, and the usual three concluding blessings. That one blessing in the middle, however, is considerably longer than any one paragraph of the weekday prayers and is a composite of various sections.

In the Amida for the Sabbath evening, the intermediate blessing has three sections: an introduction to a reading from the Torah, the reading itself (in this case, the first mention of the Sabbath in the Torah), and a concluding petition.

> You have sanctified the seventh day unto Your name.
> It is the purpose of the creation of heaven and earth.
> You blessed it above all other days.
> You sanctified it above all other occasions.
> Thus did You write in Your Torah:
> > The heaven and the earth were finished, and all their array.
> > On the seventh day God finished the work that He had been
> > doing, and He rested on the seventh day from all the work
> > that He had done. And God blessed the seventh day and de-
> > clared it holy, because God ceased from all the work of crea-
> > tion that He had done. (Gen. 2:1–3)

The Sages considered the recitation of this biblical passage so important that they wrote, "Whoever recites this section on the eve of the Sabbath is considered to be the partner of God in the work of creation."[57]

The third section is a request, a petition, that God accept our rest. It begins by addressing God in words that are common for the beginning of a prayer, "Our God and God of our fathers," and then continues:

> Accept our rest. Sanctify us by Your commandments and grant
> our portion in Your Torah.
> Satisfy us with Your goodness and make us rejoice in Your
> salvation.
> Purify our hearts to serve You in truth.
> Grant us Your holy Sabbath, O Lord our God, as a gift of love
> given willingly.[58]
> May Israel which sanctifies Your name rest thereon.
> Blessed are You, O Lord, who sanctifies the Sabbath.

This third section is truly the heart of the middle blessing for the Sabbath and appears in the Amida for each of the four Sabbath services: evening, morning, additional, and afternoon. This was probably the early, original

Sabbath blessing which was elaborated upon in a different way in each of those four services.[59]

The blessing inserted in the Sabbath morning Amida has a similar format. Here too there is a biblical passage (in this case, Exodus 31:16–17), preceded by an introduction and followed by the same petition used in the evening service. Here the introduction does not focus on the Sabbath and its holiness. Instead it stresses the role of Moses in the granting of this precious gift to the people of Israel:

> Moses rejoiced in the gift which was his portion,
> For You proclaimed him a faithful servant.
> A diadem of glory did You place upon his head
> When he stood before You on Mount Sinai.
> By his hand he brought down the two tablets of stone.
> Upon them was written the observance of the Sabbath.
> And thus is it written in Your Torah:
> > The Israelite people shall keep the Sabbath, observing the
> > Sabbath throughout the generations as a covenant for all
> > time: it shall be a sign for all time between Me and the
> > people of Israel. For in six days the Lord made heaven and
> > earth, and on the seventh day He ceased from work and was
> > refreshed. (Exod. 31:16–17)

The introduction is unusual for two reasons. The first is that it gives Moses his due. Moses' name is seldom mentioned in the prayers, which may have been Judaism's way of emphasizing that no man, no matter how important, is perfect or indispensable. Here, however, we have a lovely poem emphasizing his role in the revelation at Sinai. The second element that makes it unusual is that since it specifically mentions the "two tablets of stone," one would have expected a quotation about the Sabbath from the Ten Declarations rather that the passage that appears. This has led to the speculation that the original passage quoted was indeed the Ten Declarations and that for some unknown reason this other passage was preferred and substituted.

Following the biblical passage, a comment upon it appears:

> You did not give it, O Lord our God, to the nations of the
> world.
> You did not bestow it, O our king, upon idol worshipers.

Nor shall the uncircumcised partake of its rest.
Rather unto Israel, Your people, did You give it in love,
To the descendants of Jacob whom You chose,
The people that sanctify the seventh day,
They shall all be satisfied and rejoice in Your goodness.
The seventh day did You favor and sanctify,
The most desirable of days did You call it,
A remembrance of the act of creation.

This discussion of the exclusivity of the Sabbath is based on the idea expressed in the biblical passage that the Sabbath is a sign between God and Israel. But rather than seeing the Sabbath as we usually do—as a way for Israel to express its belief in God, the creator of all—it is taken here as a sign of God's favor, a great gift given exclusively to the people God has chosen. The Sabbath is God's chosen day and Israel is God's chosen people. They belong together. This is a kind of "midrash" or rabbinic exegesis of the biblical text. The author asks, "Why does it say, *The children of Israel* shall keep the Sabbath'?" and then answers, "To stress that only to Israel was this gift given, to no one else, emphasizing Israel's unique position with God." "Why does it say, 'For in six days the Lord made heaven and earth'? To indicate that the Sabbath is a reminder and remembrance of creation."

The middle blessing of the Musaf (additional) service is similar to this. There is an introduction, the inverse alphabetical poem *Tikanta Shabbat*, which indicates that God "instituted the Sabbath and desired its sacrifices," and a biblical passage, the command to offer special sacrifices on the Sabbath (Num. 28:9–10). This emphasis on sacrifices may have stemmed from the comment made by Rabbi Yose that one must add some new thought to the Musaf service and that "even if one said, 'And may we offer our obligatory daily sacrifice and the Musaf sacrifice before You,' one has fulfilled the obligation."[60] This section includes a request that the sacrifices be restored—a request that prayerbooks of the Conservative movement have changed into a historical remembrance of what our ancestors did, rather than a prayer that we be able to offer them again. The Reform service does not include it at all.

The section from the Bible is followed by a poem on an entirely different topic, emphasizing the joy of the Sabbath:

May those who observe the Sabbath and proclaim it a delight
    rejoice in Your kingship;
May all those who sanctify the seventh day be sated and filled
    with delight from Your bounty,
For You desired the seventh day and sanctified it,
Proclaiming it the most desirable of days,
A memorial to the creation.

The blessing then concludes with the same request as all the middle
blessings of the Sabbath Amida, that God accept our rest.

In the Amida of the afternoon service, the last of the Sabbath prayers,
no biblical passage is quoted. Instead, the middle blessing begins with
a lovely hymn based on the theme of Sabbath rest:

You are one and Your name is one,
And who is like Your people Israel,
One nation in the world?
A diadem of greatness,
A crown of salvation.
A day of rest and holiness
Did You give Your people.
Abraham will rejoice,
Isaac will celebrate,
Jacob and his sons will rest thereon.
A rest lovingly given and freely granted,[61]
A rest of truth and faithfulness,
A rest of peace and tranquillity, quiet and security,
A complete rest that You desire.
Your children will understand and know that their rest comes
    from You,
By their rest shall Your name be sanctified.

This idea of the oneness of God, stated so fervently in the Shema, is a
frequent theme of the Prophets and the rabbinic writings. The sense of
it is often "uniqueness." God is unique and so is Israel. This mutuality
of uniqueness is explained in a talmudic passage which may well form
the basis of our prayer:

The Holy One said to Israel:
You have made Me one entity in the world,
As it is said: Hear, O Israel! The Lord is our God, the Lord is
    one (Deut. 6:4).
And I shall make you one entity in the world,
As it is said: Who is like Your people Israel,
    one nation in the world (2 Sam. 7:23).[62]

In addition to the theme of uniqueness, this poem also emphasizes the
rest and peace that the Sabbath bestows upon those who observe it. The
poem found in the Musaf service placed the joy of the Sabbath at its
center. Now, in a prayer recited when the Sabbath is close to its conclusion, the dominant sensation is not joy, but the quieter one of rest and
peace. As we prepare to take leave of the Sabbath, we have surrendered
entirely to its quietude and, in a mood almost of nostalgia, we appreciate
that precious tranquillity we are about to lose.

    Once again the blessing ends with the request that God accept our
rest.

The Festival Amida

The pattern of the middle blessing of the Amida for the festivals—
Passover, Shavuot, and Sukkot—is less complex than that for the Sabbath, since here the middle blessing is the same for Maariv, Shacharit,
and Mincha. It begins with a discussion of God's love for Israel as manifested in, among other things, the granting of the festival days:

You chose us from all the peoples,
You loved us and desired us.
You exalted us from all the nations
and sanctified us with Your commandments.
You brought us near, O our king, to Your service,
and called us by Your great and holy name.
In love You granted us, O Lord our God,
festivals for joy,
holidays and seasons for rejoicing . . .

—at this point the specific festival being celebrated is mentioned, be it Passover as "the season of our freedom," Shavuot as "the season of giving the Torah," or Sukkot, Shemini Atzeret, and Simchat Torah as "the season of our rejoicing"—

a holy convocation,
a memorial to the Exodus from Egypt.

The second section of the holiday blessing asks that the remembrance of the people, of the ancestors, of Jerusalem, and of the Messiah come before God. "Remembrance" means that God will recall these things and will perform the promises He has made in regard to them.

The third section contains a request to God. On the Sabbath we asked that God accept our rest. On the festivals, which are characterized by rejoicing rather than by rest, we ask that God grant us the blessing of happiness:

Let us inherit with joy and gladness Your holy festivals,
And may Israel, who sanctifies Your name, rejoice in You.
Blessed are You, O Lord, who sanctifies Israel and the
    seasons.

The middle blessing of the Amida of the additional service, Musaf, for the holidays resembles that of the Sabbath, since it too specifically recalls the sacrifices that were brought to the Temple on this occasion. On the festivals, however, a major section is added, lamenting the exile and the destruction of the Temple, and concluding with a petition that God rebuild His house and reestablish His sanctuary so that sacrifices can be offered once again. Here, too, Conservative prayerbooks change the wording so that sacrifices are remembered but without a request to restore them.

The emphasis on the Temple during the festivals is most appropriate since the three pilgrimage holidays—Passover, Shavuot, and Sukkot— were the time when the Torah required Jews to appear in the Temple. In the days of the Second Temple, Jews, not only from the Land of Israel but from all parts of the diaspora, came to Jerusalem on those occasions, crowding the city and courts of the Temple with masses of people. If ever the Temple was missed, it would be specifically on those days when worship in the Temple was the major focus of Jewish religious life. Observance of the Sabbath might be centered around the home and the synagogue, but nothing could substitute for the pageantry of the Temple on the festivals. The sights, sounds, and excitement of those times were difficult to re-create elsewhere, and it is that longing for its restoration that is expressed in these prayers.

Insertions for the New Month, Intermediate Days of the Holidays, Hanukkah, and Purim

Even though they have a special character, the New Month (Rosh Ho-desh, celebrating the beginning of the month), the intermediate days of the festivals (the third through the sixth days of Passover and the third through the seventh days of Sukkot), Hanukkah, and Purim are consid-ered regular weekdays as far as the Amida is concerned. The weekday Amida is recited with the addition of a special prayer.

On the New Month and the intermediate days, the special prayer is inserted into the seventeenth blessing, the prayer for the Temple service. Commonly referred to by its opening words Ya-ale Ve-Yavo, it asks God to remember us for good and bring us salvation. An additional (Musaf) Amida is recited on the intermediate days and on the New Month as well.

On Hanukkah and Purim and, in the Siddur of the Conservative movement, on Israel Independence Day as well, a special paragraph is inserted into the eighteenth blessing, Modim, the blessing of thanks-giving. That blessing, Al Ha-Nissim, expresses our appreciation to God for the "miracles which are with us daily." Since these special days are times when we recall God's miracles, we add these words:

> For the miracles, for the redemption, for the powerful deeds,
> For the salvation and the battles that You performed for our
>   ancestors
> In those days and at this time.

This is followed by a description of the occurrences of the day, empha-sizing God's mercy in standing by the people of Israel and delivering them from their enemies. For Hanukkah, it concludes with a description of the entry of the Jews into the Temple, which they cleansed and where they then "kindled lights in Your holy courts and established these eight days of Hanukkah to give thanks and praise Your holy name."[63] On Purim the story of the book of Esther is recapitulated, and on Israel Independence Day the narrative tells of the return of the Jewish people to the Land and the triumph over Arab armies who sought to prevent the establishment of the State.

The Amida is the cornerstone of official Jewish worship. It is the central prayer without which there is no service. It contains the basic elements of Jewish worship: praise of God, petition, and thanksgiving. Its concern is the central concern of Judaism: the redemption of the people of Israel and the total restoration of Israel's status as a people free of foreign rule and accountable only to God. Besides the concepts it ingrains, it is also a prayer in which both individuals and the entire people can petition God for help in overcoming current problems of life, including matters of health and prosperity. It provides an opportunity to specify one's personal needs and to recite whatever thoughts and meditations one wishes to add. It provides us with the opportunity of directing our attention toward God, who is felt as a living presence, and understanding and experiencing Him daily through the eyes of Jewish history and tradition. With its flexible framework, it changes in ways that make it appropriate to every special occasion, be it the Sabbath or any of the holidays of the Jewish year. The spiritual experience of reciting it and of being in the presence of God is as important as the specific content of the words and makes it an essential element of Jewish religious life.

> To attain this sense of God's presence . . . is a goal that must be fought for anew each day, against the countless distractions of life . . . but the testimony of those who have reached the highest rung on the ladder of prayer is that it is an indescribably glorious experience.[64]

10

Concluding Prayers

*B*ringing the act of prayer to a conclusion is no easier than beginning it. The earliest services may have ended simply with the conclusion of the Amida, a prayer for peace. But just as there is a tendency to add more and more preliminary material to prepare for prayer, so there is a tendency to add to the conclusion and to linger before parting. One is reminded of the rabbinic interpretation of the eighth day added to the seven days of Sukkot, called Shemini Atzeret (the Eighth Day of Assembly), for which there is no explanation in the Torah. The rabbis said that it was a case of "parting is such sweet sorrow"; God just could not bear to part with the people of Israel who had assembled in His court. Therefore He said to Israel, *"He-atzer*—Please tarry with Me awhile longer."[1]

Prayers of Supplication

The first addition to the service is Tachanun, prayers of supplication. Although all petition is supplication, these special prayers go even further. We come before God to ask His help in utter humility, realizing our total dependency on His grace. This concept is stressed in a midrash that describes the prayers of both Moses and David, considered the two greatest leaders of Israel.

Israel had two fine leaders, Moses and David, king of Israel.
Their meritorious deeds could have sustained the whole world,

yet they begged the Holy One only for a favor. . . . How much more should a person who is not even a thousand-thousand-thousandth or a ten-thousand-ten-thousandth part of the disciples of their disciples beseech the Holy One only for a favor.[2]

The Sages here are indulging in clever word play. They are connecting the word *va-et-chanan* ("I entreat") with *chinam* ("free"), which is translated here as "a favor." We beseech God to grant our petitions freely, whether we deserve it or not, because of His quality of mercy *(chanun)*. No person has a claim on his maker. Our actions do count, and Judaism affirms reward and punishment. Nevertheless, we should come before God not to claim a reward, but to throw ourselves instead on His mercy. This concept was institutionalized in these Tachanun prayers. Portions of the Tachanun may have originated in the rites for fast days and the Day of Atonement, where the same themes of confession and atonement are found. In the daily ritual, these were originally individual prayers that eventually became part of the service. Different rites have created various versions. What they all have in common is the use of verses that stress the admission of our inadequacy and sin, and our plea for God's mercy.

When the Torah is read on Mondays and Thursdays, a longer version is recited, while a shorter one is said on other days. In the shorter version, we begin by performing the symbolic gesture of placing our head on our arm as a sign of our humility before God while saying:

> David said to Gad, "I am in great distress. Let us fall into the hands of the Lord, for His compassion is great; and let me not fall into the hands of men." (2 Sam. 24:14)

The prophet Gad has reproved David for his sins and David humbles himself, admitting his errors. He throws himself upon the mercy of God. This serves as an example for us. If David, the great king, could admit his faults, so can we. No one is too great for that. On the other hand, the motif of God's mercy is present as well. We depend upon His compassion. The ancient custom was to recite this prayer while prostrating oneself before the Lord. This was modified to the symbolic gesture of placing one's head on one's arm.

In imitation of David, we recite a confession of sins patterned after that of the Day of Atonement:

O merciful and compassionate one [*chanun*]!
I have sinned before You.
O Lord, full of mercy!
Be merciful to me and accept my supplications [*tachanunai*].

This is accompanied by Psalm 6, a penitential psalm begging for God's mercy and compassion, which concludes with words of comfort:

The Lord heeds my plea,
the Lord accepts my prayer.
All my enemies will be frustrated and stricken with terror;
they will turn back in an instant, frustrated.

The Tachanun concludes with a medieval *piyyut* featuring the word "guardian" and based on the Shema and the Kedusha.

Guardian of Israel,
   guard the remnant of Israel.
Let not Israel perish
   who say "Hear, O Israel."

Guardian of one nation,
   guard the remnant of one nation.
Let not one nation perish
   who unify Your name—"the Lord is our God,
   the Lord is one."

Guardian of a holy nation,
   guard the remnant of a holy nation.
Let not a holy nation perish
   who three times recite the threefold "holy."

The mood of the entire prayer is undoubtedly dour, which is why it is not recited on the Sabbath, holy days, or any festive occasion. A circumcision ceremony, a bar or bat mitzva, or any other joyous event is cause for eliminating it. It is not recited during the entire month of Nisan, the month of our liberation, and conversely it is not recited in a house of mourning, where the mood is already bleak and does not need additional sadness. Hassidism has always found it contrary to its mood of joy and seeks any excuse, such as the anniversary of the death of a prominent rabbi, to eliminate it. It must be admitted that it is not appealing to the modern temper. Nevertheless, there is something to be said for reminding ourselves of the need for humility and of the fact that while human beings may be the peak of creation, we were, as the Talmud says, created after the ant.[3] No one likes excessive and artificial cringing, but considering the catastrophes human pride has caused, from the Tower of Babel to the scud missiles of Iraq, it may not be a bad idea for us to admit our shortcomings from time to time and even to bow our heads in shame.

An ancient legend recounted during the thirteenth century ascribes the origin of the longer version of the Tachanun, *Ve-Hu-Rachum* ("He is merciful"), to an incident that occurred at the time of the destruction of the Temple:

> After the destruction of the Temple, Titus [or Vespasian] cast into the sea three ships filled with men and women, without a helmsman. The Almighty sent a stormy wind which drove the ships to the shores of three different kingdoms. . . . Following their safe landing, the Jews on one of the ships were subjected to terrible persecutions, from which they were miraculously delivered, and in connection with which three wise and pious men of their group composed the . . . prayer.[4]

Taken as a legend and not as history, the story nevertheless indicates to us the emotional substructure of this prayer. It vividly calls to mind the suffering and destruction that Israel has undergone, but also voices our deep faith that God's mercies are real and that asking for His care is not in vain.

Torah Service

On Mondays and Thursdays, the Torah is read at the Shacharit service. This is yet another instance of stressing the role of the Torah within Jewish worship. The weekday reading is the first section of the Torah portion that will be read in full on the following Sabbath.

The Torah service begins with the chanting of two appropriate verses:

When the Ark was to set out, Moses would say:
Advance, O Lord!
May Your enemies be scattered,
And may Your foes flee before You! (Num. 10:35)

For Torah shall come forth from Zion,
And the word of the Lord from Jerusalem. (Isa. 2:3)

Thus the remembrance of the earliest days of wandering in the wilderness, when the Ark containing the written word of God was carried at the head of the column, is combined with the hope for the future time when all nations will want to learn God's word and will hear it from Zion. Although today the Ark containing the Torah scrolls is a permanent fixture at the front of the synagogue, in early synagogues the Torah was kept in a repository in a separate room and brought in when it was to be read; it was then carried out when the reading was finished. The verses concerning the portable Ark in the wilderness would have been particularly appropriate.

Three people are called up for the reading of the Torah (*aliya*). The blessings they recite begin with the same words that commence the blessings before the recitation of the Shema:

Bless the Lord who is blessed.
Blessed is the Lord who is blessed forever.

This is followed, however, by one that explicitly relates to the Torah:

Blessed are You, O Lord our God, king of the universe,
who has chosen us from all peoples by giving us His
Torah. Blessed are You, O Lord, giver of the Torah.

God's love for us has been demonstrated by His gift of the Torah.

After the section of the Torah has been read, another blessing is recited by the person receiving an *aliya:*

Blessed are You, O Lord our God, king of the universe, who has given us the Torah of truth and planted within us everlasting life. Blessed are You, O Lord, giver of the Torah.

The idea of reciting blessings before reading the Torah is derived from the public reading of the Torah at the time of Ezra:

> Ezra opened the scroll in the sight of all the people, for he was
> above all the people; as he opened it, all the people stood up.
> Ezra blessed the Lord, the great God, and all the people an-
> swered, "Amen, Amen." (Neh. 8:5–6)

The practice of holding the scroll before the people and showing it to
them, also done at the Torah service, comes from these verses as well.

Originally each person called to the Torah read his own portion. The
first person said the blessing before the reading, and the last person
closed the reading with the second blessing. Eventually professional
readers were substituted because too many people were not able to read
the Torah properly. At the same time, each person was given the honor
of reciting blessings both before and after "his" portion.

While the Torah is out of the Ark, it is customary to recite prayers
for the welfare of those who receive an *aliya*, for the sick, and for the
welfare of the entire community. Memorial prayers for the dead are also
offered.

When the Torah is returned to the Ark, the continuation of the verse
recited when it was taken out is said:

> And when it [the Ark] halted, he would say:
>   "Return, O Lord, unto the ten thousands of the families of
>   Israel!" (Num. 10:36)

This is followed by other appropriate verses:

> For I give you good instruction;
> Do not forsake My Torah. (Prov. 4:2)
>
> It is a tree of life to those who grasp it,
> And whoever holds on to it is happy. (Prov. 3:18)
>
> Its ways are pleasant ways,
> And all its paths, peaceful. (Prov. 3:17)
>
> Take us back, O Lord, to Yourself,
> And let us come back;
> Renew our days as of old! (Lam. 5:22)

Kedusha d'Sidra

The Kedusha d'Sidra, "the Kedusha of the scriptural portion," is the last major section recited in the daily morning service. The name is derived from the fact that it includes another repetition of the biblical verses that are recited during the Kedusha prayer, the paragraph in the Amida proclaiming God's holiness.[5] *Sidra* indicates that it is connected with the recitation of biblical passages. It is also referred to by its first words, *u-va le-tzion go'el* ("A redeemer shall come to Zion"). It begins with a passage from Isaiah 59:20–21, prophetic words of consolation:

> A redeemer shall come to Zion,
> To those in Jacob who turn back from sin
> —declares the Lord.
> And this shall be My covenant with them, said the Lord: My spirit which is upon you, and the words which I have placed in your mouth, shall not be absent from your mouth, nor from the mouth of your children, nor from the mouth of your children's children—said the Lord—from now on, for all time.

Now the Kedusha verses (Isa. 6:3, Ezek. 3:12, and Exod. 15:18) are recited, together with their Aramaic translation. The "translation" of the verse from Isaiah, however, is more than that. It is also an interpretation in which any Christological reading of the verse is polemically refuted:

> "Holy"—in the heavens above where His Shechina [Presence] dwells;
> "Holy"—on earth where His power is manifest;
> "Holy"—throughout all eternity.

The three "holies" are in no way connected with a trinitarian concept of God but represent three aspects of God's holiness.

After additional verses of consolation, we conclude with an informal blessing on the theme of the truth of Torah, similar to the formal blessings of the Torah:

> Blessed is our God who created us for His glory,
> Who separated us from those who go astray

By giving us the Torah of truth
And planting within us life everlasting.
He will open our hearts to His Torah
And place His love and reverence within our hearts
So that we may perform His will and serve Him
    wholeheartedly.

The prayer also asks that God permit us to enjoy the world-to-come and the days of the Messiah, one of the few references in the Siddur to the Messiah.

Let us be worthy to live to see and inherit the goodness and blessing of the years of the days of the Messiah and the life of the world-to-come.

Following are several verses of praise, the last of which returns to the theme of the study of Torah:

The Lord desires His vindication
That He may magnify and glorify Torah. (Isa. 42:21)

The magnification of Torah comes through its study and dissemination.

The Kedusha d'Sidra was so highly esteemed in the days of the Talmud that it was credited with "sustaining the world."[6] Yet it is immediately apparent that it is very different from other sections of the Siddur. It contains the pattern of the Kedusha which we have already seen twice before, first in the blessing before the Shema and then in the repetition of the Amida. Here, however, there is no poetic setting but rather a translation into Aramaic. Furthermore, the entire section contains no rabbinic blessing. The formal structure of prayer is thus entirely missing. There is an appeal to God, but the terminology used is completely different from that of other parts of the service.

For these reasons Joseph Heinemann considers it to be one of the "prayers of the *bet midrash* (the house of study)" as opposed to prayers of the synagogue.[7] Its origins were in the schools, where prayers were not the main occupation but were recited as praise to God after the completion of study. These prayers were often in the vernacular (Aramaic) and utilized a more informal tone, so no blessing was included. This particular prayer seems to be intended to follow the study of a portion of the Prophets; such prophetic portions were read in order to convey a feeling of consolation. It was customary to then recite a prayer for the establishment of God's kingdom at the end of all sessions of study. The Kedusha d'Sidra is one version of such a prayer, the best-known being the Kaddish.[8]

Alenu

Every service concludes with a prayer that first found its way officially into the liturgy on the High Holy Days, although it may well have existed prior to that. It became so popular that it was incorporated into every service as a concluding vow and expression of hope. This prayer consists of two paragraphs written at different times, using different styles, and with different messages. The first, which is the older of the two, is a declaration of the Jewish concept of God:

> It is our duty to praise the Lord of all,
> To ascribe greatness to the creator of everything,
> For He has not made us like the nations of the world
> Nor like the families of the earth.
> He has not made our portion like theirs
> Nor our fate like that of their multitudes,
> For they bow down to nothingness and vanity
> And pray to an impotent god,
> While we prostrate ourselves and bow and kneel in
>   thanksgiving
> Before the king of king of kings,
> The Holy One, blessed is He,
> Who stretched out the heavens and founded the earth,
> Whose glorious abode is in heaven above,
> Whose magnificent Presence is in the loftiest heights.
> He is our God—
> There is no other.
> Our king is truth—
> All else is nothingness!

As it is written in His Torah:
Know therefore this day and keep in mind
That the Lord alone is God
In heaven above and on earth below—
There is no other. (Deut. 4:39)

This is an exceedingly powerful statement of Jewish belief. It is an affirmation of the existence of the God of Israel, the sole creator of everything, and a denial and denunciation of idolatry. The idols are vanity, nothingness; they do not exist. They have no power to do anything, certainly not to bring victory to their worshipers. The nations are to be pitied and we—Israel—are the fortunate ones, for God has shown us the truth and permitted us to worship Him, while they are still praying to emptiness. The Lord alone exists. Twice we are told, "There is no other," a phrase that is even more powerful in the Hebrew with its two staccato beats: *ein od.*[9]

Such a statement must have been written at the height of the conflict between idolatry and Judaism, when Judaism wished to defiantly vaunt its creed in opposition to all else. The possibility that this was composed during the era after the Maccabean revolt (second century B.C.E), a revolt in which monotheism triumphed over Hellenistic paganism, seems very plausible. This first paragraph of the Alenu is not technically a prayer. It is not addressed to God. It is a doctrinal statement, a creed and doxology in which we affirm our belief. It was undoubtedly accompanied by the ritual act of obeisance, bowing and prostrating and thus acknowledging the Lord and Him alone. It is still the practice to prostrate oneself when the Alenu is recited on the High Holy Days and to bend the knee and bow every time we say the words "While we prostrate ourselves."

The text is based on the story of creation. It constantly refers to God as creator and paraphrases the Book of Genesis. Whereas many prayers stress God the redeemer, using phrases from the story of the Exodus, this declaration concentrates on God the creator.[10] This too may be seen as a refutation of idolatry, which ascribed the creation to many gods and deified the creation itself. The sun, the moon, the earth, the sea were all gods in Greek mythology. This affirmation places the God of heaven as the creator of all that others worship as deities.

Most versions of this prayer today, including those in most Orthodox prayerbooks, omit the lines:

For they bow down to nothingness and vanity
And pray to an impotent god.

This was interpreted as a reference to Christianity and was forcibly censored by the Church. Although it was written not specifically against Christianity but against paganism, it can easily be interpreted that way. Perhaps for that reason there is little inclination to restore it. Its absence, however, could lead to a misinterpretation of the meaning of the statement. We are not praising God for creating us different from others in some absolute sense. We do not claim superiority. Our only advantage is in the fact that we recognize and worship the true God while others are misled into idolatry. The original context makes that very clear and should therefore be kept in mind.

A second paragraph has been added, which is addressed to God in the second person and includes the theme of God's kingship. Although this paragraph too lacks the rubrics of formal prayer, it is nevertheless a petition and not an affirmation of faith. It stresses the hope that just as Israel has come to recognize the true God, so, in the future, the nations will also recognize His kingship.

Therefore do we place our hope in You, O Lord our God,
That we may speedily witness Your glorious might
As idols are eradicated from the earth
And false gods are totally destroyed;
As the world is perfected in the kingdom of the Almighty
And all mortals call upon Your name,
Turning unto Yourself all the wicked of the earth.
May all the inhabitants of the world recognize and understand
That every knee must bow to You,
Every tongue vow loyalty.
They will bow and prostrate themselves before You,
And ascribe glory unto Your honored name.
All will accept the yoke of Your kingship
And You will rule over them speedily and forever.
For the kingship is Yours

And forever shall You reign in glory.
As it is written in Your Torah:
The Lord will reign forever and ever (Exod. 15:18).
And it is said: And the Lord shall be king over all the earth;
In that day the Lord shall be one and His name one
      (Zech. 14:9).

This prayer is similar to the midrashic comment that, just as at the Sea of Reeds there was a temporary acknowledgment of God by the nations who had witnessed that miracle, so "in the future the nations will renounce their idols":[11]

When idolatry and idolaters are uprooted, God will be the only [God] in the world and His kingship will last for all eternity.[12]

The combination of the two paragraphs of the Alenu makes a powerful statement about Israel's belief and her hope and vision of the future of mankind, a fitting conclusion to any service of Jewish prayer.

Idolatry in the sense of paganism may have virtually vanished from the parts of the world in which Jews live, and monotheism may have triumphed in the forms taken on by Judaism's daughter religions, Christianity and Islam, but the fight against idolatry and the need to take a stand against it remain as important as ever. The idols of humanity are no longer statues of wood or stone. They are concepts and ideologies that seek to replace the morality of God with the good of the state or of some master race. They include anything that places self-interest or gain ahead of the good of humanity. Fanatic religions are playing an ever more powerful role in our world, and they too can become idolatrous, even if they pretend to speak in the name of monotheism. The Jewish struggle against idolatry has yet to be won and the Jewish dream of mankind united in the worship of the creator of life has yet to be realized.

Daily Psalm

Included in the Shacharit service, usually at the conclusion but sometimes at the beginning, is the recitation of a special psalm which is designated as the psalm for that day. This custom is first referred to in the Mishna as part of the ritual of the Temple.[13]

The song that the Levites would recite in the Temple:
On the first day they would say:
> The earth is the Lord's and all that it holds,
> the world and its inhabitants (Ps. 24).

On the second day they would say:
> The Lord is great and much acclaimed
> in the city of our God,
> His holy mountain (Ps. 48).

On the third day they would say:
> God stands in the divine assembly;
> among the divine beings He pronounces judgment (Ps. 82).

On the fourth day they would say:
> God of retribution, Lord,
> God of retribution, appear! (Ps. 94).

On the fifth day they would say:
> Sing joyously to God, our strength;
> raise a shout for the God of Jacob (Ps. 81).

On the sixth day they would say:
> The Lord is king,
> He is robed in grandeur (Ps. 93).

On the Sabbath they would say:
> A psalm. A song: for the sabbath day (Ps. 92).

Although the rabbis of the Talmud make an attempt to connect each psalm with the events of creation recorded for that day,[14] it is difficult to understand why these particular psalms were chosen. Three of them, however, do seem to have a connection. That of the first day (Sunday) echoes the theme of creation. Friday's speaks of God ascending His throne at the conclusion of the creation, and that of the Sabbath bears the specific heading, that it is a song for the Sabbath. The practice of reciting them is another link between the synagogue and the Temple.

The sections after the Shema and the Amida that bring the daily service to a close include prayers of supplication and consolation, the reading of the Torah on Mondays and Thursdays, and the affirmation of our belief and our hope for the realization of God's kingdom. The service can be compared to the famous bell-shaped curve: we ascend through the preliminaries to the Shema and the Amida, which stand at the peak. We then descend through supplication and consolation, prepared to go on our way, pausing for one final declaration of our belief in God and our hope for the future. The intensity is past, but there is a feeling of calm contentment that all will be well.

11

Sabbath and Holidays

*T*he wonder and the beauty of the Sabbath have drawn to it the best of the liturgical talents of the Jewish people. The weekday is a time when prayer is a small island of sanctity in the midst of a sea of overwhelming concerns and occupations. On the Sabbath our burdens have been lifted, and worship can become the focus of life. Therefore, although the pattern of worship on the Sabbath and holy days is built of the same basic components as those of weekday prayer, the additions and expansions create a feeling of having entered into a new world. The major units of the Shema and the Amida remain at the center of the service, but changes and additions already described are made in order to reflect the special nature of those days, and the additional (Musaf) service is recited. There are other prayers, however, that are recited only on the Sabbath and holidays, and which are of extraordinary beauty.

Welcoming the Sabbath

One of the most moving and beautiful services of the Jewish year is Kabbalat Shabbat (Welcoming the Sabbath), which is recited Friday evening prior to the Sabbath evening service (Arvit). Unlike all the other services we have discussed, this one is relatively new, dating from the sixteenth century. Not only that, but it comes from one specific circle of Jews, the Kabbalists of the city of Safed in the Upper Galilee. At that time, Safed was the center of Jewish mystical studies. The city itself—

high in the hills, frequently covered by mist, consisting of crooked white houses perched on steep hillsides—is a perfect setting for mysticism. The service these Kabbalists originated is an example of creativity in prayer that is unexcelled. It is not a total innovation, however, since the mystics based it on ancient ideas and practices mentioned in the Talmud:

> At dusk on Sabbath eve, Rabbi Hanina would wrap himself and say, "Come, let us go out to welcome Sabbath the Queen." Rabbi Yanni would dress himself up and say, "Come, O bride; come, O bride."[1]

The Sabbath has always been so precious that it was thought of as more than a mere period of time. Instead, it became personified. Legend has it, for example, that the Sabbath complained that each day of the week had a partner: Sunday and Monday are a couple; so are Tuesday and Wednesday, and Thursday and Friday. Only the Sabbath remained isolated and alone. Therefore God bestowed on the Sabbath a most fitting partner—the people of Israel.[2] Thus the Sabbath becomes "the bride." The personification of the Sabbath is also seen in the interpretation of the psalm of the Sabbath, Psalm 92. In one of the liturgical poems for Sabbath morning, it is stated that this is the song that the Sabbath itself recites in praise of God, its creator. To all of this must be added the idea that the Sabbath is also a "foretaste—a sixtieth part—of the world-to-come."[3] When the Mishna mentions the psalm for the Sabbath, it comments:

> A psalm—a song for the Sabbath day (Ps. 92:1). A psalm—a song for the time-to-come, for the day that is entirely Sabbath and rest for all eternity.[4]

The Sabbath, a day on which human beings are completely equal—there are no rich and no poor on a day when no business can be transacted, and money is therefore useless; a day on which there are no masters and no slaves, for no one is allowed to labor; a day free of trouble and woe; a day of pure pleasure and joy—is surely a taste of what the perfected world will be.

The mystics of Safed created a liturgy for greeting the Sabbath that placed the personified Sabbath—the bride, the queen—at its center and expressed both the wonder of the Sabbath day and the hope and longing for the true Sabbath of the time-to-come. Basing themselves on the talmudic precedent, they would walk out onto the hillsides as the sun set and recite psalms appropriate to the occasion. Then they would walk back to the synagogue, accompanying the Sabbath and welcoming the mystic bride into the presence of her groom, the people of Israel. The very atmosphere of Safed is embodied in these customs.

We greet the Sabbath with six psalms, Psalms 95–99 and Psalm 29. The number six represents the six days of creation and the six days of the workday week, which lead up to the seventh day, the Sabbath. Psalms 95–99 have a common theme and form a unit within the Book of Psalms. The theme running like a thread through them is the kingship of God. Since the Sabbath celebrates creation, it is indeed the day of God's coronation. A few verses will illustrate this point:

> For the Lord is a great God,
> the great king of all divine beings. (Ps. 95:3)

> Declare among the nations, "The Lord is king!"
> the world stands firm; it cannot be shaken;
> He judges the peoples with equity. (Ps. 96:10)

> For He is coming to rule the earth;
> He will rule the world justly
> and its peoples in faithfulness. (Ps. 96:13)

> The Lord is king!
> Let the earth exult,
> the many islands rejoice! (Ps. 97:1)

> For He is coming to rule the earth;
> He will rule the world justly,
> and its people with equity. (Ps. 98:9)

> The Lord, enthroned on cherubim, is king,
> peoples tremble, the earth quakes. (Ps. 99:1)

The sixth psalm, Psalm 29, is a magnificent description of the presence of God sweeping through the world, causing all of creation to tremble, and finally taking His place in majesty as the everlasting king:

> The Lord sat enthroned at the Flood;
> the Lord sits enthroned, king forever. (Ps. 29:10)

With this, the coronation is complete and Lecha Dodi ("Come, My Beloved"), an original composition by one of the leading mystics, Solomon Ha-Levi Alkabez, is recited. As was the custom, his name is enshrined in the opening letters of each verse. At the beginning and between each verse the refrain is chanted:

Come, my beloved, to greet the bride—
Let us welcome the Sabbath.

Who is the beloved to whom this is addressed? The answer lies in another set of mystic symbols with an ancient history. Judaism has pictured Israel as the bride of the Holy One—so that in some parables we are the husband of the Sabbath and in some we are the bride of God. From the earliest times, the Torah and the Prophets utilized the language of marriage, love, and faithfulness to describe the exclusive relationship God demands of the people of Israel. Even the Shema commands, "Love the Lord your God." Worship of other gods is termed "whoring after them." Hosea learns about God and Israel from his own experience with an unfaithful wife. It is on this foundation that Rabbi Akiva built his interpretation of the love poetry of the Song of Songs, which became Judaism's accepted interpretation.[5] It is to be seen, he taught, as a song of love between God, the beloved, and Israel, the maiden. The maiden praises the beauty of her lover. He seeks her in order to rescue her and bring about total salvation. This is what lies behind the custom of reading the Song of Songs, or part of it, prior to the Kabbalat Shabbat service. It also accounts for the terminology of this magnificent hymn, Lecha Dodi, which is the crown jewel of the service. "Come, my beloved," it says, using the word—*dod*—that is found in the Song of Songs to designate the lover. God is invited to accompany Israel to greet the Sabbath.

The first verse reads:

"Observe" and "remember" were uttered as one.
Thus did the unique God proclaim them to us.
The Lord is one and His name is one
For the sake of His glory and praise.

All the verses are set in rhyme, so that in Hebrew the last word in each of the first three lines rhyme, as do the last word of each paragraph. In this verse the author refers to the midrash that explains why there are two versions of the Sabbath commandment. One verse reads, "Remember the Sabbath day" (Exod. 20:8), while the other says, "Observe the Sabbath day" (Deut. 5:12). The rabbis explained this as one of several instances when God did what no human can do—He uttered two words at the very same time.[6]

> Let us come to greet the Sabbath,
> For she is the source of blessing
> Anointed of old at the beginning,
> Last of creation, first in planning.

The Sabbath was the last thing to be created, but, says the author, it was the first in God's mind. All of creation was aimed toward it. Placing it last does not mean it is unimportant. On the contrary. Everything else exists for its sake.

> O sanctuary of the king, royal city—
> Arise and depart from your overthrow,
> Long enough have you dwelt in the valley of tears—
> He will have compassion upon you!

Suddenly the subject of the hymn changes. No longer are we dealing with the Sabbath, but with Jerusalem, the city of God. The poet, living in Safed some fifteen hundred years after the overthrow of Jerusalem, feels himself to be on the brink of the redemption. Mysticism dwelt upon the coming of the Messiah and the restoration of Jerusalem. The poet is using the weekly Sabbath, which is now being welcomed, as a symbol of the great Sabbath of redemption, and although ostensibly he is inviting God to join in welcoming the queen-bride Sabbath, his real intent is to encourage God to bring the messianic Sabbath. The rest of the hymn deals exclusively with the events of redemption, the great Sabbath of the future.

> Arise, shake off the dust!
> Put on your robes of majesty, O My people!
> Through the son of Jesse, the Bethlehemite,
> My soul's redemption is near.

This reference to the Messiah, who will be a descendant of Jesse's son David, continues the theme of redemption.

Rouse, rouse yourself!
Your light has come! Arise and shine forth!
Awake, awake! Break forth in song!
The glory of God is revealed to you.

The poet here and throughout invokes the phrases of the prophets,
especially Isaiah:

Rouse, rouse yourself!
Arise, O Jerusalem. (Isa. 51:17)

Awake, awake, O Zion!
Clothe yourself in splendor;
Put on your robes of majesty,
Jerusalem, holy city! (Isa. 52:1)

Arise, shake off the dust,
Sit [on your throne], Jerusalem. (Isa. 52:2)

He is so carried away by his theme that he speaks to Jerusalem of her
redemption as if it were already an accomplished fact. On the Sabbath,
even if redemption has not come, one feels as if it had.

You shall no more be shamed or reviled.
Why are you downcast, why are you disquieted?
In you shall the needy of My people find shelter.
The city shall be rebuilt on its mound.

Here, too, the poet takes phrases from various biblical sources and weaves
them together into a message of consolation.[7]

Those who despoiled you shall be despoiled,
Your destroyers shall stay far from you,
Your God will rejoice over you
As a bridegroom rejoices over his bride.

The dominating image of God the bridegroom comes from Isaiah 62:5,
where it is the climax of a description of God reclaiming His people and
His Land in a great royal wedding. To the Jew steeped in Scripture, each
phrase conjures up an entire prophecy and its imagery.

You shall spread out right and left
And sing the praises of the Lord—

> Through the man—the son of Peretz—
> And we shall be happy and rejoice.

The "son of Peretz" refers to the Messiah, since David was a descendant of Peretz.

Only in the last paragraph does the poet return to the theme of the weekly Sabbath, welcoming her into our midst. When chanting this verse, it is the custom for the congregation to turn toward the entrance of the synagogue as if it were actually welcoming the Sabbath bride into its midst.

> Come in peace, crown of your husband,
> In happiness and joy
> Into the midst of the believers among the treasured people—
> Come, O bride! Come, O bride!

As the verse concludes with the talmudic phrase welcoming the Sabbath bride, the congregation turns once more toward the front. The Sabbath is now in the midst of the worshipers, and the welcoming ceremony is concluded. The advent of the Sabbath can now be celebrated by reciting the psalm for the Sabbath day, Psalm 92, and Psalm 93, whose theme is that God has now assumed His kingship over the earth He created:

> The Lord is king,
> He is robed in grandeur;
> the Lord is robed,
> He is girded with strength.
> The world stands firm;
> it cannot be shaken.
> Your throne stands firm from of old.

We may no longer go out into the fields to greet the Sabbath and escort her back with song to the synagogue the way that a human bride is met and escorted to the bridal canopy with song and dance, but the service nevertheless carries with it a unique beauty, an expression of love for the Sabbath, Israel's precious gift, and a mystical longing for the time of wholeness and peace.

Sabbath Eve Service

Kabbalat Shabbat is followed by the Arvit service for Sabbath eve. Although the basic pattern of the weekday service is maintained, there are a few important additions which give it a special Sabbath flavor.

Two "anthems"—biblical descriptions of the Sabbath—have been added. The first, read before reciting the Amida, consists of Exodus 31:16–17:

> The Israelite people shall keep the Sabbath, observing the Sabbath throughout all generations as a covenant for all time: it shall be a sign for all time between Me and the people of Israel. For in six days the Lord made heaven and earth, and on the seventh day He ceased from work and was refreshed.

On a holiday, Leviticus 23:44 is read:

> So Moses declared to the Israelites the festivals of the Lord.

In each case, words from the Torah indicating that the people of Israel have been commanded to observe this sacred time set the tone for the holy day.

The second "anthem" follows the silent Amida:

> The heaven and the earth were finished, and all their array. On the seventh day God finished the work that He had been doing, and He ceased on the seventh day from all the work that He had done. And God blessed the seventh day and declared it holy, because on it God ceased from all the work of creation that He had done. (Gen. 2:1–3)

Thus the central prayer is surrounded by biblical verses emphasizing the importance of the Sabbath and its meaning.

An abbreviated version of the Amida is recited aloud by the leader of the service after the silent reading. This is unique, since at the evening service, which was considered to be a voluntary and not an obligatory service, the Amida is never repeated. Various theories have been offered to explain this pseudorepetition. Rashi, the classical medieval French commentator, wrote that Friday night was the only night when people went out to synagogues located in the fields, far from where they lived.

Since they were fearful of danger, they wished to leave together. This prayer gave latecomers an opportunity to catch up with the rest.[8] Others theorize that there once was a repetition for every evening service, but only this one has remained.[9] Whatever the case, the brief prayer is composed of seven phrases which refer to the seven paragraphs of the Sabbath Amida:

> Protector [shield] of Abraham,
> Who revives the dead by His word,
> The holy God, like whom there is no other.
> He grants rest to His people on the holy Sabbath, for He desired to grant it to them.
> We shall worship Him in reverence and awe.
> We shall acknowledge and thank His name daily.
> Source of all blessings, God of thanksgiving, Lord of peace, who sanctifies the Sabbath and blesses the seventh day, granting its holiness to the people satiated with joy in remembrance of creation.

This is then concluded with a prayer that God accept our rest and with the blessing "Blessed are You, O Lord, who sanctifies the Sabbath."

The other special feature of this service is the recitation of the Kiddush, the prayer sanctifying the Sabbath, which is pronounced over a cup of wine. Although basically a prayer recited in the home, it became customary to recite it in the synagogue because of those who used the synagogues as hostels. Another possible explanation is that there were poor people who could not afford wine at home, so the blessing was recited for them at the synagogue. This custom is practiced widely today outside the Land of Israel itself, where it was never adopted.

Sabbath Eve Home Service

Although the synagogue is the place of prayer *par excellence*, prayer is by no means confined to it. This is not only because those who are unable to attend synagogues may pray at home but because there are acts of worship designed specifically for the home and blessings whose natural setting is the home. Blessings recited before and after meals, for example, belong in the home, as do other acts of worship connected with meals. The Passover Seder is the best-known example. The Sabbath meals also take on a special importance, especially the evening meal. Prior to that meal, the Sabbath is greeted in the home by the lighting of the Sabbath candles. Two candles are lit, usually by the woman of the house. Some follow the custom of lighting an additional candle for each child in the family. After lighting the candles, she passes her hands over them three times, covers her eyes with her hands, and recites the blessing. The blessing follows the usual formula for the performance of any *mitzva*:

> Blessed are You, O Lord our God, king of the universe, who has sanctified us by His commandments and commanded us to kindle the Sabbath light.

Originally, lamps were kindled before the Sabbath began, in order to make certain that the house would be illuminated on the Sabbath. Once the Sabbath begins, it is forbidden to kindle flame, so if it was not done by that time, people would have sat in darkness during the Sabbath. This was the position held by the Sadducees during the Second Temple and later by some splinter groups in Judaism such as the Karaites, who interpreted the Torah injunction not to kindle flames on the Sabbath to mean that no fires at all should be allowed to burn then. The Sages took the opposite position and even made the lighting of lamps into a *mitzva* that one is obligated to perform. The Geonim decreed that it was mandatory to recite a blessing when kindling them, in order to demonstrate their opposition to the Karaite position.

The picture of a Jewish mother passing her hands over the flames of the candles, covering her eyes, and reciting a blessing has become a standard part of Jewish folklore. A popular musical such as *Fiddler on the Roof* could not depict Jewish life in the villages of eastern Europe without a production number featuring dozens of women performing that act, accompanied by music. The reason for that action is based on a problem of Jewish law. Whenever a blessing is recited, it is immediately followed by the action that is the subject of the blessing. On Hanukkah, for example, we recite blessings and then kindle the flames; similarly, we first recite a blessing and then put on a tallit or tefillin. On the Sabbath, one is forbidden to light a flame, yet how can a blessing for Sabbath candles be recited when it is not yet the Sabbath? The solution was to light them, cover the eyes, recite the blessing, and then uncover the eyes and look at the flame. Looking at the candles became the action performed after saying the blessing. The significance that the Sages attached to the Sabbath lights was well expressed in this midrash:

> And God blessed the seventh day and declared it Holy (Gen. 2:3). He blessed it with the lamp. . . . He blessed it with the face of man, for the light of man's face on the Sabbath is unlike that of any other day.[10]

The lights are symbolic of the light that the Sabbath brings to those who observe it.

The ceremony accompanying the meal itself consists of singing Shalom Aleichem ("Peace unto You"), blessing the children, honoring one's wife by reciting Proverbs 31:10–31 (Eishet Chayil, "A Capable Wife"), reciting the Kiddush, ritually washing the hands and reciting a blessing, and saying the blessing *ha-motzi* ("Who brings forth bread from the earth"), after which the meal is eaten. The meal is accompanied by the singing of special Sabbath songs (*zemirot*) and concluded with Birkat Ha-Mazon, the Blessing After Meals.

Shalom Aleichem ("Peace unto You") is a late poem of kabbalistic origins which was based on an early talmudic legend:

> Two ministering angels accompany a person on the Sabbath eve from the synagogue, one good angel and one bad angel. When he arrives home, if he finds the lamp lit, the table set, and the sofa made up, the good angel says, "May it be His will that it be thus on the next Sabbath." The bad angel has to answer "Amen" against his will. But if not, the bad angel says, "May it be His will that it be thus on the next Sabbath," and the good angel has to answer "Amen" against his will.[11]

The poem ignores the possibility that things would not be done properly and paints a picture of the family surrounded on the Sabbath by angelic beings, symbolic of the peace and tranquillity of the Sabbath itself.

It is customary for parents—usually but not necessarily the father—to bless their children at the beginning of the Sabbath by placing their hands upon each child's head as the Patriarch Jacob placed his hands upon his grandchildren. To a son, one says, "May God make you like

Ephraim and Manasseh," recalling Jacob's grandchildren, who received his special blessing (Gen. 48:12–20); to a daughter, "May God make you as Sarah, Rebecca, Rachel, and Leah." He then recites the Blessing of the Priests:

> The Lord bless you and keep you!
> The Lord make His face to shine upon you and be gracious to
>   you!
> The Lord lift up His countenance to you and grant you peace!
>   (Num. 6:24–26)

The wife is then honored by the reading of Proverbs 31:10–31, an alphabetical chapter which praises the virtues of the perfect wife of that time:

> What a rare find is a capable wife!
> Her worth is far beyond that of rubies.
> Her husband puts his confidence in her,
> And lacks no good thing. (Prov. 31:10–11)

> "Many women have done well,
> But you surpass them all."
> Beauty is illusory;
> It is for her fear of the Lord
> That a woman is to be praised.
> Extol her for the fruit of her hand,
> And let her works praise her in the gates. (Prov. 31:29–31)

Admittedly, some of the poem is archaic and hardly describes the modern woman, who seldom "sets her hand to the distaff" (31:19), but the overall picture is one of such virtue that it is still an appropriate way for a husband to proclaim publicly his appreciation for his wife as part of a long line of worthy Jewish wives and mothers. Thus the meal involves the entire family and serves to bind it and the generations to one another.

The Kiddush begins with a biblical anthem, the same verses of Genesis 2:1–3 previously recited in the synagogue. The blessing consists of the regular blessing recited anytime one drinks wine, blessing God who is the "creator of the fruit of the vine," and a blessing proclaiming the sanctity of the day:

> Blessed are You, O Lord our God, king of the universe, who
> sanctified us by His commandments and favors us, giving us the
> heritage of His holy Sabbath in love and favor—a remembrance
> of the work of creation. For it is the first of all the sacred occasions,
> a reminder of the Exodus from Egypt. For You have chosen us
> and sanctified us from all the nations, giving us the heritage of
> Your holy Sabbath in love and favor. Blessed are You, O Lord,
> who sanctifies the Sabbath.

The description of chosenness is strongly reminiscent of blessings of the
Torah. Like the Torah, the gift of the Sabbath is a sign of God's love
and favor to the people He singled out to serve as His priests. The
blessing also connects the Sabbath to the people Israel—both have been
sanctified by God. It recounts the purposes of the Sabbath that the two
versions of the Ten Declarations relate: to remind us of the creation and
of the Exodus from Egypt.

The wine is not "sanctified." It is the means and the occasion for
blessing God and for reciting the fact that the Sabbath has been sanctified—not by us, but by God. The use of wine is mentioned in the
Talmud, which quotes Exodus 20:8 ("Remember the Sabbath day and
keep it holy") and interprets it to mean: "Remember it over wine."[12]
Wine has always played a key role in religious ritual. The Bible says,
"Wine cheers the hearts of men" (Ps. 104:15). What better way, then,
to symbolize joyous occasions than to bless God the creator of wine and
recite the reasons for the celebration. Thus wine plays a prominent role
at the beginning and end of every holy day, at the Passover Seder, at a
wedding, and at a circumcision ceremony.

Following that Kiddush, we wash our hands and recite a blessing that
is reminiscent of the rituals of purity connected to the Temple. The
family table is viewed as a symbol of the altar itself. The bread over
which a blessing is said is sprinkled with salt the same way that sacrifices
were. On the Sabbath, two loaves are used rather than one. This is
connected with the double portion of the manna that the Israelites wandering in the wilderness received each Friday, representing not only the
special sanctity of the Sabbath but also the fact that all food for the
Sabbath must be prepared in advance.

It is customary to accompany the meal with the singing of special

Sabbath songs, *zemirot,* which were written to celebrate the Sabbath day. These songs generally praise the Sabbath day and describe the commandments and activities connected to it. There are many different melodies to these texts, coming from all over the world, and new ones are added all the time. They add to the festivity and joy of the meal. The prayer following the meal is the one recited after any meal, with the addition of a special paragraph referring to the Sabbath. It is also the custom to begin it on the Sabbath or any joyous occasion by reciting Psalm 126, which describes the vision of restoration of Zion, when "our mouths shall be filled with laughter, our tongues, with songs of joy" (126:2). Once again we experience the Sabbath as the foretaste of redemption.

Sabbath Morning Prayers

The Sabbath morning service follows the basic pattern of the daily morning service, with appropriate changes in the Amida, but it has been expanded and augmented extensively. Because of the honor due the Sabbath and the fact that people have more time to devote to prayer, nine psalms have been added to the preliminary service, Pesukei d'Zimra. Some of them, such as Psalm 19, were selected because they include a description of the heavens and earth, whose creation we celebrate on the Sabbath. Psalms 34, 90, and 91 stress God's goodness and salvation, while Psalms 135 and 136 are songs of praise similar to the "hallelujah psalms" at the end of the Book of Psalms which we read each day. Psalm 136 is called "the great Hallel" because it lists all the favors of God and follows each with the words "His faithfulness endures forever." Psalm 33 is another psalm of praise; Psalm 93, the psalm for the Sabbath, and Psalm 94, describing the coronation of God, bring this recitation to an end.

The closing blessing of the Pesukei d'Zimra is also lengthened and elaborated on the Sabbath. Before the paragraph *yishtabach,* with which the weekday section ends, a lengthy liturgical poem is inserted, beginning with the words *nishmat kol chai* ("The soul of all living"). This poem, referred to by the Sages as the Blessing of Song,[13] is prescribed for use at the Passover Seder and can also be found in the Haggadah. There is

nothing to indicate that it was written specifically for use on the Sabbath.
It consists of expressions of praise that would be appropriate any day. It
is likely that its length precluded its incorporation into the weekday
services. This liturgical poem is almost a service in itself, encompassing
all the major themes of worship. Although the Blessing of Song may be
a composite of different individual sections of praise, any one of which
could stand by itself, together they form one coherent liturgical poem of
great power and beauty, whose complex poetics place it on a par with
any of the psalms. It engages all the creatures of the world in the praise
of God, emphasizing the inability of humans to adequately praise and
thank Him. The human being stands in awe of all that exists and all that
has been done for humanity. All of one's being, every limb, every fiber,
must join in praise—exceeding even that of David, the greatest of all
poets. Even then, it will not be sufficient.

> The soul of every living thing shall bless Your name, O Lord
>   our God.
> The spirit of all flesh shall continually adore and exalt the
>   mention of You, O our king.
> You are God from everlasting to everlasting.
> Other than You we have no king, redeemer, savior, liberator,
>   and deliverer
> Who sustains and pities at all times of sorrow and distress.
> We have no king other than You.
>
> God of the first generations and of the last,
> God of all creatures,
> Lord of all generations,
> Praised through the multitude of adorations,
> Governing His world with steadfast love
> and His creatures with mercy.
> The Lord neither slumbers nor sleeps.
> He awakens the sleepers and arouses the slumberers.
> He makes the dumb speak,
> Frees those who are imprisoned,
> Sustains those who fall,
> Straightens those who are bowed down.
> Unto You alone do we give thanksgiving and acknowledgment.

Were our mouths filled with song as the sea,
Our tongues with melody as the multitude of its waves,
Our lips with praise as the expanse of the heavens,
Our eyes bright as the sun and the moon,
Our hands spread out as the eagles of heaven,
Our feet swift as the deer,
We would still be unable to adequately acknowledge You and
   bless Your name, O Lord our God and God of our fathers,
For even one thousand-thousand-myriad-myriad part of the fa-
   vors You have bestowed upon our fathers and upon us.
From Egypt You redeemed us, O Lord our God,
From the house of bondage You freed us.
In famine You fed us and in plenitude You supported us.
From the sword You saved us, and rescued us from the plague.
From malignant and chronic diseases You delivered us.
Until this very moment have Your mercies always helped us,
Nor have Your loving-kindnesses deserted us.
Never forsake us, O Lord our God!

Therefore the limbs You have planted in us,
The spirit You have infused within us,
The tongue You have put in our mouths—
They shall all thankfully acknowledge, bless, praise, laud,
   exalt, glorify, sanctify, and proclaim Your sovereignty, O
   our king.
For every mouth shall acknowledge You,
Every tongue shall pledge loyalty to You,
Every knee shall bend to You,
Every back shall bow to You,
Every heart shall revere You,
Every inward part shall sing unto Your name—
As it is written:
   All my bones shall say,
      "Lord, who is like You?
      You save the poor from one stronger than he, the poor
      and needy from his despoiler" (Ps. 35:10).

Who is like You?

Who can be compared to You?
Who is equal to You?
The great, mighty, awesome God—
Most High God,
Creator of heaven and earth!
We shall praise, exalt, and glorify You,
We shall bless Your holy name—
As it is said:
> Of David.
>> Bless the Lord, O my soul, all my being, His holy name
>> (Ps. 103:1).

God—in the greatness of Your might—
Great—in the glory of Your name—
Mighty—for all time—
Awesome—in Your awesome deeds.

The king enthroned aloft on high,
Dwelling forever,
His name is high and holy.
It is written:
> Sing forth, O you righteous, to the Lord;
> it is fit that the upright acclaim Him (Ps. 33:1).

You will be praised by the mouth of the upright,
You will be blessed by the words of the righteous,
You will be exalted by the tongue of the pious,
You will be hallowed in the midst of the holy.
By the myriad choirs of Your people, the house of Israel,
Your name will be glorified, O our king, in every generation.
For it is the duty of all creatures to thank and acknowledge,
> praise, laud, glorify, exalt, adore, bless, uplift, and acclaim
> You, O Lord our God and God of our fathers, beyond all
> the words of song and praise of David son of Jesse, Your
> anointed servant.

The last section, "For it is the duty," uses the same expressions that appear in the rabbinic legend about Moses at the Sea of Reeds (see p. 40). This was what the Israelites too were expected to do as a response to God's miraculous salvation. The section "You will be praised" spells out the name Isaac in Hebrew (Yitzhak) in the first letters of the second word of each stich. In "Who is like You," Deuteronomy 10:17, which forms the basis for the beginning of the Amida, is quoted and then each word in it is expounded: "God—in the greatness of Your might," and so on.

This is a magnificent prologue to the service, setting the stage for the blessings and praises to come.

Torah and Other Biblical Readings

Although the reading of the Torah on weekdays and its significance have already been discussed, the primary reading of the Torah is on the Sabbath. In the talmudic period there were two different methods of reading. In the Land of Israel the Torah was read over a period of three years, while in Babylonia the cycle took only one year. There are synagogues today that use a three-year cycle, but not in the same way as the ancient custom, which was to read the entire Torah consecutively. Today's practice is to read the first one-third of each portion one year, the second one-third the next, and the last one-third on the third year of the cycle. The ancient three-year cycle was eventually abandoned, and the universal tradition now is to begin and end the Torah cycle each year at Simchat Torah. Since there is a different number of Sabbaths in various years (especially because some Jewish years are leap years, which have thirteen months instead of twelve), there are certain portions that may be read together or separately.

The Torah service on the Sabbath is more elaborate than on weekdays. Not only is it longer, since an entire Torah portion is read, and not only are more people called to the Torah (seven on the Sabbath and five on festivals, as opposed to three on weekdays), but the ceremony surrounding taking out the Torah and putting it back is also expanded. Before the Torah is read, verses stressing God's kingship and concluding with "May the Lord grant strength to His people; may the Lord bestow peace upon His people" (Ps. 86:8, 145:13, and 29:11) are recited. Throughout rabbinic writings, the word "strength" is interpreted to mean

"Torah," so this last verse is understood as referring to God bestowing the Torah upon Israel.

A meditation from the Zohar, the mystical book of the Kabbalah composed by Moses de Leon in the thirteenth century in Spain, is read. The passage, written in Aramaic, is a prolonged blessing of God's name, a plea for His favor, and an affirmation of the truth of His Torah:

> I do not place my trust in man,
> Nor rely upon a son of God,
> But only upon the God of heaven,
> For He is the God of truth,
> His Torah is truth,
> His prophets are truth,
> He abounds in deeds of goodness and truth.
> In Him do I trust,
> To His holy and glorious name I utter praises.
> May it be Your will to open my heart to the Torah.
> Fulfill all the wishes of my heart
> And the hearts of all Your people Israel,
> For good, for life, and for peace.

This may well have been intended to indicate Judaism's rejection of the Christian doctrine that Jesus is the "son of God" in whom humanity is expected to believe for salvation. On the contrary, we reject all reliance on human beings and trust only in God. At the same time the reading emphasizes our acceptance of the Torah and prophetic writings as expressing the truth, the main attribute of God. Just as the blessing that follows the Shema repeats the word *emet*—truth—over and over, so this selection repeats its Aramaic equivalent.

On the festivals, the section of the Torah known as the Thirteen Attributes, because it includes thirteen variations on God's attribute of mercy, is recited:

> The Lord! the Lord!—a God compassionate and gracious, slow to anger, rich in steadfast kindness, extending kindness to the thousandth generation, forgiving iniquity, transgression, and sin.
> (Exod. 34:6–7)

This is the climax of the story of Moses' plea that God forgive the people of Israel following the sin of the golden calf. In this verse Moses receives the assurance that the very nature of God is to be forgiving. It is an expansion of the verse in the Ten Declarations: " . . . showing kindness to the thousandth generation of those who love Me and keep My commandments" (Exod. 20:6). It emphasizes the quality of mercy, going far beyond the verse in the Ten Declarations in expressing the forgiving nature of God. The entire verse reads:

> . . . forgiving iniquity, transgression, and sin; yet He does not remit all punishment, but visits the iniquity of fathers upon children and children's children, upon the third and fourth generations. (Exod. 34:7)

For liturgical purposes, the Sages cut the verse artificially. The Hebrew phrase *nake lo yinake* (literally: "remitting, not remitting"—a way of emphasizing the negative, which cannot be reproduced exactly in English) is simply cut off after the word *nake*. By eliminating the two negative words, the verse takes on exactly the opposite meaning: "remitting." This midrashic method was utilized by the Sages in order to further emphasize the forgiving nature of God, eliminating any mention whatsoever of His judgment and punishment. This emended version of the verse became the core of prayers for God's forgiveness (*slichot*) that precede them. Its recitation on the festivals was the result of kabbalistic influence. It appears first in the seventeenth century in a kabbalistic work, *The Gates of Zion*, by Nathan Hanover. Although its appropriateness for the festivals—which are times of joy and not of forgiveness—seems remote, it has become the trademark of those services throughout the Jewish world.

Much more ancient is the practice of reciting the verse "Hear, O Israel" and a rabbinic response to it, "One is our God, great is our Lord, holy is His name," when the scroll of the Torah is taken out of the Ark. This is followed by a call to proclaim the greatness of God: "Exalt the Lord with me; let us extol His name together" (Ps. 34:4).

The Torah is carried in procession from the Ark to the reader's table while verses from First Chronicles 29:11 and Psalms 99:5 and 99:9 are chanted. This ceremonial homage to the Torah emphasizes its centrality and sanctity. The Torah becomes more than a scroll. It is adorned with a beautiful cover and ornaments of silver: crowns, or "pomegranates"; silver cylinders over the handles; bells; and shields patterned after the breastplate of the High Priest. Throughout the centuries Jewish artisans have produced magnificent work in tapestry and metal to adorn these scrolls. The scrolls of the Torah have come to substitute for the fact that Judaism has no holy images. Unlike Catholics, we cannot parade statues and images through the synagogue or the streets. Unlike pagans, we cannot adorn representations of the gods with silver or gold. So our imageless religion takes the most sacred of our objects, the scroll containing the word of God, places it in a shrine, adorns it in beautiful clothing and jewels, and parades it before the people accompanied by song, much as David did when he brought the Ark into Jerusalem "with shouts and with blasts of the horn . . . leaping and whirling before the Lord" (2 Sam. 6:15–16). This joyous feeling is augmented by the fact that when the reading is completed, the Torah is lifted and shown to the entire congregation, which stands and proclaims, "This is the Torah that Moses placed before the people of Israel [Deut. 4:44] at the command of the Lord through Moses [Num. 4:37]" emphasizing both the divine origin of the Torah and the role of Moses in transmitting it to Israel. In some places it is customary to point to the Torah when saying this. When the Torah is returned to the Ark, another procession is held, beginning with another call to praise God:

> Let them praise the name of the Lord,
> for His name, His alone, is sublime;
> His splendor covers heaven and earth.
> He has exalted the horn of His people
> for the glory of all His faithful ones,
> Israel, the people close to Him.
> Hallelujah. (Ps. 148:13–14)

and the chanting of Psalm 29 or, on festivals that fall on weekdays, Psalm 24.

After the weekly Torah portion, called either the Sidra or the *parasha*, is finished, someone is called upon to read a portion, known as the Haftarah (dismissal or conclusion), from one of the books in the second section of the Hebrew Bible, the Prophets. Unlike the Torah readings that begin with Genesis and continue through the end of Deuteronomy, the prophetic portions are not consecutive. Originally there was not even a fixed list of these readings. They were selected by the person who was to expound the Torah or by some synagogue official. They were chosen for their appropriateness to the message being delivered and the Torah portion just read. Eventually specific sections were designated, which in most cases are connected in some way to the weekly Torah portion. On certain special Sabbaths—such as those before the fast of the Ninth of Av, the High Holy Days, or the weeks before Purim and Passover—there are special readings that are appropriate for the season of the year.

The reading from the Prophets is also set in a series of blessings, one preceding it and four following it. Although the sanctity and importance of the Prophets is less than that of the Torah, the blessings of the prophetic reading are much more involved. The blessing before the reading is relatively brief; it praises God, "who chose worthy prophets and favored their words which were uttered in truth. Blessed are You, O Lord, who chooses the Torah, His servant Moses, His people Israel, and prophets of truth and righteousness." Here too the word "chosen" carries with it the connotation of loving.

The first blessing following the reading is an affirmation of our belief that the words of the prophets will be realized. Since the prophetic words were chanted basically in order to bring Israel messages of comfort, this blessing stresses the fact that regardless of the reality of our lives and the great gap that exists between the promises and the actuality of the current situation, these words are true and dependable. We have hope that all will yet be well.

Blessed are You, O Lord our God, king of the universe,
Rock everlasting,
Righteous one of all generations,
Faithful God who says and does, speaks and fulfills—
For all His words are true and righteous.
You, O Lord our God, are dependable
And Your words are dependable—
Not one word of Your words will remain unfulfilled
For You are a dependable God and king.
Blessed are You, O Lord, God—all of whose words are
   dependable.

The next two blessings pray for the rebuilding of Zion and the restoration of the kingdom of David. In all likelihood these blessings are alternate versions of the prayers for the rebuilding of Zion and the Davidic kingship that are found in the Amida. How they came to be recited after the reading from the Prophets is unclear. It is possible that since the comforting message of the Prophets concerned the end of exile and the restoration of Zion, these blessings seemed appropriate. These are the "words" everyone hopes will be fulfilled by the dependable God.

Have mercy upon Zion. . . .
Blessed are You, O Lord, who makes Zion rejoice in her
    children.

Make us rejoice, O Lord our God, in Your servant, Elijah the
    prophet
And in the kingdom of the house of David Your anointed
    one—
    may he come speedily and gladden our hearts!

Let no stranger occupy his throne. . . .
Blessed are You, O Lord, shield of David.

The final paragraph is a blessing for the Sabbath day itself:

For the Torah, for the service, for the prophets,
For this Sabbath day which You have given us, O Lord our
    God,
    for sanctity and rest, for honor and glory—
For everything do we thankfully acknowledge You,
O Lord our God, and bless You—
May Your name be blessed by all living beings forever and
    ever!
Blessed are You, O Lord, who sanctifies the Sabbath.

Of the three sections of the Hebrew Bible—Torah, Prophets, and Writings—readings from the first two are part of the service each Sabbath. The third is not read on a regular basis, but five books from it, known as the Chamesh Megillot (Five Scrolls), are chanted at various appropriate occasions. The Book of Esther, commonly called *the* Megilla, recounts the pseudohistorical story that Purim commemorates and is read on that holiday. Over the centuries a place has been found in the synagogue ritual for the other four *megillot* as well. Lamentations, a collection of dirges concerning the destruction of Jerusalem in 586 B.C.E., is read on Tisha B'Av (the Ninth of Av), the fast day that commemorates the destruction of the First and Second Temples. The Song of Songs, a book of love poems, is read on the Sabbath that occurs during the holiday of Passover. Its depiction of the flowering of nature in the springtime is appropriate for Passover, which is known as the Spring Festival. More importantly, the rabbinic interpretation of the book as a love song between God and Israel, in which God, the lover, seeks His beloved in order to rescue her, is intertwined with the idea that the future redemption of Israel will take place on Passover. The Sages taught that, as Israel was redeemed from Egypt on Passover, so in the future Israel will be redeemed on Passover as well. The Book of Ruth is read on Shavuot both because its harvest theme matches the season and because it is the story of a woman who accepted the Torah—i.e., converted—paralleling Israel's acceptance of the Torah on Shavuot. Finally, the Book of Ecclesiastes is read on the Sabbath during Sukkot. This book is a collection of the sayings of an anonymous teacher of wisdom who assumes the role of Solomon in order to depict the emptiness and vanity of the pursuits of wealth, wisdom, and power. When all is said and done, he finds that there is nothing of value in life aside from enjoyment. Time and time again, he returns to the theme of rejoicing. "Go, eat your bread in gladness, and drink your wine in joy" (Eccles. 9:7); "O youth, enjoy yourself while you are young! Let your heart lead you to enjoyment in the days of your youth" (Eccles. 11:9). There is little of lasting value; all is vanity; therefore one should rejoice in whatever one has, for that is the will of God. Sukkot is termed by the Sages "the holiday of our rejoicing," so the theme of rejoicing as stated by Ecclesiastes is appropriate for it.

Havdalah

Just as the chanting of Kiddush ushers in the Sabbath, so the recitation of Havdalah ("separation") ceremonially parts from it. This prayer too is basically a home ceremony which has found its way into the synagogue.

According to tradition, there is an entire category of worship known as *"havdalot"* (prayers of separation) of which the ceremony at the end of the Sabbath is the best-known.

> The Men of the Great Assembly decreed blessings, prayers, sanctifications (*kedushot*), and distinctions (*havdalot*) for Israel.[14]

Blessings are words of praise for what God has done. Prayers are requests for God to help us. Sanctifications are those prayers that hallow the name of God—*kiddush ha-shem*. *Havdalot* would be those in which a distinction is drawn between categories such as light and darkness, day and night, the holy and the profane.

Judaism constantly makes distinctions, and the conclusion of the Sabbath, which marks such a differentiation in a sharp and sudden manner, becomes the occasion for stressing this fact. The original formula, recorded in the name of Rabbi Judah the Prince, is "He who distinguishes between holy and profane," to which people were free to add whatever categories of distinction they wished.[15] The Hebrew word for "profane" (*chol*) means that which pertains to the weekday or that which is not sacred. The Sabbath is holy; other days are *chol*. That which is dedicated to God or to the Temple is holy; everything else is *chol*. Israel belongs to God and therefore is holy; all others are *chol*, but with the potential of becoming holy when they recognize God. In the words of Isaiah: "In that day, Israel shall be a third partner with Egypt and Assyria as a blessing on earth; for the Lord of Hosts will bless them, saying, 'Blessed be My people Egypt, My handiwork Assyria, and My very own Israel' " (Isa. 19:24–25).

The text of Havdalah used today reads:

> Blessed are You, O Lord our God, king of the universe, who distinguishes between holy and profane, between light and darkness, between Israel and the nations, between the seventh day and the six days of activity. Blessed are You, O Lord, who distinguishes between sacred and profane.

These same "distinctions" are inserted into the fourth blessing of the Amida of the evening service following the Sabbath. Havdalah is also recited at the end of a festival, even though the festivals are not specifically mentioned. It is the recognition of distinctions in general that is the subject.

Havdalah is a particularly beautiful ceremony. Three blessings are recited over three different items—wine, spices, and flame—each of which appeals to a different sense: taste, smell, and sight. These are ancient practices, predating the schools of Hillel and Shammai, who already debated the exact order of their use.[16] Wine is commonly used for the recitation of special prayers. Spices and flame may have come into use because immediately following the Sabbath it is again permissible to light a fire and prepare food, which is accompanied by the fragrance of spices. This rather prosaic beginning has developed over time in more spiritual directions. Spices have been connected with the idea that each person has an "extra soul" on the Sabbath. This is a way of saying that on the Sabbath we live more fully and on a higher plane than during the week, so that the existence of the human being is doubled. When this soul departs at the conclusion of the Sabbath, the person is weakened and needs the scent of spices to revive him. This can be seen as a reflection of the sadness we feel at the conclusion of the Sabbath, during which life has been so good, as opposed to the difficulties of facing the "real" weekday world of need and work.

The rabbis have also connected the flame to a legend concerning Adam, the first human being.

> When it grew dark after the Sabbath, primal Adam became frightened. . . . God provided him with two stones which he rubbed together until light emerged, over which he pronounced a blessing. What blessing did he pronounce? Creator of the lights of flame.[17]

Another Sage suggested that "we recite a blessing over flame because it was the beginning of God's creation."[18] God's first command was "Let there be light." Therefore, the moment the first day of the week begins at the conclusion of the Sabbath, we celebrate the creation, which began on the first day, by imitating the act of God and creating light. In a sense we are like Adam, who received the gift of fire from God Himself. If the Greeks thought that Prometheus had to steal fire from the gods for the benefit of mankind, the Sages taught that Adam was guided in making fire by God, who wanted to help him. When the Sabbath ends, we counteract our sadness at its departure by celebrating the creation of the world.

The three blessings recited are those for wine ("Creator of the fruit of the vine"); spices ("Creator of various spices"), after which we inhale the aroma; and lights ("Creator of the lights of flame"), after which we stretch out our hands toward the flame, bend the fingers, and look at the shadows, at the contrast between light and darkness. The blessing speaks of "lights" in the plural. Therefore the special braided candle used for Havdalah has at least two wicks, so that there are two lights. Many use candles with six wicks, symbolic of the six days of the week. At the conclusion of a festival that does not fall on the Sabbath, the spices and flame are omitted.

Before reciting these blessings and the Havdalah prayer, we chant a collection of verses that give expression to an important emotional component of Havdalah:

> Behold the God who gives me deliverance!
> I am confident, unafraid;
> For Yah the Lord is my strength and might,
> And He has been my deliverance.
> Joyfully shall you draw water
> From the fountains of deliverance. (Isa. 12:2–3)
>
> Deliverance is the Lord's;
> Your blessing be upon Your people! (Ps. 3:9)
>
> The Lord of hosts is with us;
> the God of Jacob is our haven. (Ps. 46:12)
>
> The Jews enjoyed light and gladness,
> happiness and honor. (Esther 8:16)
> So may it be for us!
>
> I raise the cup of deliverance
> and invoke the name of the Lord. (Ps. 116:13)

The common theme of these verses is the assurance of God's help and deliverance. Standing in the dark of evening, we are confident that our lives will be full of light. Following the victory of Esther and Mordecai over their enemies, the Jews of Shushan enjoyed "light and gladness."

Our prayer is: "So may it be for us!" May the coming week be a time of joy and honor for us. The very cup we are to use becomes "the cup of deliverance." We require such assurance when we face the uncertainties of the coming week. Like Adam, we are overcome by fear. We know what has been, but not what will be. Night is always a time of fear, as witness the prayer for protection in the Maariv service, *hashkivenu*. The end of the Sabbath is even more a time when we feel the need of protection. The Sabbath was worry-free. The week is filled with confrontation and struggle. At such a time we require reassurance, and these verses grant it to us.

Havdalah is both a farewell to the Sabbath and a celebration of the challenge of the new week. It symbolizes all the distinctions Judaism draws between the holy and the profane, and assures us that God will help us to cope with the difficulties of the week ahead. God has created a world of light and blessing for us. The light He created has been granted as a gift to humankind. We can kindle flame as He created light and thus become partners in the creation. The week, a time of creation and creativity, is no less a part of the divine plan than is the Sabbath.

The Hallel

The recitation of the Hallel—Psalms 113–18—is unique to the holidays and festivals. This is one of the oldest prayers in our liturgy, not only because the text is from the Bible, but because we know that it was recited as a unit in the Temple during Second Temple times. Before other prayers had been fixed, these particular psalms had been singled out to be recited on certain festival days. After the destruction of the Second Temple, this practice was transferred to the synagogue and became part of the obligatory services to be recited by Jews. We have no way of knowing whether or not these psalms were used similarly during the days of the First Temple, when many psalms were recited there on different occasions. Of the various types of psalms that exist, the ones chosen for this recitation are the ecstatic "hallelujah" compositions, which are exalted in praise of God, plus a thanksgiving psalm (*hodu*). The Sages explained that of all the various forms of prayer found in the Book of Psalms, "hallelujah" is the finest, because it contains "both praise and the name of God."[19] The word "hallelujah" is composed of two words: *hallelu* ("praise") and *jah* ("the Lord").

The original recitation in the Temple was confined to the pilgrimage festivals.[20] It was said twice on the first day of Passover—in the evening when the lamb was slaughtered and in the morning to mark the festival day itself. On Sukkot, however, when special ceremonies were conducted daily with the four species (the citron, the willow, the palm, and the myrtle), it was recited every day. As the Talmud remarks, "Could one imagine that Israel would slaughter the Passover offering or wave the lulav [palm branch] without reciting the Hallel?"[21] It was recited also on Shavuot and every day of Hanukkah.

In later generations, the fact that it was not said every day of Passover was thought strange, and midrashic explanations were suggested:

> Why is "rejoicing" not written [in regard to Passover]? Because the Egyptians died then. And thus you find that on all seven days of Sukkot we recite the Hallel, but on Passover we do not, except on the first day and first evening. Why? As Samuel said, quoting the verse, "If your enemy falls, do not exult" (Prov. 24:17).[22]

The musical renditions of these psalms by the choir of Levites were accompanied by other special events, such as the playing of the flute before the altar.[23] One can imagine the excitement and the beauty of these festivals, when multitudes of people ascended to Jerusalem from all over the country and even from the diaspora, thronging into the Temple compound to bring their offerings and listen to the singing of the Hallel. The Mishna and Talmud indicate that by the time dawn broke, the Temple court was already filled with people.[24]

The inclusion of Hanukkah with the three festivals came about when that holiday was created by the Maccabees in 164 B.C.E. to celebrate their victory and their rededication of the Temple to the service of the God of Israel. According to Second Maccabees 10:5–8, the dedication celebration was patterned after Sukkot, because they remembered how "a little while before, during the Sukkot festival, they had been wandering in the mountains and caverns like wild animals" and had been unable to celebrate the festival properly. Therefore, they actually carried the lulav during the celebration and sang the same songs of praise that were usually sung on Sukkot—i.e., the Hallel. Although in future years the celebration of Hanukkah did not retain most of the specific features of Sukkot, two remained: the duration of eight days (Sukkot and Shemini Atzeret) and the recitation of Hallel each day.

This pattern of reciting the Hallel became part of the synagogue service. In the diaspora, where a second day is added to the festivals, it is said on the first and second days of Passover, two days of Shavuot, every day of Sukkot (including Shemini Atzeret), and Simchat Torah, as well as every day of Hanukkah. In certain rites and in Israel, it is also recited on the first evening of Passover. It is also the practice now to recite the Hallel on two new holidays that have been added in our time to the cycle of the Jewish year, Israel Independence Day (Yom Ha-Atzmaut) and Jerusalem Day (Yom Yerushalayim).

On Sukkot, the lulav and etrog (citron) are held during the recitation of the Hallel and waved in six directions—up, down, east, west, north, and south, indicating the presence of God everywhere in the universe—during the recitation of verses from Psalm 118.

A departure from the Temple practice is that the "partial Hallel"—the regular reading from which two sections have been deleted—is now recited on the remaining days of Passover and on Rosh Hodesh (the beginning of the month). The "partial Hallel" was created in Babylonia long after the Temple had ceased to exist. The idea of omitting the recitation of the opening sections, of Psalm 115 (verses 1–11) and Psalm 116 (verses 1–11) seems strange. The story is related that the great Sage Rav visited one of the academies in Babylonia at the beginning of the third century C.E. "and saw that they were reading Hallel on Rosh Hodesh. He intended to stop them, but when he saw that they skipped parts, he realized that it was their ancestral custom."[25] This practice was adopted throughout the entire diaspora but was unknown in the Land of Israel and made its way there only much later. The probability is that while the synagogue pattern for Hallel was taken over from the practice of the Temple, some Jews in Babylonia, farther removed from the Temple than those in the Land of Israel, found it difficult to understand why there was no Hallel on the other days of Passover or on Rosh Hodesh. These were also times of rejoicing, no less important than the intermediate days of Sukkot. Therefore they began to recite Hallel on them as well, but, being aware that this was an innovation, they found a way of differentiating between the older practice and the new one by leaving out certain verses.[26]

The Sages added a blessing before and after the recitation of these psalms. We might have expected that since Hallel is basically a reading from a biblical book, it would be treated similarly to readings from the Torah or the Prophets, with a blessing praising God for giving us the books of the Bible. It does not. Instead it follows the pattern of blessings recited before the performance of any *mitzva*:

> Blessed are You, O Lord our God, king of the universe, who has sanctified us by His commandments and commanded us to recite the Hallel.

Saying the Hallel thus becomes a ritual commandment to be performed, much like the lighting of candles, the use of the lulav, putting on a tallit, or eating matza at the Passover Seder. It seems that we are commanded to chant these particular psalms on these specific days not in order to recite Scripture but because we are required to acknowledge through their words the mercies of the Lord and the miracles that He performed for us at these seasons. Thus the Sages taught:

> Who determined the saying of the Hallel? Prophets of Israel determined that they should recite it section by section whenever trouble comes or whenever they are redeemed.[27]

Fanciful explanations were offered as to exactly when this collection of psalms was recited for the first time. "Moses and Israel said it when they emerged from the sea." Some suggest that it was said before the sea was split, as a plea to God, or that it was uttered by Joshua when the people of Israel were threatened by the kings of Canaan, or by Deborah and Barak when they were endangered by Sisera, or by Hezekiah when they were besieged by Sennacherib, or by Hananiah, Mishael, and Azariah when Nebuchadnezzar threatened them, or by Esther and Mordecai when Haman wanted to destroy them.[28] These explanations are especially centered on Psalm 115, which is a plea before God.

On these festive occasions, then, Israel celebrates the miracles God performed for us at the Exodus, at Mount Sinai, and during the years of desert wandering. It would be thankless indeed to remember those times and not to praise God for His wonders.

The concluding blessing is similar to other blessings following the reading of songs of praise:

All Your creations shall praise You, O Lord our God, and Your faithful ones, the righteous who do Your will, and all the household of Israel will acknowledge and give thanks, bless, praise, glorify, exalt, reverence, sanctify, and proclaim Your sovereignty in song, O our king. For it is good to thank and acknowledge You; it is pleasant to sing unto Your name—for You are God from everlasting to everlasting. Blessed are You, O Lord king, praised with words of glorification.

It is doubtful that these psalms were written as a unit to be recited together. Indeed, each seems to have its own individual theme, composed for a specific occasion. Nevertheless, when taken together, they form an appropriate unit.

The first psalm in the group is a call to the people to perform the act of praise, an elaborate call to prayer:

Hallelujah.
O servants of the Lord, give praise;
praise the name of the Lord.
Let the name of the Lord be blessed
now and forever.
From east to west
the name of the Lord is praised. (Ps. 113:1–3)

It praises God both for His exalted qualities and for His concern with human beings:

Who is like the Lord our God,
who, enthroned on high,
sees what is below,
in heaven and on earth? (Ps. 113:5–6)

This is the paradox of God, that He is both transcendent and immanent. This praise, however, is not connected to the theme of the festivals, but speaks in terms of the needs of each individual.

He raises the poor from the dust,
lifts up the needy from the refuse heap. (Ps. 113:7)

Psalm 114 describes the event that lies at the historical core of all the festivals, the Exodus from Egypt:

> When Israel went forth from Egypt,
> the house of Jacob from a people of strange speech,
> Judah became His holy one,
> Israel, His dominion.
> The sea saw them and fled,
> Jordan ran backward. (Ps. 114:1–3)

Psalm 115 is a liturgical composition written for a particular occasion, a time of peril when the people flocked to the Temple to seek assurance of their triumph. It is in the form of a dialogue between the people and the Levites, probably originally recited by antiphonal choirs:

> Not to us, O Lord, not to us
> but to Your name bring glory
> for the sake of Your love and Your faithfulness.
> Let the nations not say,
> "Where now is their God?"
> when our God is in heaven
> and all that He wills He accomplishes. (Ps. 115:1–3)

The people plead with God for action. Their destruction would be an act of desecration of God's name. Let Him therefore intervene and bring them victory. The Levites assure Israel that the gods of the nations are worthless and nonexistent. Those who worship them are similarly powerless:

> Their idols are silver and gold,
> the work of men's hands.
> They have mouths, but cannot speak,
> eyes, but cannot see;
> they have ears, but cannot hear,
> noses, but cannot smell;
> they have hands, but cannot touch,
> feet, but cannot walk;
> they can make no sound in their throat.
> Those who fashion them,

all who trust in them,
shall become like them. (Ps. 115:4–8)

What then does Israel have to fear?

O Israel, trust in the Lord!
He is their help and shield.
O house of Aaron, trust in the Lord!
He is their help and shield.
O you who fear the Lord, trust in the Lord!
He is their help and shield. (Ps. 115:9–11)

Idolaters trust in worthless fetishes. Israel must trust in the Lord, who can and will help and shield them. The people accept this reassurance. They believe that God will remember their needs and help them. He will extend His blessing, His salvation, upon them. Blessing also refers to the blessing that the priests recite at the end of the sacrificial ceremony. They will leave doubly blessed:

The Lord is mindful of us.
He will bless us;
He will bless the house of Israel;
He will bless the house of Aaron;
He will bless those who fear the Lord,
small and great alike. (Ps. 115:12–13)

May the Lord increase your numbers,
yours and your children's also.
May you be blessed by the Lord,
Maker of heaven and earth. (Ps. 115:14–15)

The Levites tell the people that they can indeed expect God's blessing. In gratefulness and full of trust, the people now praise God, blessing His name, assured that they will triumph in the trial they face:

The heavens belong to the Lord,
but the earth He gave over to man.
The dead cannot praise the Lord,
nor any who go down in silence.
But we will bless the Lord

now and forever.
Hallelujah. (Ps. 115:16–18)

They had come to the Temple worried and concerned. The words of assurance they have heard permit them to leave full of confidence and trust.[29]

Psalm 116 is a magnificent composition in which an individual who has been saved from death and oblivion describes a terrible ordeal and the way in which God came to the rescue. Within the liturgical framework of the Hallel, this can be seen as a metaphor for the people of Israel at their time of trouble. In Egypt, at the sea, they came close to death and destruction. They called upon the Lord and He saved them. Worshipers come to the Temple—or today to the synagogue—to acknowledge His salvation.

> The bonds of death encompassed me;
> the torments of Sheol overtook me.
> I came upon trouble and sorrow
> and I invoked the name of the Lord,
> "O Lord, save my life!" (Ps. 116:3–4)

> You have delivered me from death,
> my eyes from tears,
> my feet from stumbling. (Ps. 116:8)

In order to repay the Lord, this person wishes to acknowledge God's goodness "in the presence of all His people" (Ps. 116:14) and comes to the Temple:

> I will sacrifice a thank offering to You
> and invoke the name of the Lord.
> I will pay my vows to the Lord
> in the presence of all His people,
> in the courts of the house of the Lord,
> in the midst of Jerusalem.
> Hallelujah. (Ps. 116:17–19)

This is followed by Psalm 117:

Praise the Lord, all you nations;
extol Him, all you peoples,
for great is His steadfast love toward us;
the faithfulness of the Lord endures forever.
Hallelujah.

This brief psalm introduces the theme of giving thanks to God for His mercies, which is the core of Psalm 118, the triumphant conclusion of the Hallel. Written in the first person singular, like the Song of the Sea after which it is patterned, it depicts the thanksgiving of the people after having emerged triumphant from a time of danger and peril. They come to the Temple in order to perform a ceremony of thanksgiving, acknowledging God's wondrous actions on their behalf. What could be more fitting for the festival, when God's past salvation of Israel is recounted:

Acknowledge the Lord, for He is good.
His steadfast love is eternal.
Let Israel declare,
"His steadfast love is eternal."
Let the house of Aaron declare,
"His steadfast love is eternal."
Let those who fear the Lord declare,
"His steadfast love is eternal." (Ps. 118:1–4)

The recitation of the formula "His steadfast love is eternal" is the official act of thanksgiving and acknowledgment they have come to perform. They explain what happened to them to cause them to give thanks:

In distress I called on the Lord;
the Lord answered me and brought me relief. . . .
All nations have beset me. . . .
They have beset me like bees;
they shall be extinguished like burning thorns;
by the name of the Lord I will surely cut them down. . . .
I nearly fell;
but the Lord helped me.
The Lord is my strength and might;
He has become my deliverance. . . .
I shall not die but live

and proclaim the works of the Lord. . . .
Open the gates of victory for me
That I may enter them and praise the Lord. (Ps. 118:5–19)

The procession that has been standing at the gates of the Temple is now admitted through the gates:

This is the gateway to the Lord—
the victorious shall enter through it. (Ps. 118:20)

Once inside, the ceremony of thanksgiving is conducted. It consists of public acknowledgment of God's actions on behalf of Israel:

I acknowledge [*hodu*] You, for You have answered me,
and have become my deliverance.
The stone that the builders rejected
has become the chief cornerstone.
This is the Lord's doing;
it is marvelous in our sight.
This is the day that the Lord has made—
let us exult and rejoice on it. (Ps. 118:21–24)

They call on God to deliver Israel in the future as He did in the past and the present:

O Lord, deliver us!
O Lord, let us prosper! (Ps. 118:25)

The Levites—or the priests—then refer to the Priestly Blessing which ended every service:

May he who enters be blessed in the name of the Lord;
we bless you from the house of the Lord.

The psalm concludes with a reiteration of the ceremony of thanksgiving and acknowledgment, repeating the declaration of belief in the Lord three times:

The Lord is God;
He has given us light;
bind the festal offering to the horns of the altar with cords.

You are my God and I will praise You;
You are my God and I will extol You. (Ps. 118:27–28)

The climax is a repetition of the formula of thanksgiving:

Acknowledge [*hodu*] the Lord for He is good.
His steadfast love is eternal. (Ps. 118:29)

"This is the day the Lord has made—let us rejoice and exult on it" (Ps. 118:24) summarizes the meaning of the festivals, and nowhere is that feeling better manifested than in the chanting of the Hallel, the highlight of the festival service. The synagogue service cannot rival the color, pageantry, and excitement of the festival celebrations in the Temple, but the words of the Hallel assisted by beautiful melodies and spirited singing can give us at least a little touch of ancient rejoicing. Reciting these ancient words helps transport us back to the time of the First Temple, when such words were first recited, to the excitement of a people saved from disaster come together to acknowledge the greatness of the Lord. It places us with the pilgrims who thronged to the Second Temple from all over the world to hear these words recited on the festival days when Jerusalem was at her height and the Temple was one of the great wonders of the world. The closest that one can come to actually re-creating this is to come to the Western Wall on one of the festivals, especially at dawn on Shavuot, when thousands flock to the plaza from all parts of Jerusalem, following a night of study. Streams of people come together and the plaza is crowded as, standing before the remnant of the Temple complex, the worshipers repeat the same words that were said there two thousand years ago or more. The synagogues in which we recite these psalms are far removed from the Temple in time and place, but the words can help us to recapture those feelings of excitement and profound rejoicing. Thus, the ancient images are superimposed upon present realities.

Garments of Prayer: Tallit and Tefillin

Words and music are the basic ways we use to express our devotion to God. There are, however, nonverbal means of communication that can be no less meaningful or important. The times when we sit or stand, the reclining of the head in sorrow or contrition, the bending of the knees, the steps backward we take when concluding the Amida are all bodily symbols of emotions or ideas. Objects can also be part of worship. The lulav, etrog, and shofar are integral parts of prayer. The mezuza on the doorpost is a declaration no less meaningful for being silent and static.

Garments are also an integral part of our approach to God. The descriptions of the clothing worn by the priests who officiated in the Temple and especially the garb of the High Priest, which included such items as a breastplate with twelve precious stones representing the twelve tribes and a golden plate worn on the forehead with the words "Holy to the Lord" cut out of it, are elaborately detailed in Exodus 28:6–43 and 39:2–31. What was important for the priests is also important for the individual Jew. The entire people of Israel is considered "a kingdom of priests and a holy nation" (Exod. 19:6), and this is expressed both through our high standards of ethics and morality and through ritual actions and garments. These garments are in themselves statements concerning our relationship with God:

Beloved are Israel, for the Holy One has surrounded them with *mitzvot*—tefillin on their heads and tefillin on their arms, [four]

tzitzit on their garments, mezuzot on their doorways. Concerning
them, David said: I praise You seven times each day for Your
just rules (Ps. 119:164).[1]

In Judaism today the concept that all Jews are holy and the democratic
basis of the synagogue have resulted in the fact that, unlike the Temple,
special garments are not required by those who lead services in synagogues, while the ordinary Jew at prayer, no matter where, does use
special garments. In the Temple, the officiants were clearly differentiated
from the populace; in the synagogue, there is no differentiation and all
are equally privileged to wear special garments. The use of special rabbinical robes, which was common in Europe even among Orthodox rabbis,
was a practice borrowed from non-Jews in order to clearly demonstrate
the status of "Jewish clergy."

In their origins, both the special garments of prayer were intended
not merely for times of prayer but as part of the daily costume. The tallit
and the tefillin, as well as the head covering (kippa) which is of much
less importance in Jewish law, were to be worn the entire day. Thus
Abraham Ibn Ezra, the medieval Spanish commentator, indicated that
the wearing of the tzitzit (fringes), the main component of the tallit,' was
more important when *not* praying, since during prayer one was unlikely
to be tempted to sin.[2] Temptation occurs during the course of our everyday life, and it is then that we need to be reminded of our obligations
to God. Although there are some who wear tzitzit in the form of an
undergarment called *arba kanfot* ("four corners") or *tallit katan* (a small
tallit) at all times, both the tallit and the tefillin have come to be thought
of as appurtenances of prayer and are identified with the act of worship.

Covering the head is mentioned first in the rabbinic writings, where
its use is an act of piety which seems to have been confined to the Sages
and was not common usage.[3] Although it later became customary to cover
one's head when praying or reading sacred texts, and among some to do
so at all times, this has never been considered a *"mitzva"* in the technical
sense. While there are blessings to be recited when putting on a tallit or
tefillin, there is no such blessing for donning a head covering. It has
become, however, both a distinctive sign of Judaism and a symbol of
modesty and humility.

Both the tzitzit and the tefillin can be traced back to the Bible. In the case of tefillin, we cannot be certain that the verses in the Torah that we identify as describing them were meant to be taken literally. Even if they did refer to some specific object, we do not know that those used during the biblical period were similar to the tefillin of later times. The tzitzit, however, are quite definitely of biblical origin. The commandment is found in a paragraph that became the third section of the Shema:

> Speak to the Israelite people and instruct them to make for themselves fringes on the corners of their garments throughout the generations; let them attach a cord of blue to the fringe at each corner. That shall be your fringe; look at it and recall all the commandments of the Lord and observe them, so that you do not follow your heart and eyes in your lustful urge. Thus you shall be reminded to observe all My commandments and to be holy to your God (Num. 15:38–40).

The description here is obviously of actual garments, and we are told exactly how these fringes were to be made. We are also given clear reasons for doing so: to keep us faithful to God and His commandments, and to help us remember that we have been commanded to be holy.

The biblical scholar Jacob Milgrom has shown that this practice was based on the custom in the ancient Near East of using elaborately decorated hems of garments as signs of status.[4] The more important the individual, the more elaborate the hem. Deep blue or purple dye was expensive, being derived from the murex snail and requiring large quantities of snails for a small amount of dye. It was associated therefore with nobility, and adding blue thread to the fringe signified the worth and status of those who wore it. The dye was also used in priestly garments (Exod. 28:6) and in the inner curtain of the sanctuary (Exod. 26:1). Thus the wearer was elevated to a status similar to that of priesthood: holiness and nobility. Garments with such fringes were a visible sign of the status that Rabbi Akiva later characterized so astutely when he said, "Beloved are the people of Israel for they are called the children of God."[5] Rabbinic Judaism also connected the color to God:

> Rabbi Meir said: Why is blue [techelet] different from all other colors? Because blue resembles the sea, the sea resembles the sky, and the sky resembles the throne of glory, as it is said,

"Under His feet there was the likeness of a pavement of sapphire" (Exod. 24:10).[6]

Rabbi Meir even went so far as to say that since the verse that commands the fringes says, "Look at *it*" (Num. 15:39), in the singular, rather than, "Look at *them*," it indicates that when one fulfills this commandment it is as if one were granted a glimpse of God Himself.[7]

In early biblical days there was no special garment such as the tallit of today. Rather, the garments worn by Israelites were made with a fringe in each place where the hem came to an end, and a blue thread was incorporated into the trim bordering the hem. In this way the Israelite was designated as part of God's noble and holy retinue. This was an outward sign of Israel's designation as a kingdom of priests, intended not so much so that others would recognize their position, but so that they themselves would be conscious of who they were and would not ignore the covenant made with God.

During the period of the Second Temple, the form of the tzitzit seems to have changed. Fringes were attached to any garment that had only four corners. Specific regulations came into existence as to how the white threads should be inserted or attached to the garment, together with a blue thread, but even then this was part of the normal garment rather than a special one. In addition, the way in which the thread was to be wound took on special significance. Each corner has one long thread and three short ones, folded to make eight threads. Since there are 613 commandments, the twists and knots are designed in such a way that, taken together with the numerical value of the word tzitzit itself (600), they add up to 613. Thus the very form of the fringes reminds one of the obligation to observe the commandments.

We also know for certain that women as well as men put such fringes on their garments. Rabbi Judah put fringes on the garments worn by all the women of his household.

The Sages taught: All are obligated to observe the *mitzva* of tzitzit: priests, Levites, and Israelites, converts, women, and slaves.[8]

Rabbi Simeon disagreed, believing that since they are worn only during the day, they fall into the category of commandments that are time-connected, and women are exempt from such commandments.[9] The Sages had ruled that since the Torah mentions that the tzitzit should be seen, they are to be worn only in the daytime. Night is not a time when things are visible. The only exception to this is the eve of Yom Kippur, Kol Nidre, when the extraordinary holiness and uniqueness of the occasion calls for the wearing of this symbol of holiness. Gradually the wearing of tzitzit became a male practice, although it was never actually forbidden to women. Today, the practice of women wearing a tallit is becoming more common outside of Orthodox circles.

A rabbinic tale, based on the biblical wording that the fringes are to help us curb our "lustful urges," illustrates the way in which the Sages thought the tzitzit were to assist us. A student spent a fortune to go to a world-renowned harlot. She had prepared seven beds, one on top of another, six of silver and the seventh of gold. She awaited him on the golden bed, and as he climbed up to reach it the four tzitzit of his garment hit him across the face, whereupon he shamefacedly lowered himself and sat down on the ground. When she asked him what was wrong, he explained that the tzitzit were witnesses which had reminded him of his obligations and his wrongdoing. The woman was so impressed, the story goes on, that she sought out the academy he was attending, studied Judaism, converted, and married the student.[10]

Eventually a garment developed, resembling a cloak, that is worn over regular clothing when prayers are recited. The fringes and not the garment itself are the essence of the commandment. The blessing recited when putting it on makes it clear that the commandment being fulfilled is the one the Torah mentions: wearing fringes. It is: "Blessed are You, O Lord our God, king of the universe, who has sanctified us by His commandments and commanded us to wrap ourselves in tzitzit."[11]

Tefillin

Judaism lays great stress upon actions and tries to achieve the fullest expression of its beliefs and ideals through actions that concretize our faith, as well as through thoughts and words. Thus the tradition was not content with reciting the words of the Shema but devised an action symbol to concretize it and all that it represents: the tefillin. The tefillin, wound around the forehead and the arm, consecrate our entire body, indeed our entire being, to the service of God.

The practice of wearing tefillin was derived from the rabbinic interpretation of the verse "Bind them as a sign on your hand and let them serve as frontlets between your eyes" (Deut. 6:8). The tefillin in use today consist of two small, square, black leather boxes containing four sections from the Torah, to which are attached black leather straps. The sections are Exodus 13:1–10, Exodus 13:11–16, Deuteronomy 6:4–9, and Deuteronomy 11:13–21. The materials that go into the construction of the tefillin are taken from clean animals that were suitable for Temple sacrifice or food, as prescribed in the dietary laws. The words are written on parchment by a scribe (*sofer*), tied with animal hair, and sewn with tendons.

Although rabbinic law insists that the boxes (*batim*) and the outer side of the straps be black, there were some who made themselves ostentatious tefillin plated with gold.[11] The authorities strongly disapproved of this.

Tefillin are decorated with the Hebrew letter *shin*, which stands for the word *Shaddai* (Almighty God). On one side of the head tefilla, the letter *shin* has four instead of the three strokes that usually form it, possibly to signify that the passages inside are written on four separate parchments, while the same passages in the hand tefilla are on one continuous scroll. This practice is ascribed to the fact that the Torah says, "As a sign upon your hand," in the singular, while the passage referring to the head is in the plural: "And they shall be frontlets between your eyes" (Deut. 6:8).

We have no way of knowing if the original intent of that verse was to indicate the wearing of some actual sign or if it is merely poetic language for making the words of the Torah an integral part of one's thoughts and deeds. We do know that the High Priest wore a plate on his forehead inscribed with the name of God:

> You shall make a plate of pure gold and engrave on it the seal inscription: "Holy to the Lord." (Exod. 28:36)

Furthermore, the custom of wearing some object around the neck or near the heart is an ancient one, so the possibility exists that this is the intent of the verse. Recent findings in graves in Jerusalem from the time of the First Temple of small metal scrolls on which were written the Priestly Blessing (Num. 6:24–26) have led to speculation that these were pro- totefillin, worn during life and then buried with the individual.[12] In any case, by the period of the Second Temple, no later than the third century before the Common Era, tefillin similar to ours were worn. These tefillin became for the layman the equivalent of the High Priest's plate, adorning the individual with the name of God and conferring upon him the status of membership in a priestly people. As with the tallit, these tefillin were not intended to be worn only at times of prayer, but all during the day. During the rabbinic period, the Sages at least wore them all day. This was feasible because the boxes then were not hard leather, which would be difficult to wear continuously, but small, soft leather pouches into which the scrolls were inserted. Although these bear an outer resemblance to protective charms and magical amulets, neither the verses from Deu- teronomy on which the Sages based their laws of the tefillin nor the rabbinic interpretations themselves give them any such meaning. They are reminders and signs, part of the system of action symbols with which we surround ourselves. Furthermore, the passages contained within them have no superstitious connotations.

The first two sections, Exodus 13:1–10 and 13:11–16, were chosen because they contain verses that could be seen as referring to wearing tefillin:

> And this shall serve you as a sign on your hand and as a reminder
> between your eyes—in order that the teachings of the Lord may
> be in your mouth—that with a mighty hand the Lord freed you
> from Egypt. (Exod. 13:9)

This follows the commandment to observe the feast of Passover, but it was understood by the Sages as further referring to writing the passage itself and placing it on one's person. The purpose is so that it may serve as a sign and a reminder of God's redemptive actions.

The second section contains a similar verse:

> And so it shall be as a sign upon your hand and as frontlets
> between your eyes that with a mighty hand the Lord freed us
> from Egypt. (Exod. 13:16)

This follows the laws concerning the status of the firstborn: "Every firstborn male among your children you shall redeem" (Exod. 13:13). All the firstborn are consecrated to God because of the fact that they were saved when the firstborn of Egypt were slain. Although it would seem that this passage applies only to the firstborn, it should be remembered that the entire people of Israel is designated as God's firstborn: "Thus says the Lord: Israel is My firstborn son" (Exod. 4:22). Just as the firstborn of Israel were consecrated specifically to God, so too the entire Jewish people has been consecrated to His service, a consecration expressed by our wearing of tefillin.

The third and fourth passages, Deuteronomy 6:4–9 and 11:13–21, are also the first and second sections of the Shema. They too repeat the command to write these words so that they may serve as a sign of our relationship to God. Thus all four passages were selected because they contain the verses that were interpreted as meaning that words of Torah are to be worn on the head and hand and explain their significance as being signs of the unique relationship between God and Israel and the dedication of our lives to His service. This dedication, *kabbalat ol malchut shamayim* (taking upon oneself the yoke of God's kingship), is expressed verbally through the recitation of the Shema and concretely through the wearing of tefillin.

The way in which the straps (*retzuot*) are traditionally wound is a further indication of our subservience to God. They are designed to form the three letters of the word *Shaddai* (Almighty God): *shin, dalet, yod.* The letter *shin* is formed by the strap wound around the middle finger and again by the strap wound around the back of the hand. The *dalet* is formed by the knot of the tefilla at the back of the head, and the *yod* by the knot on the hand tefilla. Thus each person bears the name of God, no less than does the High Priest, literally following the practice in which a servant had his master's name inscribed upon him, as Isaiah indicated in his prophecy:

One shall say, "I am the Lord's,"
Another shall use the name "Jacob,"
Another shall mark his arm "the Lord's,"
And adopt the name "Israel." (Isa. 44:5)

By inscribing God's name upon ourselves, we make quite clear to all the unique relationship between ourselves and God. As the rabbis said,

"And all the peoples of the earth shall see that the Lord's name
is proclaimed over you, and they shall stand in awe of you" (Deut.
28:10). This refers to the tefilla for the head.[13]

Tefillin are not merely a sign of subservience. There is more than that
in our relationship with God. The Shema, which is the acceptance of
God's kingship over us, begins with the word "love": "You must love
the Lord your God" (Deut. 6:5). The tefillin too represent the close
intimacy of love and affection. This is best indicated by the way in which
the straps are wound around the fingers and by the verses that are recited
at that point. The straps wound around the fingers remind us of a wedding
band, and the seven windings around the arm have been taken as symbolic of the seven wedding blessings. During the seventeenth century
it became customary to recite the magnificent wedding formula of God
and Israel found in the Book of Hosea:

> And I will espouse you forever:
> I will espouse you with righteousness and justice,
> And with goodness and mercy,
> And I will espouse you with faithfulness;
> Then you shall know the Lord. (Hos. 2:21–22)

Hosea's daring symbolism depicts Israel as the wife of God who went
astray. In the end, however, there will be another marriage ceremony
more binding and effective than the first, in which God will dower Israel
with all the desirable qualities she had lacked: righteousnes, justice,
goodness, mercy, and faithfulness. From then on, Israel will "know the
Lord," that is, be in a relationship of intimacy with God which represents
the fullest expression of closeness and love between them. Donning the
tefillin, the Jew assumes the role of God's bride and pledges eternal
faithfulness and love to Him. Thus, when the magnificent love poetry
of the Song of Songs was interpreted by the Sages as a symbolic representation of the relationship between God and His people Israel, they
interpreted the Shema and the tefillin as the two great seals of love,
intended to bind them together:

> Set me as a seal upon your heart, as a seal upon your arm (Song
> 8:6). Rabbi Berachia said: "As a seal upon your heart" refers to
> the Shema, as it is written, "Take to heart these words" (Deut.

6:6). "As a seal upon your arm" refers to the tefillin, as it is written, "Bind them as a sign on your hand" (Deut. 6:8).[14]

The mutuality of this relationship was emphasized by another midrash in which God is depicted wearing tefillin. The passages written in His tefillin indicate His love and affection for Israel, paralleling those in our tefillin, which demonstrate our love for Him. Our tefillin say, "The Lord is one."

> What is written in the tefillin of the master of the world? "And who is like Your people Israel, one nation on earth" (1 Chron. 17:21). Said the Holy One to Israel, "You have made Me one unique entity in the world, therefore I will make you one unique entity in the world."[15]

Just as reciting the four passages in the Shema is symbolic of our aspiration to study the entire Torah, so wearing the tefillin with their four Torah passages serves to demonstrate our love of Torah and our desire to learn. This is the spirit of another midrash:

> Israel said to the Holy One, "Master of the world, we want to busy ourselves with Torah day and night, but we are not free to do so." The Holy One replied, "Fulfill the *mitzva* of tefillin and I will account it to you as if you were busy with Torah day and night."[16]

As Maimonides summed it up, the tefillin "remind us continually of God and of our duty to revere and love Him, to keep all His commandments, and to believe concerning God that which every religious person must believe."[17]

Wearing Tefillin   Although the ancient practice was to wear tefillin all day, today they are usually worn only on weekday mornings while the Shacharit prayers are being recited. They are not worn on the Sabbath or holy days,[18] since those times are designated as being a "sign" (*ot*), just as tefillin are a sign. When the entire day is a reminder of God, one needs no further external sign of devotion to God. On weekdays, however, when one's thoughts and energies are likely to be directed toward other matters, we need that additional reminder of our relationship to God. On Rosh Hodesh (the beginning of the month), which is a kind of holiday but is basically a weekday, they are worn until the recitation of Musaf.

The tefilla for the hand is put on first. Right-handed people put it on the left arm, left-handed people on the right arm. The box is placed on the upper arm facing the heart, thus symbolizing that one's strength and one's thoughts are dedicated to God. The following blessing is then recited:

> Blessed are You, O Lord our God, king of the universe, who has sanctified us by His commandments and commanded us to put on tefillin (*l'haniach tefillin*).

The strap is then wound around the arm seven times and the remainder is wound temporarily around the palm.

The tefilla for the head is then placed on the head, the box on the forehead near the hairline and the two straps hanging down in front of the chest. Another blessing is then recited, which concludes with the words ". . . and commanded us concerning the commandment of tefillin [*al mitzvat tefillin*]." This is followed by the same response spoken during the Shema: "Blessed is the name of His glorious Majesty forever and ever."

Thus our attention is focused on the connection between the tefillin and the Shema, and on the idea that wearing tefillin is another way of accepting the kingship of God.

The strap is then unwound from the palm and wrapped three times around the middle finger and once around the fourth finger, reminiscent of a wedding band, and the remainder is wound around the hand to form a *shin*. It is then that the verses from Hosea are recited. When taking the tefillin off, the reverse procedure is followed. Both when putting them on and when taking them off, one stands in order to indicate their importance.

Tefillin are put on while reciting the morning prayers once one has reached the age of fulfillment of the commandments, which is thirteen years for a male and twelve for a female. They are symbolic of mature responsibility and, like all commandments, are not obligatory until the time of maturity. Although until modern times generally only males used tefillin, the Talmud indicates that at least some of the Sages considered tefillin permitted for women:

> Michal the daughter of Kushi put on tefillin and the Sages did not object.[19]

Just as some women today wear a tallit as an expression of their religious beliefs, so some put on tefillin to indicate their full participation in Jewish worship.

Ironically enough, it was one of modern Judaism's most iconoclastic poets, Saul Tchernichovsky, who, in his epic poem *Baruch Mi-Magentzah,*[20] best expressed the religious meaning of the tefillin. The hero, who has been forced by the Crusaders to renounce Judaism, recalls the first time he donned tefillin:

> For the very first time
> In my life now I bind
> To my arm the black box
> And I fear lest it slip,
> For my tender soul knows
> That the synagogue men
> Will watch me with care
> As I enter their midst.
> My father's face I see
> Shining with joy;
> Joyful tremors, holy tremblings
> Surge through my flesh.
> The yoke of the Torah I take on myself,
> The Torah of God, my Rock, my creator.
> My soul fills with strength;
> In all the world none is happy as I.
> And I count: one, two . . .
> Five . . . seven times wound.
> The strap binds my flesh,
> The blood swells beneath.
> My arm aches with pain
> Yet my heart leaps within
> Like a fish in a stream.

The smell of leather fills my nostrils,
A smell sharp and sweet.
"And I will espouse you forever."
Yet I have broken the covenant . . .
"I will espouse you with goodness and mercy."
After strangers have I strayed . . .
"And I will espouse you with faithfulness
And you shall love your creator."

The moving contrast that the poet draws between Baruch's forced disloyalty to God and the first time he expressed his loyalty through the donning of tefillin reveals the depth of feeling the tefillin can evoke. Alienation from God or from Judaism is difficult to overcome. Closeness to God and tradition is difficult to attain. An action that is beyond words, which involves our feelings and senses, which indeed surrounds and encompasses us, may help us to achieve those "joyful tremors, holy tremblings" that define the religious experience.

13

The Blessing After Meals

The opportunity of addressing God is both an obligation and a privilege. The experiences of daily life present us with just such opportunities. The tripartite division of the day, for example, is an experience that invites us to recognize the power behind the universe and to address Him in words of praise, petition, and acknowledgment. Other events in life that occur with less regularity also call for a response. Thus the tradition prescribed blessings to recite upon seeing certain things, eating food, or encountering new or unusual experiences. In this way, experiences are lifted from the ordinary and endowed with special significance. They become moments in which we sensitize ourselves to the presence of God. They move us to declare to others and to ourselves that there is a God and that He alone rules the universe. This is certainly the case when we are confronted either with wondrous sights and experiences or with events that bring us happiness and satisfaction. When seeing magnificent vistas of nature, such as great mountains, we bless God "who makes the creation." If we see the ocean, we say, "Who made the great sea." Hearing thunder elicits a blessing of God "whose might and strength fill the world." A rainbow is both an object of natural beauty and a symbol deriving from the story of the promise made to Noah after the flood. Its appearance is the moment to speak of God "who remembers the covenant, is faithful to His covenant, and fulfills His word." The blessing that for many elicits the most profound emotional reaction is the *shehecheyanu*. Recited at every holiday, at every special new occasion, this blessing is attached to the experience of life itself. To be able to say, "Who has kept us in life, sustained us, and allowed us to reach this moment," means having survived to reach yet another season, another milestone. We bless God, whose sustaining force keeps us alive.

Perhaps the most natural occasion for blessing concerns food. Reciting a blessing before eating has been likened to paying the price to acquire what one is about to consume. This should be interpreted not in the crass sense that God requires us to pay for whatever we take from the world He has created, but rather that it is important for us to realize how much we are dependent upon God. Ultimately, everything we have comes from the sustaining environment He has provided. By acknowledging this, we train ourselves to be grateful, to take nothing for granted, and to properly value the world and its bounty. Were we to pause long enough to recognize this before consuming the products of the earth, perhaps we would not be so quick to abuse and pollute it.

The essence of such a blessing is the acknowledgment that God has created all of this for us. This awareness is much more important than the specific wording. Rabbi Meir taught that even if one did not say the correct blessing ("Who brings forth bread from the earth") but used such expressions as "Blessed is He who created this bread. How pleasant it is!"—that would be an acceptable blessing.[1]

A blessing recited before eating, such as the blessing for bread which is to be said before any meal at which bread, the staple of life, is consumed, is not a biblical command. The Sages derived it by logical reasoning from the Torah's command to bless God after eating (Deut. 8:10). If we bless God when we are satiated, surely we must do so when we are hungry![2]

This Blessing After Meals, Birkat Ha-Mazon (literally, the Blessing of Food), is one of the more well known prayers today because it is recited at so many public occasions, be it weddings, celebrations of a bar or bat mitzva, or dinners sponsored by various organizations. Even groups such as the United Jewish Appeal have issued their own benchers—pamphlets containing the prayer. Lively melodies have also been devised for it, so it can sometimes be a spirited affair. It is, however, more than a community sing. It is a beautiful series of blessings embodying Judaism's philosophy of life.

One might have thought that after eating is precisely the moment when we need say no blessings at all. Does not a blessing imply some need which must be met? In this case, the opposite is true. It is when we do not "need" God for something that we should take the time to remember what we have received from Him. God should be connected in our consciousness with the experience of having fulfilled basic human needs. Such an experience should lead immediately to words of praise. It is not when we are hungry that the most important blessings are recited, but when we are sated. Having eaten enough, it is all too easy to forget the source of all we have and to take our comforts for granted. The Jewish tradition utilizes that moment for driving home the lesson that what we have is not the product of our own might but the result of God's beneficence. The Sages connected having an abundance of material comforts, especially food, with rebellion against God. That was what caused the Israelites to build the golden calf and the generation of the flood to rebel:

> Thus you shall eat your fill. Take care not to be lured away to serve other Gods (Deut. 11:15–16). He said to them: Beware lest you rebel against God, for one does not rebel against God except out of satiety.[3]

The immediate experience of comfort is precisely the time for articulating our indebtedness to God. Thus the midrash teaches:

> Abraham would entertain travelers passing by and, after they ate and drank, he would say to them, "Bless!" They would say to him, "What shall we say?" He would say to them, "Blessed is the eternal God from whose produce we have eaten."[4]

The Birkat Ha-Mazon is fully as important in the regimen of home or community worship as the Amida is in synagogue prayer.

The Sages connected the blessings with the verse "When you have eaten your fill, bless the Lord your God for the good land which He has given you" (Deut. 8:10). They interpret each section of the verse as referring to a different paragraph of the blessing:

> "When you have eaten your fill, bless" refers to the invitation to bless. "The Lord your God" refers to the first blessing. "For the land" refers to the blessing of the land. "Good" refers to

[the blessing of] Jerusalem. "Which He has given you" refers to
the blessing "Who is good and does good."[5]

By dividing the verse in this way, they were able to provide a biblical
basis for the five sections of the Birkat Ha-Mazon which had developed
by the second century c.e.: an invitation to recite the prayer and four
blessings, to which special sections are added in order to signify the
Sabbath, festivals, and holidays, just as such additions are made to the
Amida.

The invitation is used when three or more people have eaten together.
It is a call to bless God, similar to the *barchu* that precedes the Shema.
No minyan is required, however, and the more informal words "Gentle-
men [or Friends], let us say the blessing" are used, to which the others
respond, "May His name be blessed forever." The leader repeats this,
under the principle that one does not ask others to praise and not do so
oneself. The leader then adds, "With your permission, let us bless Him
from whose possessions we have eaten and whose goodness gives us life."
When there are ten who have eaten together, the word *eloheinu* ("our
God") is added to the invitation to bless, and the response becomes:
"Let us bless our God." Although it did not become the practice, the
Mishna suggested adding the name "the Lord" if there were one hundred people present and gave more elaborate formulas for increasing
numbers.[6]

The first blessing is an immediate response to the experience of
eating, which causes us to realize that God has created a world in which
our needs for sustenance can be met. Such a realization brings us to feel
that God is merciful and good, that He relates to humanity with love.[7]
The paragraph opens and closes with a blessing:

Blessed are You, O Lord our God, king of the universe, who
sustains the entire world with His goodness. With grace, loving-
kindness, and mercy He gives bread to all flesh, for His loving-
kindness is everlasting. Because of His great goodness, we have
lacked nothing; because of His great name, we shall never lack
food. For He is God who sustains and nourishes all and is good
to all and prepares food for all creatures that He created. Blessed
are You, O Lord, who sustains all.

There could hardly be a blessing more universal in nature than this, expressing belief in the God who created the world as an act of love, whose relationship to humanity is one of mercy and faithfulness. All His creatures are beloved to Him. There is no mention here of any particular relationship with either the people or the Land of Israel. It is rather the loving father of all who is celebrated in a blessing that could be recited by any human being who believes in God the creator.

The nature of the second blessing is quite different. The main subject is the Land. As indicated in the biblical verse we have discussed (Deut. 8:10), God is to be blessed for food and sustenance, but also specifically for the Land of Israel, which He bestowed upon His people. Just as food is a sign of His goodness, concern, and love, so the Land that produces it is proof of these same qualities. The biblical phrase "for the good land" quoted in this paragraph, then, is not a general reference to the earth but one specific to the land given to the Jewish people, the Land of Israel.

> We thankfully acknowledge You, O Lord our God,
>   for granting our ancestors the inheritance of a pleasant, good,
>   and spacious land,
>   for taking us out of the land of Egypt, O Lord our God, and
>   redeeming us from the house of bondage,
>   for the covenant which You have implanted in our flesh,
>   for the Torah which You have taught us,
>   for the laws which You have revealed to us,
>   for life, grace, and kindness which You have bestowed upon
>   us,
>   and for the food with which You always provide us, every day,
>   at all seasons and times.
> For all this do we thankfully acknowledge You and bless
>   You
> —may Your name be continually blessed by all living beings
>   forever and ever—
> as it is written: When you have eaten your fill, bless the Lord
>   your God for the good land which He has given you
>   (Deut. 8:10).
> Blessed are You, O Lord, for the land and for the food.

Wherever a Jew resides, no matter in what country the food he has eaten was grown, he must acknowledge the gift of a specific land bestowed by God upon a homeless people. Later, the Sages insisted that the themes of Torah and the covenant also be mentioned. In the end, this blessing becomes an opportunity to express gratitude to God for His particular relationship to the Jewish people. It is a means of fostering Jewish national identity and strengthening the bonds of Jewish peoplehood. Thus, the first two blessings constitute complementary expressions of universality and particularity.

The third blessing introduces an entirely new and different theme. It does not refer to the role of God as our provider and sustainer. Strictly speaking, it is not even a blessing, since it does not give thanks or acknowledge God's past actions, but a request, a prayer, a plea that God act mercifully toward Jerusalem and toward the house of David. Thus it is yet another version of the prayer for the restoration of Jerusalem and the kingship of David that appears in the Amida and the similar one recited in the blessing after the Haftarah. In different words, they all ask God to show His mercy by restoring Jerusalem and reestablishing Jewish sovereignty through the house of David, God's anointed.

> Have mercy, O Lord our God, upon Your people Israel, upon Your city Jerusalem, upon the the dwelling place of Your glory, Zion, upon the kingship of the house of David, Your anointed one, and upon the great and holy House which is called by Your name.

Since the context and the setting for this recitation is a meal, the idea of sustenance is introduced here and interpreted in a novel way, one that reflects the reality of life and especially of the difficulty of living on the sufferance of others, which was the common Jewish condition for so many centuries. Not being able to provide for oneself but having to depend on others is a condition of shame and embarrassment. The most important thing that God can do for us is to help us to be independent, indebted only to Him:

> Our God, our father, care for us, provide for us, sustain us, give us our needs, prosper us—and speedily relieve us of all our sorrows. Let us not be in need of the generosity of human beings

nor of their loans, but only of Your full, open, abundant, and spacious hand, O Lord our God, so that we shall never be ashamed or embarrassed.

This last section is a later addition which does not appear in the Siddur of Saadia Gaon. The concluding blessing (*hatima*) returns to the earlier theme:

Rebuild Jerusalem the holy city speedily in our days. Blessed are You, O Lord, who in His mercy rebuilds Jerusalem. Amen.

Thus the paragraph that began with "mercy" ends with it as well.

Although the wording of this blessing was undoubtedly revised after the fall of Jerusalem and the destruction of the Temple in 70 C.E., all these Jerusalem-centered prayers have a much more ancient origin. It has been suggested that they were composed during the Maccabean era, when there was great danger for Israel, Jerusalem, and the Temple.[8] The Book of Ben Sira, written in the second century B.C.E., already contains a very similar prayer for Israel, Jerusalem, Zion, and the Temple:

Have mercy on the people called by Your name,
Israel Your firstborn.
Have mercy on Your holy city,
Jerusalem Your dwelling place.
Fill Zion with Your splendor
And Your Temple with Your glory. (Ben Sira 36:17–19)

Thus Jews prayed for Jerusalem and the Temple when these existed at their height and were in the hands of the Jewish people. As long as the world remained unredeemed, Jerusalem had not reached its full glory. This theme was so important that it was included whenever a major prayer was recited, be it the Amida or the Birkat Ha-Mazon. God, who is so beneficent and supplies our needs, can certainly be counted upon to supply this need as well and to fulfill His word concerning Jerusalem. The very recitation of such a request creates the sense of assurance that it will be fulfilled. Thousands of years elapsed, during which the ruins of Jerusalem testified to the fact that this request had not been answered, yet Jews continued to recite it and come away with the belief that there was still hope. As the midrash put it in a comment to Psalm 31:24 ("The Lord guards those who believe"):

> This refers to Israelites who say, "Blessed is He who revives the dead," and answer, "Amen," for they believe with all their strength that the Holy One revives the dead—even though the dead have not yet been revived. They say, "Redeemer of Israel," even though they have not been redeemed. They say, "Blessed is He who rebuilds Jerusalem," even though it has not yet been rebuilt![9]

Perhaps this was the source of strength that permitted the Jewish people to survive and provided the energy for the ultimate realization of those hopes.

This blessing concludes the basic format that had evolved by the first century C.E. It consisted of only three blessings, which explains why the word "amen" is inserted here. A fourth blessing was eventually added. Although we do not know the actual reason for this, later teachers offered an explanation as part of their attempt at tracing the origins of the entire Birkat Ha-Mazon. While not historical, it is nevertheless of interest:

> Rav Nachman said: Moses instituted the blessing "Who feeds" for Israel at the time when the manna descended. Joshua instituted the blessing of the Land for them when they entered the Land. David and Solomon instituted the blessing "Rebuilds Jerusalem," David instituting "For Your people Israel and Your city Jerusalem" and Solomon "For the great and holy House." The blessing "Who is good and does good" was instituted in Yavneh because of those who were slain at Bethar . . . because they did not rot and because they were brought to burial.[10]

The last reference is to the fall of the final fortress at the time of the Bar Kochba rebellion, in 135 C.E., which resulted in a terrible slaughter and the end of Jewish independence until our own time. In the rabbinic memory, Bethar was the bloodiest of all Jewish defeats and symbolized the tragedy of that ill-fated rebellion. The killing of men, women, and children in huge numbers dwarfed the tragedy of the destruction of Jerusalem or the fall of Massada.[11] Even though the evidence indicates that this fourth blessing was actually known to Sages who lived before that time, it has always served as a reminder of those terrible events.[12]

The essence of this fourth blessing can be summed up in the words that give it its name and which probably constitute its original core:

> . . . Who is good and does good unto all . . . who rewarded us, rewards us, and will reward us. . . .

This is based on the blessing "Who is good and does good," said whenever one hears good tidings, the opposite of the blessing "the true judge" (*dayyan emet*), recited when hearing bad news.[13] Although the massacre at Bethar could by no stretch of the imagination be called "good tidings," the fact that, according to the Talmud, the bodies were brought to proper burial was cause for blessing God. In Jewish tradition, proper burial according to the rites of Israel is an important *mitzva* and an act of kindness toward the dead. We are, of course, not the only ones to be concerned with giving the dead a respectful burial. In Sophocles' play, Antigone risks her life to bring the body of her brother to proper burial and not permit it to rot in the field. Indeed, she loses her life because of her deed. In Judaism, this concern takes on added importance. Not only is the thought of bodies strewn upon the earth repugnant, but it detracts from the honor due to the body, which is, after all, created in the image of God.[14] The horror in our minds when we think of the way in which bodies were disposed of in the Holocaust makes our generation particularly sensitive to this and capable of understanding the thinking of the rabbis.

Whatever the actual impetus that caused it to be added to the three-fold blessing, this blessing serves to remind us of that historic occurrence, to reinforce the main theme of the Birkat Ha-Mazon—God's goodness experienced in the meal—and to assure us that our request for His mercy is as good as answered. His rewards in the past and the present give us reason to believe that they will extend to the future as well.

Over the years this fourth blessing has become a kind of catchall to include a number of more informal prayers that begin not with *baruch* but with *ha-rachaman*—"the Merciful One." Just as it was common to conclude the Amida with private prayers or requests, so here, when the formal blessing comes to an end, individual requests are added. Different rites have included such requests as:

> Enlighten our eyes in Your Torah and let us succeed in all our endeavors.

> Save us from poverty.

> Remove the evil inclination from within us.

None of these appear in the version commonly used today, in which we ask God the merciful to bless the host of the meal and all those assembled, and to hasten the messianic era. This last is unusual, since the more formal prayers carefully avoid references to the Messiah. Today, many have added prayers for the State of Israel and for Jews unable to leave lands of oppression.

In keeping with the general principle that all blessings must end with "peace," here too the theme of peace is inserted toward the end, through the recitation of the last line of the Kaddish—"He who makes peace in the heavens will make peace for us and for all Israel"—and of Psalm 29:11:

> May the Lord grant strength to His people;
> May the Lord bestow on His people peace.

The verse that is recited just prior to this has always been problematic:

> I have been young and am now old,
> but I have never seen a righteous man abandoned,
> or his children seeking bread. (Ps. 37:25)

The lines come from a pietistic psalm whose entire theme is that the righteous man need not worry. God will care for him and reward him while punishing the wicked. As other sources in Judaism have frequently acknowledged, the world is unfortunately not so simple, and there is ample suffering of the righteous and rejoicing by the wicked. Some recite the verse quietly, in recognition of that sad truth. It is also possible to view it as an admonition to us. When the righteous are abandoned and their children must seek bread, we should not stand by and witness it but do something about it. It has been remarked that there are times when we should act as if there were no God and do those things ourselves that need to be done. Feeding the hungry is one of them. As Isaiah put it when he denounced those who fast in order to seek God's forgiveness while continuing acts that cause human suffering:

No, this is the fast I desire:
To unlock the fetters of wickedness,
And untie the cords of the yoke
To let the oppressed go free;
To break off every yoke.
It is to share your bread with the hungry,
And to take the wretched poor into your home;
When you see the naked, to clothe him,
And not to ignore your own kin. (Isa. 58:6–7)

It may be that the entire Birkat Ha-Mazon has to be recited in the light of Isaiah's message. The blessing makes us aware of the resources that God has provided which make it possible for us to sustain life. At the same time, we see a world in which these resources are not properly utilized, in which there are those who have and those who have not, in which all too often exploitation is the rule, with little thought given to either immediate or long-range effects. Birkat Ha-Mazon states the situation from God's point of view: the raw materials are there; the potential for a prosperous humanity exists; but human beings must become the partners of the Almighty and take the proper actions in order to make God's dream a reality.

During the sixteenth century, the custom evolved of chanting Psalm 126 before reciting the Birkat Ha-Mazon on the Sabbath, holidays, and other happy occasions. This psalm expresses the great joy that will come with salvation and the return to Zion:

When the Lord restores the fortunes of Zion
—we are veritable dreamers—
our mouths shall be filled with laughter,
our tongues, with songs of joy. (Ps. 126:1–2)

Chanting the psalm on the Sabbath as an introduction to the Blessing After Meals was another indication that on that day one feels a foretaste of the redemption and of the world-to-come. Today, with the return of

Israel to its land, the words are not simply a pious hope for the future but a description of an event that has taken place in the lifetime of many of us and can be experienced fully. Thus on festive occasions the Blessing of Food also becomes an opportunity for Jews everywhere to express wonder and thanksgiving at the modern miracle of the restoration of Zion.

14

Rites of Mourning

*G*rief is one of the strongest and most natural of all human emotions. When confronted with death, especially of those with whom we had special ties of love, we need not be told what to do in order to mourn.

What need is there, then, for rites of mourning, for special words to say and actions to take? Would we not be better off simply expressing ourselves spontaneously or, better yet, experiencing these feelings within and forgetting Hamlet's "trappings and . . . suits of woe"? Yet there are times when the grief remains so deep inside that it finds insufficient outward expression and cannot be dealt with in a way that helps the bereaved to find his or her way back to the path of living. The Jewish tradition has evolved a liturgy of mourning that permits the expression of natural feelings and yet channels them into the process of healing. As a religious tradition, it endeavors to help the mourner place the experience of grief within the context of belief.

In this chapter we will deal primarily with those aspects of mourning that are connected to prayer. These include the prayers recited at a burial, the Mourners' Kaddish, the additions and deletions to the service at a house of mourning, the Yizkor service, and the observance of the *yahrzeit*, the anniversary of a death.

Prayers at the Burial

Although Jewish law requires the mourner to tear his or her garment as
a sign of grief and to recite a blessing prior to the funeral, this blessing
was not instituted specifically for mourners or for funerals but is the one
to be recited whenever hearing bad news: "Blessed are You, O Lord our
God, king of the universe, the true judge" (*dayyan emet*). When viewing
any evidence of catastrophe, one recites this blessing.[1] This includes
specifically the death of a parent.[2] The Sages taught that "one is required
to bless God for the bad, just as one is required to bless Him for the
good."[3] The requirement is connected with the verse "You shall love
the Lord your God . . . with all your might [*meod*]" (Deut. 6:5), which
was interpreted by the rabbis as meaning: "with whatever measure [*mid-
dah*] He metes out to you, acknowledge Him greatly."

This concept is illustrated by the Sages in a midrash concerning Job:

> The Lord has given, and the Lord has taken away; blessed be
> the name of the Lord (Job 1:21)—for the measure of good and
> for the measure of punishment. What did his wife say to him?
> "You still keep your integrity? Blaspheme God and die!" But he
> said to her, "You should speak as did the shameless women (of
> the generation of the flood). Shall we accept only good from God
> and not accept evil?" (Job 2:9–10). The people of the generation
> of the flood were vile during good times, yet when punish-
> ment came upon them, they accepted it, whether they liked
> it or not. . . . Should not we be well behaved also during
> punishment?[4]

Since there is only one God, Judaism cannot divide good and evil and
say that only the good comes from God and the evil has another source.
Ultimately everything comes from Him. This is the problem that has
vexed religious thinkers from the time of the author of Job through our
own day, when the Shoah (the Holocaust) has rendered the concept of
God as the direct source of all that happens obscene and blasphemous.
The author of Job does not deny that all comes from God, but he does
make two very important statements: that one cannot assume that human
suffering is a sign of human sin and that understanding the ways of God
is beyond our human abilities.

Reciting this blessing does not mean that one must not be unhappy about terrible things that happen, but that even such times can be transformed into an occasion to acknowledge and bless God. Blessing God is not the same as thanking Him. One would have to be particularly masochistic to thank God for things that we wish with all our hearts had never happened. To bless God when tragedy occurs is to express ultimate faith in His existence and goodness and in the value of life despite what has happened. The blessing is recited not because I thank God for what has happened, and not even because I believe that He wished it so, but in order to assert my continuous belief even under difficult circumstances. Suffering is a time to affirm God, just as is rejoicing. Despite my questions, I hold on to my belief not only that God exists, but that there is ultimate meaning in life and value in upholding morality.

Milton Steinberg, a brilliant rabbi who died at the age of forty-six, wrote of the way in which belief in the existence of God can enable one who is to die to take comfort:

> Given God, everything becomes more precious, more to be loved and clung to, more embraceable; and yet at the same time easier to give up. . . . For these belong to the universe and the God who stands behind it. . . . I let go of them the more easily because I know that as parts of the divine economy they will not be lost. . . . When they slip from my hands they will pass to hands better, stronger, and wiser than mine. For only when He is given, can we hold life at once infinitely precious and yet as a thing lightly to be surrendered.[5]

This same belief can invest the recitation of the mourning blessing with the power to help us bear our grief.

The words recited at the burial are an elaboration on the same theme. Known as *tziduk ha-din* (the Justification of Judgment), they represent the willingness of the mourner to accept what has happened and not to challenge God's justice. The roots of this ceremony are to be found in the stories of Jewish martyrs who, at the hour of death, would recite verses indicating their belief in God despite what was happening to them.

The Rock!—His deeds are perfect, yea, all His ways are just (Deut. 32:4). When they apprehended Rabbi Hanina ben Ter-

adion, he was condemned to be burned, together with his Torah
scroll. When he was told of this, he recited this verse: The
Rock!—His deeds are perfect.[6]

This same verse is also interpreted to mean that Moses told Israel, "I
do not tell you merely that He does not justify the guilty or punish the
innocent, but that He does not even exchange one for the other,"[7] i.e.,
merit and guilt are not exchanged, but each deed is rewarded or punished
appropriately. God's judgments are perfect. In view of these interpretations, it is no wonder that this same verse is the first to be recited in
the burial service, which consists entirely of similar verses and verse
fragments, together with explanations and poetic expansions, written in
rhyming stanzas.

> The Rock!—His deeds are perfect,
> Yeah, all His ways are just;
> A faithful God, never false,
> True and upright is He (Deut. 32:4).
> The Rock! Perfect in all His deeds.
> Who can say to Him, "What are You doing?"
> He rules what is below and what is above.
> The Lord deals death and gives life,
> Casts down into Sheol and raises up (1 Sam. 2:6).
> The Rock! Perfect in all actions,
> Who can say to Him, "What are You doing?" (Eccles. 8:4).
> He decrees and acts, freely acting faithfully toward us.
> Because of the merit of him who was bound as a lamb,
>   listen and act! (Dan. 9:19).
> Righteous in all His ways (Ps. 145:17).
> The Rock! Perfect, long suffering, filled with mercy.
> Have pity and mercy upon fathers and sons,
> For forgiveness and mercy belong to You, O Master.

The *piyyut* continues in this vein, repeating the key words "righteous,"
"judge," and "true," and then concludes with two well-known verses:

> The Lord has given, and the Lord has taken away;
> Blessed be the name of the Lord (Job 1:21).

But He, being merciful, forgave iniquity
    and would not destroy;
He restrained His wrath time and again
and did not give full vent to His fury (Ps. 78:38).

The sum total of this burial prayer is an affirmation of God's quality of
mercy. Even though we have experienced His quality of justice, of harsh-
ness, we accept this and reaffirm our belief in His essential love. The
reality of death is not to be allowed to annul our ability to believe in
goodness as a divine quality.

The *piyyut* is not couched in the form of a blessing. It never uses the
terminology "Blessed are You, O Lord." It was composed at a time when
the basic blessings had already come into being and nothing of that sort
was being added to the liturgy. Strangely enough, there is such a thing
as a "Blessing of the Mourners," which is mentioned often in the Mishna
and the Talmud but which eventually ceased to be used.[8] This was a
series of blessings that was recited first in the synagogue or in the town
square and then in the house of the mourners. It was recited not by the
mourners themselves but by others in the mourners' presence. Its main
purpose was to strengthen and comfort the mourners. This was not done
prior to the burial, when it was considered improper to try to comfort a
person, the grief being still too intense. Rather, it was recited after the
burial had taken place. These blessings are unusual in that they do not
address God but speak directly to the mourners and then to those who
comfort them.

Although these blessings are not in current use, it is worth looking
at them in order to understand Judaism's approach to mourning. The
first blessing spoke of the greatness of God and concluded with "Blessed
are You, O Lord, who revives the dead," the same blessing that appears
in the *gevorot*, the blessing in the Amida that stresses God's might and
wonders.[9] Thus the process of healing begins by reaffirming the belief
that in some way human existence continues after death.

The second blessing was directed at the mourners themselves.

Our brothers who are worn out and crushed by this mourning,
    let your hearts consider this: this is the path that has existed from

the time of creation and will exist forever. Many have drunk from
it and many will yet drink. As was the first meal, so shall be the
last. Our brothers—may the master of comfort comfort you.
Blessed is He who comforts the mourners.

The act of comforting is performed through helping the mourners realize
that what they are undergoing, terrible and personal as it is, is part of a
universal process. To know and experience sorrow and loss is part of the
human condition. Death has been part of life since the beginning and
will continue to be part of life until the end of the world as we know it.
To quote Shakespeare:

Thou know'st 'tis common; all that lives must die,
Passing through nature to eternity. . . .
But you must know, your father lost a father;
That father lost, lost his. . . .
From the first corse till he that dies today,
This must be so.[10]

This same sentiment is voiced today when the mourners follow the
practice of walking between two rows of friends upon leaving the grave
and again when they enter the synagogue for the first time. We say to
them, "May God comfort you among the mourners for Zion and Jerusalem." This is also said whenever one departs from a mourner during
the week of mourning.

On the one hand, there is an inclination to say, "What does it matter
who else has suffered a loss? Mine is unique to me." On the other hand,
it may help to place one's sorrow into proper perspective. Certainly the
very fact that others come to offer words of comfort is helpful. The very
stylized words have a value in placing what is happening into a ritual
framework that elevates it from the everyday. Yes, it happens to
everyone, but that does not mean that it is to be passed over and has no
significance.

The third of the ancient blessings addresses itself to those who have
come to comfort:

Our brothers who perform acts of loving-kindness,
children of those who perform acts of loving-kindness—
who follow the way of our father Abraham. . . .
Our brothers—may He who rewards goodness reward you.
Blessed are You who rewards deeds of goodness.

One of the basic concepts of rabbinic Judaism is *gemilut hasadim*, the performance of acts of loving-kindness. That which characterizes the Jew is an attitude of active mercy, of care for other human beings. Loving-kindness, the willingness to help others not only through charity but through personal concern, is the mark of a descendant of Abraham. Such acts as visiting the sick, burying the dead, and comforting the mourner are classified as *gemilut hasadim*. This blessing stresses that value concept and takes the opportunity to emphasize the importance of the help that the community is offering to the mourner. Thus people are encouraged to go and comfort the mourner so that this important practice will not be abandoned.

Judaism is not a solitary religion. It places the experiences of life within a context of living in a community. These blessings are evidence of that. The community comes together at this time of personal loss in order to affirm its belief, and to speak words of consolation to the bereaved, putting the sorrow into a universal context, demonstrating the concern of all for the suffering of each one, and praising those who fulfill this act of kindness.

The Mourners' Kaddish

The Mourners' Kaddish is undoubtedly one of the best-known prayers of Judaism. Regardless of its title, its words have no connection to death or mourning. Not a syllable expresses any concept whatsoever of Jewish belief concerning life after death or resurrection, themes that are dealt with in other Jewish prayers. The Kaddish is a prayer for the sanctification of the name of God, a petition asking that the kingdom of God be established on earth and that this be done speedily so that we ourselves may witness it. The origins of the Kaddish also have nothing to do with death or mourning. It began as a popular prayer recited at the conclusion

of a biblical discourse, expressing the hope that the biblical words of
hope and comfort would be speedily fulfilled. The Mourners' Kaddish
is but one version of this basic prayer that God's kingship be revealed.
The opening words, *yitgadal ve-yitkadash*, are taken from Ezekiel 38:23:
ve-hitgadilti ve-hitkadishti—"Thus will I manifest My greatness and My
holiness, and make Myself known in the sight of many nations. And they
shall know that I am the Lord." This is the rabbinic concept of *kiddush
ha-shem* (sanctifying the name of God). To sanctify God's name is to bring
honor to God in a public way. Since a quorum of ten constitutes a "public"
in Jewish law, any act of sanctification can be recited only when this
quorum, called a minyan, is present.

The sanctification of God's name is more than a ritual act. Whenever
a Jew does anything that causes others—Jews or non-Jews—to praise God
or to recognize the wonders of God, His deeds, His Torah and commandments, that person has performed an act of *kiddush ha-shem*. The
ultimate act of *kiddush ha-shem* is martyrdom, and indeed that is frequently
the meaning ascribed to the term itself. To be willing to die rather than
transgress God's will is the supreme manifestation of sanctifying His
name in the world. *Kiddush ha-shem* and the concept behind it have several
liturgical expressions, including the Kedusha and the Kaddish. Sanctity,
however, is not the main subject of the Kaddish. The word "holy" appears
only once. The central idea is that God's kingship be revealed, that all
the words of the comforting prophecies be realized during our own days
and not in some distant millennium.

Although the Kaddish appears in many variations, its ancient kernel
is to be found in lines which are in Aramaic, the vernacular of rabbinic
times:

May His great name be magnified and sanctified
According to His will in the world which He created.
May He establish His kingship in our lifetime, in our days,
    and in the lifetime of all the house of Israel—speedily and
    soon—and say: Amen.

May His great name be blessed forever and for all eternity.
And may He be blessed for all eternity.[11]

May the name of the Holy One, blessed is He, be lauded,
    glorified, exalted, raised, honored, uplifted, and praised.

He is above all blessing, song, praise, and words of consolation
recited in this world—and say: Amen.

May there be great peace from heaven
And life for us and for all Israel—and say: Amen.

The prayer thus concludes with a request that God bless Israel with
peace, as does the Priestly Blessing.

Amram Gaon said that the seven words of praise—lauded, glorified,
exalted, raised, honored, uplifted, and praised—represent the seven
heavens, and indeed this suggestion gives us some hint at the origins
and intentions of this prayer. We have already discussed the mystical
prayers recited by those who wished to ascend to heaven (see pp. 171–
72). The Kedusha clearly resembles them. So does the Kaddish, with
its repetition of words of praise and exaltation. It is characteristic of such
prayers that they use words and repetitions in a way that is far beyond
the rational semantic content of the words. Such words of glorification
of God could well accompany mystical exercises.

This prayer was originally used not in the synagogue but in the house
of study, where it was recited after a discourse on the Torah had been
expounded.[12] These are the words of consolation which are referred to
in the fourth paragraph. After listening to a discourse, what can be more
spontaneous and appropriate than praying that the hopes voiced in it be
speedily realized? The antiquity of the prayer can be seen in the fact
that it is extremely similar to the so-called Lord's Prayer found in the
Christian Bible: "Our father in heaven, / Sanctified be Your name. / May
Your kingdom come. / May Your will be done on earth as it is in heaven."[13]

The popularity of the Kaddish was such that it came to be used not
only upon the conclusion of sermons but as a conclusion of almost every
section of the service. When recited after the conclusion of the Amida,
a paragraph was added asking that prayer be accepted:

Accept the prayers and supplications of all Israel before their
father in heaven—and say: Amen.

When recited at the conclusion of other portions of the service, a short-
ened version is used, consisting of the first few sections. This is known
as the *"chatzi* (partial) Kaddish."

More sections were added to make a unique recitation when concluding the study of a portion of rabbinic texts, asking God's blessing upon the Sages of Israel.

The best-known version is called the Mourners' Kaddish. When and how this prayer became associated with death and mourning is not entirely clear. The Talmud contains a statement indicating that the response said in the Kaddish was considered helpful in annulling any heavenly decrees against a person.

> Rabbi Joshua ben Levi said, "If one answers, 'Amen. May His great name be blessed,' decrees against him are nullified."[14]

This idea is then reflected in a legend concerning Rabbi Akiva which is found in several late sources:

> Rabbi Akiva was walking in a cemetery when he encountered a man naked and black as coal, with a great bundle of thorns on his head. . . . Rabbi Akiva tried to stop him. . . .
>
> He said to [Akiva], "I beg you—do not delay me—lest those in charge of me become angry!"
>
> He said to him, "What is this, what is your work?"
>
> The dead man said to him, "Every day I am sent to cut wood."
>
> He said to him, "What was your work in this world?"
>
> He said to him, "I was a tax collector, and I favored the wealthy and was stringent with the poor."
>
> He said to him, "Have you not heard from those in charge of you how you may assuage this punishment?"
>
> He said to him, ". . . I have heard something from them which does not sound possible . . . that if one has a son who stands in the congregation and says, 'Bless the Lord,' and they reply to him, 'May His great name be blessed,' he is immediately released from punishment." . . .
>
> Therefore it is the custom to have an orphan recite *barchu* or Kaddish at the conclusion of the Sabbath.[15]

The conclusion of the Sabbath was thought to be the time when souls resume their punishment after having been released for the Sabbath. These superstitious folk beliefs were opposed by many authorities, who insisted that prayers cannot in any way help the dead.[16] The better motivation for the prayer is to bring honor to the dead by demonstrating the knowledge and piety of their children who can lead the congregation in prayer and cause the name of God to be blessed. It has also been suggested that the connection to mourning may have been that learned discourses were given in the house of mourning in honor of the dead and that the mourner was then the one given the honor of reciting the prayer for God's kingship which always followed those words.

The requirement of the tradition that those in mourning for parents recite this prayer for eleven months minus one day and not longer stemmed from the idea that punishment for the wicked in Gehenna was no longer than twelve months.[17]

The recitation of the Kaddish during the period of mourning serves an important purpose for the mourner. Precisely at the time when faith is most fragile, the individual recites the words that express the hope of all Israel that God's name will be exalted in the world and that His kingdom will be established. Even without consideration of the meaning of the words, the very act of repeated recitation of a prayer in public helps restore equanimity and leads the mourner back to a place within the community of believers.

Yizkor

The Yizkor service in memory of the dead is held on Yom Kippur and on the last day of each of the three festivals, Passover, Shavuot, and Shemini Atzeret. Its name derives from the first word of its central prayer, which means "May He remember." Although it is variously elaborated with the recitation of psalms and other prayers, it is basically the recitation by individuals of a prayer for remembrance of those they mourn and by the collective community for all who have died. The text is simple:

> May God remember the soul of . . . who has gone to eternity.
> May his/her soul be bound up in the bond of life with the souls
> of Abraham, Isaac, Jacob, Sarah, Rebecca, Rachel, and Leah,
> and with those of all the righteous in the Garden of Eden.

"Remember" has the connotation of "act for their benefit." Thus the Almighty is asked to care for the souls of those who have departed and place them in paradise. This service appears first during the Middle Ages in Europe, where it was recited on Yom Kippur in order to remember the many martyrs slain during the Crusades. Such a memorial list was recited in Nuremberg in 1295, and the custom soon spread. Later, the practice began of saying it on the festivals as well. There were those who opposed this, since grieving over the dead is not in the spirit of the festivals, which are days of joy and gladness. Popular custom and desire overcame rabbinic reluctance in this as in many other cases, and the recitation became strongly rooted.

Many people erroneously believe that only those whose parents are dead should recite this prayer and that others should leave the synagogue at that time. This superstitious practice both vitiates the original intent of the prayer, which was for the community to pay homage to the martyrs of Judaism, and ignores the need to commemorate the terrible tragedy of our own day, the Holocaust. Surely the entire people of Israel, young and old, should commemorate those six million, many of whom are unknown or left no relatives to remember them.

Another prayer was written specifically concerning the martyrs of the Black Death and the Crusades and inserted into the Sabbath prayers. The Crusaders killed Jews in the Holy Land as well as in the European lands they passed through on their way to Jerusalem. Accusations of ritual murder were rife and resulted in the slaughter of entire communities. In many instances Jews gathered together and committed suicide rather than fall into the hands of the mobs. Known as Av Ha-Rachamim (Father of Mercies), the prayer asks both for rest for the dead and for vengeance on the perpetrators of those horrible massacres. Originally recited twice a year on the Sabbaths near the times when the massacres in Mainz and Cologne took place, before Shavuot and before Tisha B'Av, this custom too spread until in many places the prayer is recited every Sabbath.[18]

Yahrzeit

The custom of observing the day of death as a yearly day of mourning also seems to have come into Judaism in the Middle Ages, possibly as another way of memorializing the martyrs of the Crusades. All in all, that era cast its black shadow on Jewish liturgy, introducing many memorial customs to a religion that had not previously developed a highly sophisticated liturgy of death. The conjuncture of Jewish tragedy and an environment in which prayers and masses for the dead were common produced these practices, which became an important and integral part of Judaism.

At first the mourner was honored on the Sabbath closest to the date of death by being called to the Torah, and reciting a prayer in memory of the dead.[19] This prayer is also recited at the time of burial. Known as El Malei Rachamim (God of Mercies), it too asks God to grant rest to the dead and shelter them in the Divine Presence. Customs have varied, however, since many felt that the Sabbath was inappropriate for prayers concerning the dead. Today the mourner observes the Hebrew date of death itself as a day of mourning and is given the honor of reciting the Kaddish. In some synagogues the mourner is also honored on the Sabbath before the *yahrzeit*.

Prayers in the House of Mourning

During the week of mourning, the period of *shiva*, it is customary for daily prayers to be held in the house of mourning and for the mourners not to go to the synagogue. The services held at home are the same as regular daily services, with a few deletions and additions.

The main omission is the Tachanun prayers. These are prayers for God's mercy, prayers of sadness in which the individual puts himself in the hands of God's mercy and expresses his sense of unworthiness. Although that might seem to be exactly the correct mood for a house of mourning, the tradition takes the opposite position: if there is one thing that is not needed at such a time, it is prayer that would emphasize the mood of sadness and the feelings of guilt held by mourners. We need not rub salt into a wound. Similarly omitted is Psalm 20, which is recited toward the conclusion of the morning service. Like the Tachanun, it speaks of times of troubles and of asking God to help us.

The one addition to the service is Psalm 49, which is recited evening and morning, followed by the Mourners' Kaddish, recited only by the mourners of the household. This psalm contains numerous reference to the grave:

Shall he live eternally,
and never see the grave?

Their grave is their eternal home,
the dwelling place for all generations.

Sheeplike they head for Sheol,
with death as their shepherd. (Ps. 49:10–15)

It also contains a verse that could be seen as indicating a reward of paradise instead of oblivion:

But God will redeem my life from the clutches of Sheol,
for He will take me. (Ps. 49:16)

The rites of mourning, then, are simple and not elaborate. Although they include many practices that reflect folk belief and many occasions for remembering the dead that grew up during the Middle Ages—fed both by the tragedies of the time and, possibly, by the many practices of praying for the dead in the surrounding non-Jewish culture—the liturgy of mourning remains modest. It recognizes the need for the mourner to regain faith and to come to terms with grief without denying the belief in a merciful God and in a future of hope.

Perhaps we are all like Job. Our suffering—and the death of a beloved person is a source of great suffering—causes us to question and not merely to accept passively what has happened. Our belief is called into question, our concept of God becomes problematic, yet reflection enables us to come to terms not merely with reality but with our values. At the end we may find ourselves able to say the same traditional words that we have questioned. Yet their meaning is not exactly what it was prior to this experience. Now we can find a source of strength in their new and deeper meaning at a time when it is badly needed. Even at such a moment, we reaffirm value and meaning. With all the doubts and hesitations we may have, we bless the name of the Lord.

15

Getting Started

*A*lthough most of this book has been concerned with acquiring an understanding of Jewish prayer and the format it takes in the Siddur, we should remain aware of the fact that prayer does not necessarily mean formal prayer, and we need not feel constrained to remain solely within the traditional framework. We can deviate from it, add to it, and find appropriate ways to pray outside of it. Following the destruction of the Temple in 70 c.e., Jewish law (*halacha*) made these daily prayers into positive *mitzvot* which we are required to perform, but it did not negate the fact that there is also a *mitzva* of prayer itself, which simply means to turn in praise, petition, and thanksgiving to God in whatever way we can. One can pray without ever saying Arvit, Shacharit, or Mincha, without ever reciting the Amida or the Shema, even without opening the Book of Psalms.

The Jewish tradition not only recognizes but encourages the utterance of personal, individual prayers in words that come from the heart. The Bible records many such prayers, from Moses' brief but poignant petition on behalf of his sister Miriam—"O God, pray heal her!" (Num. 12:13)—to the lengthy prayer of Solomon at the dedication of the Temple (1 Kings 8:23–53). The Talmud also records many personal, individual prayers recited by the Sages, some of which eventually found their way into the Siddur. It also speaks about blessings formulated by individuals who did not know the standard texts or did not choose to use them. In the third century c.e., a shepherd named Benjamin, using Aramaic, the vernacular language of his day, simply said, "Blessed is the master of this bread" before eating. According to the Sages, he thereby fulfilled the obligation to say a blessing before eating bread, even though it contained none of the usual elements of an official *beracha*.[1] There is a direct line from that shepherd to the shepherd in the well-known hassidic story who plays his flute and offers God the melody because he knows no prayers at all. There was no need to wait for modern Hassidism to tell us that the sincere outpouring of the heart is always acceptable to God. Formal prayers are not superior to the simple act of opening oneself to God. As the Talmud put it, basing itself on the verse "The Lord sees into the heart" (1 Sam. 16:7), "The Merciful One desires the heart."[2] All of this encourages us to pray informally and not to confine ourselves to words that have been formulated for us by others.

> Said the Holy One to Israel, "I have told you that when you pray, you should do so in the synagogue in your city. If you cannot pray in the synagogue, pray in your field. If you cannot pray in your field, pray in your house. If you cannot pray in your house, pray on your bed. If you cannot pray on your bed, meditate in your heart."[3]

Personal, individual prayer is important both for those who accept the statutory prayers as an obligation and for those who do not. For the former, it is a way of constantly refreshing what could otherwise become mere routine. For the latter, it is a way to begin on the path that leads to ever increasing participation in the full measure of traditional prayer. Lack of knowledge may be an impediment to formal prayer, to Jewish communal prayer, but not to prayer itself. One may begin without the slightest knowledge of traditional prayers and thus enter the world of prayer. Once the way is open, traditional forms can and indeed must be acquired if one is to partake fully in Jewish worship.

One who wishes to pray can do so, quietly, privately, by taking a moment to react to his or her situation. Although the impetus to do this frequently comes at a time of sorrow or need, prayer need not be confined to moments of darkness. The heart that God desires need not be a broken one. Moments of joy abound in life, in our relations with people, in our confrontation with nature, in the good news—scarce as it is—in the world. These can all be occasions for prayer. Blanche DuBois, the heroine in *A*

Streetcar Named Desire, experiencing a moment of happiness and hope, says, "Sometimes there's God—so quickly." In the Bible, Jacob had the same experience when he woke from his dream and said, "God is in this place and I did not know it!" (Gen. 28:16). The recognition of the presence of God is the impetus for prayer; conversely, prayer brings about our recognition that God is present and causes us to feel, as did Jacob, "How awesome is this place! This is none other than the house of God and that is heaven's gate" (Gen. 28:17). How terrible to be in God's house and not know it.

One should never be ashamed to pray by uttering the feelings of one's heart. What are many of the psalms, if not the record of such feelings? Of course, few if any of us can reach the heights of beauty that are contained in those psalms or in the other treasures of Jewish prayer. But then we do not have to. What we say need never be recorded. No one else need ever use it or see it. Our words are not for human ears or human judgment. Since God "searches the heart" (Jer. 17:10), it is not the poetic formulation that is important, but meaning and intent—*kavana.* The silent sigh, the exclamation of wonder, the tear—these are surely as eloquent to God as the prayers of Judah Ha-Levi.

The Siddur itself has been an open book to which one could add personal prayers or create new prayers to enhance the traditional framework. Throughout the ages, from rabbinic times until the modern period, poetic masters and leaders of prayer have created new poetic prayers, *piyyutim,* first in Israel and Babylonia, then in Italy, Spain, and wherever Jews lived and worshiped. Closer to our own time, the hassidic masters were famous for their ability to create new prayers. Rabbi Levi of Berditchev and Rabbi Nachman of Bratzlav have left us magnificent outpourings of the soul in Yiddish and in Hebrew. The renowned chief rabbi of the Yishuv (the Jewish settlement in Palestine) at the beginning of the twentieth century, Abraham Isaac Kook, was also a master of prayer, and his published prayers give an indication of how the individual can express himself—not for the sake of self-expression, the goal of poetry—but in order to reach out to God, the essential purpose of prayer.[4]

The fact that we can and should pray anywhere, at any time, in our own words, should not cause us to neglect or minimize the importance of the set framework of prayer that Jewish tradition provides. Informal prayer, for all its importance, is no substitute for the pattern of prayer the Siddur sets out for us and for the prescribed routine of daily prayer which is an obligation of traditional Judaism. The regular use of the set forms creates a pattern of life that constantly emphasizes that we stand before God, forcing us to recognize this even when we would be inclined to forget it. The prayers of the Siddur sensitize us to the world of Jewish values and Jewish concepts, and thus create a moral and spiritual milieu that enriches us and causes us to measure ourselves against a standard outside of ourselves. That is the ancient and original meaning of the word *l'hitpallel* ("to pray"): placing oneself in a situation of being judged and measured. If our personal prayers refresh our traditional devotions, our traditional prayers give weight and structure to our personal devotions.

We may begin to pray by using our own words, or we may find it easier to come to prayer through traditional, formal prayer, either with others or alone, reciting at their prescribed times the prayers and formulas found in the Siddur. It is foolish not to take advantage of the paths that others have walked before us. It is all very well for a fledgling playwright to say that reading Shakespeare might stifle his creativity, but it is also rather silly. Culture is created by building upon the past. Words have echoes and are enriched by them. Therefore, if we have difficulties in expressing ourselves through prayer, we can find help in the prayers of those who went before us. Sometimes a prayer written hundreds or thousands of years ago will express exactly what is in our hearts. Sometimes an ancient phrase will help us to say what we mean or will evoke new thoughts within us. As we incorporate the insights of others into our own minds, we enlarge our horizons and deepen our capacity to think and feel. We need not imitate mechanically or limit ourselves artificially in order to be inspired and enriched by the past.

Where does one begin? There are many possibilities. One could start the day, for example, by reciting parts of the Shacharit service at home. If time is a problem, as it frequently is in our busy world, one can begin with brief selections. The prayer that is found at the very beginning of the morning service, *modeh ani*, provides a meaningful way to start the day:

I acknowledge You, ever-living king,
and give thanks that You have mercifully restored
my soul unto me.
Great is Your faithfulness.

The recitation of the Shema or even a part of it affirms our loyalty and
sets a tone for the day, reminding us of our true obligations and the
essence of our Jewishness. The eventual goal should be to say the Amida,
in which the ultimate aspirations of Judaism for ourselves and for the
world are expressed.

Those who have been in the habit of prayer for some time might
begin by pausing to give more thought to what they are doing. They
should consider, for example, breaking old habits, for habit is the enemy
of prayer. Pray more slowly, look at the words, understand what they
mean. Say less but say it with more *kavana*: "Know before Whom you
stand." Spend a little time in preparation and add some thoughts of your
own. The ancient advice of Rabbi Yose—"Let there be a novelty in your
prayer every day"[5]—is an excellent idea. The Sages warned that prayer
should not be made a fixed thing. It should not be treated as a burden;
something new should be continually added.[6] Both those who are familiar
with the prayers and those who are coming to worship for the first time
should keep this in mind. Prayer is more than a set of sounds to be
uttered in fulfillment of some obligation. Meaning, intent, direction are
indispensable if our words are not to become magical litanies. One takes
aim—the root meaning of *kavana*—trying to reach the mark, in this case
God. There is no prayer unless there is something new, something that
expresses immediate feelings.

Choosing a Synagogue

Prayer may take place anywhere, but Jewish prayer without a synagogue
is incomplete. It is not the building that is significant, but the presence
of a congregation. Praying with others symbolizes membership in the
community and concretizes the feeling of being part of the Jewish people.
One prays with the community, is part of the community, prays for the
community, and shares values and a common history with the community.

Many find that it is easier and more satisfactory to enter the world of prayer not only by using the traditional words created by Judaism through the centuries but by participating in organized prayer in the synagogue. Coming together with other Jews can be a helpful way to experience Jewish worship. Since the destruction of the Second Temple, Jewish prayer has always been basically a community affair. Throughout the generations, wherever Jews came to live—and this is as true within the Land of Israel as in the lands of the dispersion—one of the first institutions the community would establish was the *bet knesset* (the house of gathering together), which was known by the Greek name of synagogue. In America and Europe today, one cannot imagine a Jewish community without a synagogue at its center. Synagogue affiliation is one of the major criteria for assessing a person's commitment to Judaism. To enter the world of Jewish prayer, one must find an appropriate synagogue.

Theoretically, if one is prepared for prayer, the setting should make little difference. Actually, it does influence our ability to pray. The type of service that is held there, the Siddur that is used, the amount of congregational participation—all of these make a difference. Synagogues today are usually identified with one of the organized religious movements within American Jewry: Orthodox, Conservative, Reform, and Reconstructionist. Although each of these groups has its own approach to Judaism and its own version of the Siddur, the variations within each group are great. Knowing which group a synagogue is affiliated with will not necessarily tell you what you want to know about that particular congregation and its worship services. Orthodox synagogues may range from the *shtiebel*—a small, disorganized place in which strictly Orthodox prayer is conducted in an informal atmosphere that some would find warm and meaningful, and others would consider to be merely chaotic and lacking in esthetics—to the large and formal synagogue in which the singing of the *hazzan* (the cantor) dominates. Conservative congregations also differ greatly from one another. Some are small and informal; others are very large. In some, the service is participatory; in others, it is more geared to leaders conducting the service. The role of women will also differ from one to another. Reform congregations range from the magnificent structure holding several thousand people—with a service conducted by a rabbi, perhaps a *hazzan*, and a choir accompanied by an organ, in which the Hebrew language plays a minor role and decorum is a high priority—to synagogues that are almost indistinguishable from Conservative ones. Since what appeals to one may not appeal to another, the only way to tell is to try out a synagogue and see how you feel there and how it measures up to the standards you set for worship, both ideologically and emotionally.

I obviously have my own theological preference, and there are some synagogues and prayerbooks with which I am more comfortable than others, but beyond that I usually seek out a synagogue that is concerned with prayer. I prefer participation to spectatorship and try to worship with a congregation where those leading the service know the difference between prayer and performance and welcome my participation. It may not even be so much a question of the text of the prayers, but rather of the attitude toward them and the mode in which they are recited. I can always say what I want to say, but I need an atmosphere that I find comfortable and conducive to prayer.

On the basis of your criteria, choose a synagogue whose level and mode of observance matches your own and which can also help you to increase your knowledge and involvement. Public prayer is a communal experience, and one can learn from the other participants, as well as from the professional staff of the synagogue and those who lead the services. Many find therefore that they are happiest praying with a group of like-minded people to whom they can relate in friendship and commonality. It is important to be part of the community and to pray with a community. That in itself helps one to attain the necessary concentration. Today there are many such groups which form within the larger structure of a congregation. Usually called *havurot,* from the word for fellowship or friendship, these independent study and prayer groups are especially sensitive to the needs of the individual. They encourage each person to participate as much as possible and to constantly increase his or her knowledge and ability to lead the services. In such a setting, there is no sharp dichotomy between active leaders and passive worshipers. All are responsible for the running of the service. Obviously there are practicalities involved. Not every community is large enough to sustain many varieties, and you may have no choice but to attend whatever synagogue exists where you live.

The role of women in the synagogue will also influence one's choice of a congregation. Today this varies from the synagogue in which women sit behind a curtain (*mechitza*) and play no role either in the conduct of the services or in the running of the congregation, to the egalitarian synagogue in which no distinction is made between the sexes in anything pertaining to worship. Even those who strictly adhere to Jewish law (*halacha*) are divided on the question as to what is and is not permitted. Again, you will have to decide what your position is on this matter and attempt to find a place that corresponds to your point of view.

Choosing a Siddur

Just as there are a variety of synagogues, so there are a variety of Siddurim. Each of the major streams in modern Jewish religious life has issued its own version of the Siddur. With the exception of the Orthodox, these undergo frequent revision. Prayerbooks of the Reform movement are much closer today to a traditional framework than they were previously. Nevertheless, major parts of the service are missing and texts that do not meet the theological criteria of the movement have been extensively revised. The newer Conservative prayerbooks are also different from those issued a generation ago. Although much closer to the traditional than are the Reform, and retaining the basic structure and prayers, here too certain revisions have been made, mainly in connection with sacrifices and with questions of gender. The new Conservative prayerbook also offers alternative versions of certain texts, including the Amida, in an atttempt to meet the needs of the variety of congregations within that movement.

No matter what Siddur is used where you pray, you may find it difficult to accept some of the prayers. I suspect that this problem cuts across denominational lines. Even Orthodox leaders who criticize attempts to rewrite the prayerbook point out that in using old prayers, one can use one's imagination to invest them with alternative meanings.[7] Indeed, it is true that to satisfy everyone would be impossible. That would require a Siddur tailored to each individual. One should, therefore, remember that the traditional text, like any text, has always been and will always be susceptible to multiple interpretations. Jews may have used the same words, but they did not always mean the same thing. I doubt if Maimonides and Judah Ha-Levi had the same ideas in their minds when they prayed. The Baal Shem Tov certainly understood the prayers differently than the Gaon of Vilna. Wherever possible, therefore, invest the words with meanings you can accept. Remember that, like poetry, prayer has layers of meaning, and the most superficial is not always the best. Remember, too, that what you think today may change in the future. You may come to accept ideas or language that you question now or even reject, so keep an open mind. Let the prayers challenge you, as well as you challenging the prayers.

If something is absolutely unacceptable, change it, eliminate it, ignore it. You need not change the printed page in order to change the words you utter. The tyranny of the printed page can be overwhelming. Because someone once decided that that was what was to be said is no reason for you to say it. Our ancestors allowed themselves a great deal of flexibility in their prayers. There is no reason for us to allow ourselves any less. The emergence of the printed prayerbook has in many ways stultified the previous flexibility of prayer within Jewish communities. The Siddur, for all its unquestioned greatness, is not like the Bible. The Bible is a fixed text. In order to derive new meaning from it, one utilizes the method of interpretation (midrash). The Siddur was never intended to be that. It is simply the record of the prayers in use at a certain place and a certain time. Jewish law may have fixed parameters to these prayers, but within that framework prayers changed to fit the needs of the community and the conditions of the time. They were enlarged, altered, eliminated. It would be unfortunate if that feature of Jewish prayer were to disappear.

One of the most vexing problems of prayer today is that of sexist language. The easiest part of that problem to solve is the blessing "Who has not made me a woman," which, as we have seen, has been changed in the Siddur of the Conservative movement to "Who made me in His image." More problematic is the fact that most references to God are masculine. "He" is the common pronoun. God is referred to as "king" or "father"— never queen or mother. The few feminine references to God that exist are due to the fact that rabbinic Judaism personified the indwelling presence of God as the *Shechina* (Presence), a feminine word requiring a feminine verb. Radical solutions have been proposed for the problem of masculine language,[8] but most prayerbooks have not made such changes. Many people who recognize the problem find the solution in their own awareness of the fact that, regardless of language, Judaism does not and never has assigned gender to God, but has merely used the common human words available. God is beyond sexual definition, just as God is beyond physical form. Whatever the eventual solution, greater sensitivity to the problem is called for, as is the clear understanding that God is neither "He" nor "She," no matter what terminology we use.

Another aspect of the problem is the overwhelming predominance of masculine references to our ancestors in the prayers. Occasionally Sarah, Rebecca, Rachel, and Leah are mentioned, but not in the major prayers. The first blessing of the Amida is called "The Fathers" and not "The Mothers." God is described as the "protector of Abraham" and not of Sarah. Suggestions have been made that there be more feminine references in the prayers through the inclusion of the mothers along with the fathers. In some cases this is not a radical change, but in others, such as the opening section of the Amida, it is. Here the objection is twofold: first, that the line is a specific quotation from the Bible. When God reveals Himself to Moses at the burning bush, He says, "I am the God of your father, the God of Abraham, the God of Isaac, and the God of Jacob" (Exod. 3:6). The mothers do not appear in any such quotation. The second theological objection is that God "chose" the fathers specifically, granting them a unique blessing, which was passed from father to son, but not the mothers, so that the factual basis for mentioning them is lacking. To include them in that context requires a rewriting of sacred history. The problem is not one of how we view the role of women and their place in current Jewish practice, but one of preserving the integrity of a historical tradition. This problem is not easy to solve, but it is important that we be aware of it and develop sensitivity to it.

A balance must be found between changes and continuity, just as there must be such a balance between spontaneity and adherence to fixed forms. To be true to the history and the spirit of Jewish worship, one must recognize that we cannot and should not make radical changes that divorce our prayers from their history, but at the same time we must acknowledge that flexibility and change are inherent within it, so that the inability to alter anything is a falsification of prayer.

It is unthinkable, for example, that Jewish worship should not reflect the major events of Jewish life in this century: the tragedy of the Holocaust and the triumph of the establishment of Israel. On the other hand, abandonment of basic forms and changes that eliminate the framework and language of prayer are equally objectionable.

These problems are especially vexing for those individuals and rabbinic and synagogue bodies who edit and print Siddurim. They are also difficult for those who must decide what prayer formula is to be adopted in a particular synagogue or service. But the individual who prays must also confront these issues personally. No matter in what setting you pray, at home or in a synagogue, it is your decision as to what words you utter or do not utter, what you alter, eliminate, or add. Knowing more about the prayers and their history, understanding their meaning and the pattern, structure, and themes of Jewish prayer should make it easier to make such decisions.

In all organic change the process is continuous but gradual, so that, for all the alterations, the organism remains what it was. A good case can be made for growth as opposed to radical surgery.

We have come now to the end of our discussions, but it is an end that is really a beginning. Lest we think that whatever we have learned is sufficient, we discover that it is really little more than a prologue to the subject. There is always so much more to consider, so many more questions to ask. That is all to the good, as long as we feel that we know enough to know what to ask and feel comfortable with our ability to deal with the subject. As long as the Siddur is no longer a closed book to us, the synagogue a foreign institution, and worship an uncharted journey, we are equipped to continue. At the conclusion of the words of the Sage Kohelet, who frequently raised more questions than he answered, it is written:

The sum of the matter, when all is said and done: Revere God and observe His commandments! (Eccles. 12:13)

In a sense, that too is what prayer is all about. Its main purpose is to sensitize us to the awareness of God's presence in all we do and help us determine how to live so as to be in harmony with God. To quote Leo Baeck:

> Whenever the hidden and unfathomable is experienced, man can react either with the devoutness of silence, that most intimate feeling of the living God, or with poetry and prayer which sings of the ineffable.[9]

Most of us want to be able to sing, to celebrate life with joy. Through the medium of prayer, the human being is made aware of the extra dimension of holiness that exists in the world and is enabled to express the widest possible range of reactions, feelings, desires, and aspirations. Reaching beyond the self, the individual aspires to communicate with the source of being. The Jew uses the language of prayer devised by the Sages and poets of Israel from the earliest times until today in order to attain that goal. In addition, the Jew finds that his or her life is significantly enriched by being joined to the community, both that which exists today and that which stretches backward into history and forward into the days to come. The concepts of Judaism in regard to God, human life, the Jewish people, righteousness, and morality are all conveyed in the traditional prayers that form the core of our devotions when we pray as Jews. Hopefully that liturgy has now begun to speak to us and we know enough to engage it in creative dialogue so that we can find meaning within it. The liturgy is intended to serve us in our quest for the ability to pray, not the other way around. It serves us so that we in turn can perform that service of the heart which is our path toward God and Jewish living.

It is only fitting that a book about prayer conclude with a prayer. The Talmud records a prayer to be recited when embarking on a journey.[10] Since the end of this book marks the beginning of the journey of prayer, perhaps it is appropriate.

> May it be Your will, O Lord my God,
> to lead me in peace,

to guide my steps in peace,
to uphold me in peace,
to save me from any enemy or entrapment along the way,
to bless the works of my hands
and permit me to find grace, favor, and mercy in Your eyes
and in the eyes of all who behold me.
Blessed are You, O Lord, who hears prayer.

AMEN

Notes

References to talmudic tractates are generally to the Babylonian Talmud. References to the Jerusalem Talmud are indicated by "Y" (Yerushalmi).

Chapter 1. What Is Prayer?

1. Sifre Deuteronomy 41.
2. Franz Rosenzweig, *The Star of Redemption* (New York, 1970), p. 184.
3. Pesikta Rabbati 22.
4. Abraham Joshua Heschel, *Man Is Not Alone* (New York, 1951), p. 289.
5. Louis Jacobs, *Hasidic Prayer* (New York, 1973), p. 17.
6. Tanchuma Mikez 9.
7. Leo Baeck, *The Essence of Judaism* (New York, 1948), p. 244.
8. Avot d'Rabbi Nathan B 27.
9. Deuteronomy Rabba 2:1.
10. Nahum N. Glatzer, *Franz Rosenzweig: His Life and Thought* (New York, 1953), p. 251.
11. Sotah 7:1.
12. Glatzer, *Franz Rosenzweig*, p. 102.
13. Y. Berachot 5:1.
14. Berachot 6a.
15. Avot 2:5.
16. Berachot 8a.
17. Shabbat 33b.
18. Abraham Joshua Heschel, *Man's Quest for God* (New York, 1954), p. 45.
19. Megilla 32a.
20. Jacobs, *Hasidic Prayer*, p. 68.
21. Taanit 16a.

22. The Shema in the Kedusha of the Musaf service, for example, may have been introduced there before 634 c.e. because of Byzantine persecutions which did not permit the regular recitation of the Shema. See Jacob Mann, "Changes in the Divine Service of the Synagogue Due to Religious Persecutions," *Hebrew Union College Annual* 4 (1927), pp. 241–310.
23. Sifre Numbers 42.

Chapter 2. Using the Liturgy

1. Ernst Simon, "On the Meaning of Prayer," in Jakob J. Petuchowski, ed., *Understanding Jewish Prayer* (New York, 1972), p. 109.
2. Heschel, *Man's Quest for God*, p. 13.
3. Simon, "On the Meaning of Prayer," p. 106.
4. Abraham Joshua Heschel, *God in Search of Man* (Philadelphia, 1956), pp. 375, 63.
5. Simon, "On the Meaning of Prayer," pp. 100ff.
6. Milton Steinberg, *A Believing Jew* (New York, 1951), pp. 19ff. See also his *Anatomy of Faith* (New York, 1960), pp. 88–100.
7. Avoda Zara 54b.
8. Berachot 9:3.
9. Jacobs, *Hasidic Prayer*, p. 26.
10. *The Guide for the Perplexed* 3.35.
11. Mordecai M. Kaplan, *The Meaning of God in Modern Jewish Religion* (New York, 1937), p. 33.
12. Ibid., p. 107.
13. Milton Steinberg, *Basic Judaism* (New York, 1947), p. 118. See also Robert Gordis, *A Faith For Moderns* (New York, 1960), pp. 246ff.
14. Emil L. Fackenheim, *What Is Judaism?* (New York, 1987), p. 183.
15. Ibid., p. 196.
16. Heschel, *Man Is Not Alone*, pp. 239–40.
17. Heschel, *Man's Quest for God*, p. 5.
18. Quoted in Gordis, *A Faith for Moderns*, p. 252.
19. Glatzer, *Franz Rosenzweig*, p. 209.
20. Martin Buber, *Tales of the Hasidim*, vol. 1: *The Early Masters* (New York, 1947), p. 73.
21. *Hamlet*, act 3, scene 3.
22. Quoted in Simon, "On the Meaning of Prayer," p. 105.
23. Heschel, *Man's Quest for God*, p. xii.

Chapter 3. Prayer in Early Israel

1. *Mekilta de-Rabbi Ishmael*, ed. Jacob Z. Lauterbach (Philadelphia, 1949), vol. 1, p. 215 (Beshallah 3).

2. See Ps. 118:14–16. See Reuven Hammer, "Two Liturgical Psalms: Salvation and Thanksgiving," *Judaism* 40, no. 4 (Fall 1991), pp. 491ff.

3. The entire song is quoted in the preliminary service recited each morning. Verses from it are found in the second blessing following the Shema morning and evening.

4. Gen. 8:20. Noah is depicted in the Bible as a monotheist. His entire story, however, is an adaptation of pagan stories. See below, n. 12.

5. The command to offer sacrifices appears immediately following the Ten Declarations in Exod. 20:21. Sacrifices themselves are offered in Exod. 24:5 as part of a covenantal ceremony. The description of the Tabernacle which was to be built begins in Exod. 25. Amos 5:25 may reflect a different tradition:

Did you offer sacrifice and oblation to Me
Those forty years in the wilderness,
O House of Israel?

6. Heschel, *Man's Quest for God*, p. 5.

7. "In the course of time, Cain brought an offering to the Lord from the fruit of the soil; and Abel, for his part, brought the choicest of the firstlings of his flock. The Lord paid heed to Abel and his offering, but to Cain and his offering He paid no heed" Gen. 4:3–5.

8. See, for example, Bronislaw Malinowski: "Divinities when approached are given their due, their share sacrificed from the general plenty. . . . By sharing in food sacrificially with his spirits or divinities the savage shares with them in the beneficial powers of his Providence" (*Magic, Science and Religion* [New York, 1954], p. 43).

9. See Amos 5:22–24, Jer. 7:1–26, Isa. 1:10–17. See Shalom Spiegel, *Amos and Amaziah* (New York, 1957), pp. 42–47; Abraham Joshua Heschel, *The Prophets* (Philadelphia, 1962), pp. 195–98.

10. Yehezkel Kaufmann, *The Religion of Israel* (Chicago, 1960). See especially pp. 7–121.

11. Ibid., pp. 40–42. See also Martin Buber, *Moses* (New York, 1958), pp. 52–53.

12. James B. Pritchard, ed., *Ancient Near Eastern Texts* (Princeton, N.J., 1955), p. 95.

13. Kaufmann, *Religion of Israel*, p. 303.

14. Moshe Greenberg, *Biblical Prose Prayer* (Berkeley, Calif., 1983).

15. Sunday: Ps. 24; Monday: Ps. 48; Tuesday: Ps. 82; Wednesday: Ps. 94; Thursday: Ps. 81; Friday: Ps. 93; Saturday: Ps. 92. See Mishna Tamid 7:4.

16. Tosefta Sukkah 3:2.

17. Greenberg, *Biblical Prose Prayer*, pp. 33–36.

18. Hammer, "Two Liturgical Psalms," pp. 489–97.

19. Berachot 4b.

20. See Reuven Kimelman, "Psalm 145 and the Liturgy," *Proceedings of the Rabbinical Assembly 54* (1992), pp. 97–128.

Chapter 4. The Origins of the Synagogue

1. Berachot 6a.
2. Ibid.
3. Lee I. Levine, "The Second Temple Synagogue," in Levine, ed. *The Synagogue in Late Antiquity* (Philadelphia, 1987), p. 17.
4. Ezra Fleischer, "On the Antiquity of Prescribed Prayer in Israel" [Hebrew], *Tarbitz* 59 (1990), pp. 406ff.; Levine, "The Second Temple Synagogue," pp. 15ff.
5. Women were the exception to this, since they were not recognized as authorized teachers, even though they had functioned as prophets during the First Temple and before.
6. See Lee I. Levine, ed., *Ancient Synagogues Revealed* (Jerusalem, 1981).
7. "There were 480 synagogues in Jerusalem, each one with its own school and academy, a school for teaching Scripture, an academy for teaching Mishna. All of them, as well as the Temple, were destroyed by Vespasian" (Y. Megilla 3:1). Note that even in this legendary account, the teaching of Torah is singled out as the function of the synagogue.
8. See Eric M. Meyers, "The Current State of Galilean Synagogue Studies" in Levine, ed., *The Synagogue in Late Antiquity*, pp. 127–37.
9. Oral communication to the author.
10. Yehezkel Kaufmann, *The Religion of Israel*, pp. 162, 176ff.
11. Num. 32. Clearly the land on the other side of the Jordan was not considered part of the land of Canaan which Israel was to possess.
12. Kaufmann, *The Religion of Israel*, p. 176.
13. Louis Finkelstein, "The Origin of the Synagogue," in *Pharisaism in the Making: Selected Essays* (New York, 1972).
14. Genesis Rabba to Gen. 25:27.
15. *Vita Mosis* 3.27.
16. *Against Apion* 11.27.
17. Levine, "The Second Temple Synagogue," p. 10. Shaye J. D. Cohen, "Pagan and Christian Evidence on the Ancient Synagogue," in Levine, ed., *The Synagogue in Late Antiquity*, p. 112.
18. Cohen, "Pagan and Christian Evidence," pp. 160–81.
19. Luke 4:16–22; Acts 13:13–16.
20. Megilla 29a.
21. Elias Bickerman, *From Ezra to the Last of the Maccabees* (New York, 1962), pp. 35–40.
22. Kaufmann, *The Religion of Israel*, pp. 423–24.

23. Bickerman, *From Ezra*, pp. 6ff.
24. Ibid., pp. 41–42.
25. Ezek. 1, 3, 10:18, 11:22.
26. Shalom Spiegel, "On Medieval Hebrew Poetry," in Louis Finkelstein, ed., *The Jews: Their History, Culture, and Religion* (Philadelphia, 1960), p. 865.
27. Fleischer, "Antiquity of Prescribed Prayer," p. 403.
28. Ibid., p. 413.
29. Tosefta Sukkah 4:6.
30. "Whoever has not seen Herod's Temple has never seen a beautiful building. Of what did he build it? Rabba said: yellow and white marble. Others say: blue, yellow, and white marble. Alternate rows projected out in order to leave room for cement. He intended to cover it with gold but the rabbis told him not to, since it was more beautiful as it was, resembling the waves of the ocean" (Bava Batra 4a). See Josephus, *Wars of the Jews* 1.21.1.
31. Cohen, "Pagan and Christian Evidence," p. 175.
32. Fleischer, "Antiquity of Prescribed Prayer," p. 414.
33. S. Talmon, "Order of Prayers of the Sect from the Judean Desert" [Hebrew], *Tarbitz* 29 (1960), pp. 1–20. See also Lawrence H. Schiffman, "The Dead Sea Scrolls and the Early History of Jewish Liturgy," in Levine, ed., *The Synagogue in Late Antiquity*, pp. 33–48.
34. See, for example, Ben Sira 35:22–36:22.
35. Matt. 6:5–13, 26:36, 26:41–42; Mark 14:32–39; Luke 5:33, 11:1–4.
36. Tosefta Rosh Ha-Shanah 2:17.
37. Berachot 5:1. "The early pious ones would wait an hour and then pray in order to direct their hearts toward God."
38. Megilla 29b.

Chapter 5. The Creation of the Siddur

1. Heschel, *Man's Quest for God*, pp. 82–83.
2. Berachot 26b.
3. Megilla 17b.
4. Fleischer, "Antiquity of Prescribed Prayer," pp. 401ff.
5. Louis Ginzberg, "Tamid: The Oldest Treatise of the Mishnah," *Journal of Jewish Lore and Philology* 1 (1919).
6. Berachot 11b; Y. Berachot 1:8.
7. Brevard S. Childs, *The Book of Exodus* (Philadelphia, 1974), p. 328.
8. See chapter 8 for a full discussion of the Shema.
9. Berachot 12a.
10. Geza Vermes, "The Decalogue and the Minim," in Matthew Black and

Georg Fohrer, eds., *In Memoriam Paul Kahle* (Berlin, 1968), pp. 232–40. Vermes believes that the Minim were antinomian Hellenistic Jews. Reuven Kimelman, "The Shema and Its Blessings," in Levine, ed., *The Synagogue in Late Antiquity*, pp. 71ff., questions the historicity of this explanation.

11. Ginzberg ("Tamid," pp. 207 and 278) calls the phrase "blessed the people" an archaic one meaning "to recite a blessing for the people." "Praying for somebody," he writes, "is really identical with asking God's blessing upon him." Fleischer ("Antiquity of Prescribed Prayer," p. 420) disagrees and believes that the blessing recited was the actual Priestly Blessing consisting of Num. 6:22–27. This seems unlikely, however, if only priests were present. Furthermore, the Priestly Blessing was recited later, at the conclusion of the sacrificial rite (Tamid 6:5). In general Fleischer questions the authenticity of the list of blessings in the Mishna.

12. See Reuven Hammer, "What Did They Bless?" *Jewish Quarterly Review* 81, no. 3–4 (January–April 1991), pp. 305–24, for a detailed discussion of this entire mishna.

13. Rule Scroll of the Dead Sea sect, in *Megillat-ha-Serakhim*, ed. Y. Licht (Jerusalem, 1965), pp. 277–79.

14. Taanit 27b.

15. See Fleischer, "Antiquity of Prescribed Prayer," pp. 398ff., and Solomon Zeitlin, "The Shemone Esreh: An Historical Study of the First Canonisation of the Hebrew Liturgy," *Jewish Quarterly Review* 54 (1963–64), pp. 208–49.

16. Sifre Deuteronomy 41.

17. Megilla 17b. "Ha-Pakuli" may be a description: "the cotton maker." His exact role in this is the subject of dispute. Naomi G. Cohen believes that he was a layman, invited by Rabban Gamliel to demonstrate that even a common man could recite the prayer properly: it would therefore be possible to require everyone to recite it completely. See her article "The Nature of Shimon Hapekuli's Act," *Tarbitz* 52, no. 4 (1983), pp. 547–55. Others, such as Fleischer ("Antiquity of Prescribed Prayer," pp. 398ff.), see him as a Sage who actually formulated the text of the prayer under Rabban Gamliel's supervision.

18. In Ben Sira 51:12, for example, we find: Redeemer of Israel, Gatherer of the scattered of Israel, Builder of His city and His Temple, He causes the horn of the house of David to grow, and Shield of Abraham, all of which are similar to sections of the Amida. See Fleischer, "Antiquity of Prescribed Prayer"; I. Elbogen, "Eighteen Benedictions," *Universal Jewish Encyclopedia*, vol. 4 (New York, 1939), pp. 22ff.; Joseph Heinemann, *Prayer in the Talmud* (Berlin, 1977), p. 219.

19. Elias Bickerman, "The Civic Prayer for Jerusalem," in *Harvard Theological Review* 55 (1962).

20. Fleischer, "Antiquity of Prescribed Prayer," p. 425. See Rosh Ha-Shanah 5:17.
21. Berachot 4:3–4.
22. Berachot 29a. Known as *Havinenu* from the first word of the prayer— "Grant us understanding"—the text is attributed to the Babylonian Amora Samuel. His contemporary Rav thought that the abbreviated form should contain a short version of each blessing. Samuel's prayer mentions the content of each of the middle blessings but does not repeat a blessing formula for each paragraph. This brief text is to be preceded by the first three paragraphs of the Amida and followed by the three concluding sections. Of course we do not know what kind of abbreviation Rabbi Joshua actually had in mind. See also Y. Berachot 4:3. The text can be found in most Siddurim.
23. Y. Berachot 4:3.
24. Berachot 29b.
25. Avot d'Rabbi Nathan 4.
26. Fleischer argues persuasively that it would have been impossible to expect the common person to compose his own text for such a prayer; therefore the version Rabban Gamliel fixed (Berachot 28b) was a complete text ("Antiquity of Prescribed Prayer," p. 427). Other authorities, as we have seen, disagreed with Rabban Gamliel and called for flexibility and innovation. Some modern scholars, such as Lawrence Hoffman, believe that the entire text was not fixed but that "the blessing topics were settled upon and even some sample eulogies [concluding blessing formulae—R.H.] which seemed more representative of the prayer's basic intent than others" (*The Canonization of the Synagogue Service* [Notre Dame, Ind., 1979], p. 50ff.). This is also the position of Heinemann, *Prayer in the Talmud*, pp. 31, 48.
27. The paragraphs of the Amida are mentioned in Megilla 17b, and each is given a designation (*avot, gevurot, kedushot,* etc.) and explained, but no text is given. See also Y. Berachot 2:4.
28. See Hoffman, *Canonization.*
29. Shabbat 115b: Those who write blessings are considered as if they burnt a Torah. Berachot 5:5 speaks of the leader of the service who "errs" and of the need for the leader to be careful lest he become confused (5:4). These problems arose because of the prohibition against written texts. This was part of the general prohibition of writing down anything but the Written Torah, which was kept in force until the geonic period. See Saul Lieberman, *Hellenism in Jewish Palestine* (New York, 1950), p. 84.
30. David Abudraham, who composed a commentary to the Siddur in Spain in the fourteenth century, mentions that no two communities have the same text.

31. "Rabbi Yohanan says: Who inherits the world to come? One who recites the evening Prayer immediately following the Blessing of Redemption. Rabbi Joshua ben Levi says: the Prayers were arranged to be recited in the middle [between the two recitations of the Shema]" (Berachot 4b). Rabbi Joshua thought that the Shema should precede the Amida in the morning, but follow it at night. See also Berachot 9b for a series of statements on the importance of attaching the Blessing of Redemption to the recitation of the Amida. Eventually this idea led to the custom of having the leader of the service recite the last few words of the Blessing of Redemption quietly, so that the congregants would not have to respond "Amen" but could begin the recitation of the Amida immediately and thus literally join the words of redemption to the Amida.

32. Solomon Zeitlin, "The Morning Benediction and the Readings in the Temple," *Jewish Quarterly Review* 44 (1953–54), p. 334.

33. The Book of Chronicles is considered to have been redacted very late, during Second Temple times. Therefore its language could very well reflect the fact that this blessing was already in existence. See W. S. Towner, "The Modulation of a Biblical Formula," *Catholic Biblical Quarterly* 30 (1968), p. 386: "The language of late OT writers was being influenced by the independent and evolving liturgical tradition of the Jews."

34. The Hebrew word YHVH is considered the proper name of God and stems from the root "to be." In Second Temple days the name was considered too sacred to be pronounced except by the priests as part of the Temple ritual. All others substituted the title *Adonai* ("Lord"). Since the destruction of the Temple it has been the practice never to pronounce the name.

35. Berachot 12a. See Y. Berachot 9:1, Berachot 46a, and Tosefta Berachot 1:5–7 on the blessing formula. Joseph Heinemann, "Once Again Melekh Ha Olam," *Journal of Jewish Studies* 15 (1964), pp. 149ff.

36. Tosefta Berachot 4:1.

37. Max Kadushin, *Worship and Ethics* (Evanston, Ill., 1964), pp. 63–69.

38. Ibid., pp. 159–85.

39. Saul Lieberman, "Light on the Cave Scrolls from Rabbinic Sources," *Proceedings of the American Academy of Jewish Research* 20 (1951), pp. 395–404.

40. See Y. Licht, *Megillat ha-Hodayot* [Hebrew] (Jerusalem, 1951), pp. 16–17 and 3:19, 3:37, 4:5, 5:5, 7:6, 7:26, 7:34, 8:4, 9:38, and 11:3 for prayers beginning with "I will thankfully acknowledge You [*odecha*], O Lord"; see Ben Sira 51:12.

41. Max Kadushin, *The Rabbinic Mind* (New York, 1952), p. 270.

42. Menachot 43b.

43. Yochanan Muffs, *Love and Joy* (New York, 1992), p. 57.

44. *Machzor Vitry* (Nuremberg, 1923; reprinted New York, n.d.), p. 56.
45. Megilla 31a.
46. Megilla 25a.
47. The first blessing preceding the Shema contains numerous poems concerning light and creation. See chapter 8, below.
48. Ezra Fleischer, *Eretz-Israel Prayer and Rituals* [Hebrew] (Jerusalem, 1988), pp. 109ff.
49. See Shalom Spiegel, "On Medieval Hebrew Poetry," in Finkelstein, ed., *The Jews.*
50. Louis Ginzberg, *Gaonica* (New York, 1909), 1:144.
51. Hoffman, *Canonization*, p. 166.
52. Herman Kieval, *The High Holy Days* (New York, 1959), p. 34.

Chapter 6. The Daily Order of Prayer

1. In his *Commentary on the Palestinian Talmud* (New York, 1941), vol. 3, Louis Ginzberg explains that the original pattern of prayer consisted of two daily prayers, recited at the same time as the two sacrificial rituals took place. Individuals may have recited three prayers, but that was only a "pious custom" (see Taanit 27b). Later, he believes, a Sabbath evening prayer was introduced, and eventually a daily evening prayer as well, but they remained optional. This explains why the Amida of the evening was not repeated aloud by the leaders of the service (pp. 170ff.). See Berachot 27b and Y. Berachot 4:1 on the question of whether or not Maariv (the evening service) is compulsory.

Chapter 7. Preparation for Prayer

1. Berachot 5:1.
2. Berachot 60b.
3. Tosefta Berachot 6:18.
4. Menachot 43b.
5. See Jacob Mann, "Genizah Fragments of the Palestinian Order of Service," *Hebrew Union College Annual* 2 (1925), p. 277. The text blesses God who "made me a man and not a beast, a man and not a woman, an Israelite and not a non-Jew, circumcised and not uncircumcised, free and not a slave. . . . Blessed are You . . . who created primal Adam in His image and His likeness." The Roman rite also uses "who made me an Israelite" rather than "who has not made me a non-Jew." See also Menachot 43b. Joseph Heinemann discusses this in *Studies in Jewish Liturgy* [Hebrew] (Jerusalem, 1981), pp. 190–91.
6. Plato is quoted as giving thanks that he was created a man and a Greek

rather than a barbarian or an animal with no understanding. For this and similar Greek sayings and prayers, see A. A. Ha-Levi, *Concepts in Jewish Law and Lore in Light of Greek and Latin Sources* [Hebrew] (Tel Aviv, 1981), vol. 3, p. 157.

7. Berachot 60b.

8. Berachot 16b.

9. Yoma 87b.

10. Solomon B. Freehof, "The Structure of the Birchos Hashachar," *Hebrew Union College Annual* 23 (1950), p. 348. On times for reciting the Shema, see Berachot 1:1–2.

11. The first line of the Shema is called "Rabbi Judah the Prince's recitation of the Shema. . . . When he places his hand over his eyes, he accepts upon himself the yoke of the kingship of Heaven" (Berachot 13b).

12. Shabbat 118b. The text reads: ". . . those who complete the Hallel every day." In view of the fact that the collection of psalms and blessings which we call "Hallel" has never been recited daily, but only on certain holidays, the assumption is that he was referring to completing the recitation of the entire Book of Psalms, which may be characterized as "the book of praise (Hallel)."

13. *Abudraham Ha-Shalem* [Hebrew] (Jerusalem, 1963), p. 63.

14. Elihayu Zuta 4:9.

15. Midrash Psalms 100:4.

16. Berachot 4b.

17. See the discussion of Psalm 145 on pages 55–57.

18. The importance of the word *baruch* frequently led to the composition of prayers in which the word is repeated over and over. See above, page 109.

19. *Mekilta*, ed. Lauterbach, vol. 1, p. 223.

20. e.e. cummings, *Complete Poems* (New York, 1972), p. 663.

Chapter 8. The Shema

1. Josephus, *Antiquities* 4.8.13; Luke 10:27.

2. Menachot 99b.

3. Ibid. Rabbi Simeon bar Yochai said not to reveal this to the common or ignorant people, as he did not want them to feel they need not learn. Later, the Amora Rava said that it should be revealed to them to thus encourage them at least to recite the Shema.

4. Sifre Deuteronomy 32. The reward for one who performs the commandments from love rather than fear is doubled. Fear will lead one to abandon the one he serves the moment that fear vanishes. Love knows no reasons.

5. Sifre Deuteronomy 33.
6. Sifre Deuteronomy 32. The teaching is based on the fact that the word "heart" (*levavcha*) is spelled with two *bet*s rather than one. This was taken to indicate both parts of the person: the inclination to good and the inclination to evil.
7. Ibid.
8. Ibid.
9. Avoda Zara 54b.
10. Sifre Deuteronomy 40.
11. Act 4, scene 1.
12. Ethics of the Fathers 4:19.
13. Leviticus Rabba 28:1.
14. Megilla 4:3. See Louis Finkelstein, "The Meaning of the Word PRS," in his *Pharisaism in the Making*. See also Ezra Fleischer, "Toward a Clarification of the Expression *Pores Al Shema*" [Hebrew], *Tarbitz* 41 (1972), pp. 133–44.
15. Sifre Deuteronomy 33.
16. "When they heard the actual name of God uttered by the High Priest, they would bow, kneel, and prostrate themselves, saying: Blessed be the name of His glorious Majesty forever!" (Yoma 6:2).
17. Sifre Deuteronomy 31.
18. Deuteronomy Rabba, ed. S. Lieberman (Jerusalem, 1964), pp. 68–69.
19. *Mekilta*, ed. Lauterbach, vol. 2, pp. 229ff.
20. Ibid., pp. 237ff.
21. Berachot 2:2.
22. Berachot 13b, 16a.
23. Berachot 13b.
24. Ibid. When Rabbi Jeremiah saw that Rabbi Hiyya bar Abba prolonged the word "one" excessively, he said to him, "Once you have proclaimed His kingship over what is above and below and over the four sections of the heavens, no more is required."
25. Sifre Deuteronomy 32.
26. See 2 Macc. 7.
27. Sifre Deuteronomy 307. When Rabbi Hananiah was being martyred, he recited Deuteronomy 32:4. His wife recited the last part of that verse. His daughter recited Jeremiah 32:19 when told that she was to be consigned to a brothel. These verses justify and accept the ways of God.
28. Berachot 61b.
29. Berachot 1:4.
30. Sifre Deuteronomy 306. The verse "For the name of the Lord I proclaim; give glory to our God!" (Deut. 32:3) is interpreted by Rabbi Yose to mean: When I (the leader of the service) proclaim God's name, you (the congregation) should give glory to our God. The *barchu* formula is

found first in connection with the blessings said when reading the Torah and is then applied to the opening of the Blessing After Meals. See Berachot 7:3, where Rabbi Akiva teaches that in the synagogue one says, "Bless the Lord," while Rabbi Ishmael prefers "Bless the Lord who is blessed [*ha-mevorach*]," the formula we use. Both of these are based on Psalm 135:19–20: "O house of Israel, bless the Lord; O house of Aaron, bless the Lord; you who revere the Lord, bless the Lord." Rabbi Ishmael would add words found in Psalm 113:2: "Let the name of the Lord be blessed [*mevorach*] now and forever." See Reuven Hammer, "What Did They Bless?" p. 321.

31. See Jakob J. Petuchowski, "The Creation in Jewish Literature," *Judaism* 28, no. 3 (Summer 1979), p. 309.

32. Berachot 11b. It has been suggested that the real reason for the change was technical: rabbinic law does not permit a blessing to be composed simply of a verse; therefore a change was made.

33. Porton sees this as part of a philosophy of "totality," i.e., the desire to emphasize the inclusive nature of God, His creation, His concern, and the response to Him which all creatures should make—a philosophy that has definite messianic overtones. He points out the number of times that the Hebrew word *kol* ("all") appears in various forms in this blessing, especially in the poetic additions found in the Sabbath service, as well as in other parts of the liturgy. Bezalel Porton, "Midrash Tefilla: The Literary-Ideological Continuum from Pesukei d'Zimra to Alenu," *Tarbitz* (not yet published). A midrash in the Sifra to Lev. 26:6 seems to indicate that this change from "evil" to "everything" was commonly accepted as the basic meaning of the text:

> If there is not peace, there is nothing. The verse says, "I will grant peace in the land" (Lev. 26:6). This teaches us that peace is as important as everything [i.e., all else]. Thus it says, "He makes peace and creates evil" (Isa. 45:7). This teaches that peace is as important as everything.

The reading in Numbers Rabba 11:6 is: "Great is peace, for it is as important as everything. We say, 'He makes peace and creates everything.'"

34. Sifre Deuteronomy 306.

35. Hullin 91b.

36. Berachot 11b. See Max Kadushin, *Worship and Ethics*, pp. 89ff.

37. Berachot 11b.

38. Yochanan Muffs points out that "love" implies willingness and spontaneity. God gives His gift of the Torah "freely and spontaneously to Israel," and Israel, in turn, "gives gifts and offerings freely and spon-

taneously to God." Thus the declaration discovered in the Geniza to be recited before the Shema is particularly appropriate: "Blessed are You . . . who has commanded us with the obligation to recite the Shema—to proclaim His kingship with a full heart and declare His unity with a joyful spirit, and to worship Him with a willing soul" (*Love and Joy*, p. 187).

39. Y. Berachot 1:9.

40. This translation is based on the suggestion of Stefan C. Reif that *"kiyyam"* indicates that God has kept His promise to be our God. See Reif, "Liturgical Difficulties and Geniza Manuscripts," in S. Morag, ed., *Studies in Judaism and Islam* (Jerusalem, 1981), p. 121.

41. *Mekilta*, ed. Lauterbach, vol. 1, pp. 135–36; Y. Berachot 1:9.

42. Ibid., vol. 2, p. 24.

43. Ibid., pp. 59–60.

44. In Pesachim 117b, the Babylonian Amora Rava states that the blessing at the end of the Shema should be in the past tense—"who redeemed Israel"—while the blessing of redemption recited as part of the Amida (see chapter 9) is in the present tense: "Redeemer of Israel." The reason given is that since the Amida is a petition, this is appropriate. The blessing following the Shema, however, is praise, not petition, and therefore speaks in the past tense, referring to the historical redemption. The peculiarity of this is striking, since all blessing formulas are in the present (imperfect) tense; they are taken as descriptions of God and His continuous deeds. This is the only exception. The Jerusalem Talmud records that the Amora, Rabbi Joshua ben Levi of Israel, said that the blessing should conclude with "Rock of Israel and its redeemer," which is in the perfect tense (Y. Berachot 1:9). The versions of the blessing found in the Geniza do indeed use the present tense: "Rock of Israel and its redeemer." See Solomon Schechter, "Geniza Specimens," *Jewish Quarterly Review*, o.s. 10 (1898), p. 655, and Mann, "Genizah Fragments," p. 307. The Babylonians changed this in accord with the teaching of Rava; see Ismar Elbogen, "Studies in Jewish Liturgy," *Jewish Quarterly Review*, o.s. 18 (1906), p. 587.

Chapter 9. The Amida

1. "One stands to pray only in a serious mood" (Berachot 5:1).

2. "The School of Hillel says that everyone may recite [the Shema] in whatever position he happens to be" (Berachot 1:3). "Workmen may recite it on the top of a tree or standing on the top layer of stones [of a wall being built], which they are not permitted to do when reciting the Prayer" (Berachot 2:4).

3. Yoma 53b. The Talmud compares this to the way in which a disciple would take leave of his teacher and adds that if one did not show this respect, "it would have been better for him not to have prayed at all."

4. Thus Solomon declared, "I have now built for You a stately House, a place where You may dwell forever" (1 Kings 8:13).

5. Ps. 135:21. At the dedication of the Temple, Solomon says, "When he spreads his palms toward this House, oh, hear in Your heavenly abode" (1 Kings 8:38–39). God is in the House, yet in reality heaven is His abode. Nevertheless His eyes "are open day and night toward this House" (1 Kings 8:29). A midrash in Sifre Deuteronomy 29 teaches that "those who are outside the Land must face toward the Land of Israel. . . . Those who are in Jerusalem must face toward the Temple when they pray. . . . Those who are in the Temple must direct their hearts toward the Holy of Holies when they pray. . . . Thus those who are in the north must face the south, those in the south must face the north, those in the east must face the west, those in the west must face the east; thus all Israel will pray toward the same place." See also Tosefta Berachot 3:15, Berachot 30a, Berachot 4:5.

6. Megilla 17b.

7. Tosefta Berachot 3:1.

8. "It is a positive commandment to pray daily. . . . The number of prayers is not derived from the Torah. . . . The time of prayer is not fixed in the Torah. . . . Everyone prayed according to his ability. . . . Thus it was from our teacher Moses until the time of Ezra" (Maimonides, Mishneh Torah, Laws of Prayer 1:1–3). He then explains that the exile caused such a confusion of language that people did not know how to pray properly in Hebrew. Therefore Ezra "and his court" ordained the Eighteen Blessings and the number and times of prayer (ibid., 1:4–6).

9. Berachot 26b; Tosefta Berachot 3:1–2.

10. Berachot 26b. According to the Tosefta Berachot 3:2, some authorities connected the evening prayer with the closing of the Temple gates at dusk so that it would have to be recited during daytime.

11. Berachot 26b.

12. Genesis Rabba 68:9.

13. Berachot 34a.

14. Sifre Deuteronomy 343.

15. See Megilla 25a quoted above on page 96.

16. It appears in the prayer that concludes the preliminary service before the Sabbath morning prayer. There each word describing God is commented upon.

17. Y. Berachot 7:4.

18. See notes 6–8 above.

19. Simon the Righteous said, "Upon three things does the world stand: on

the Torah, on the Temple service, and on acts of loving-kindness" (Avot 1:2).

20. Sanhedrin 10:1. See also Sanhedrin 91a–b, 92a.

21. As Yehezkel Kaufmann puts it, "That the spirit of the deceased lives on apart from the body is the belief of the people, but biblical faith draws no religious or moral inferences from this notion" (*The Religion of Israel*, p. 311). The Sages, on the other hand, often found "the doctrine of the resurrection of the dead in the Torah" (Sifre Deuteronomy 47).

22. 2 Macc. 7:9; see also 12:43–45.

23. Walter Jaeger, *Paideia: The Ideals of Greek Culture*, 2nd ed. (New York, 1943), vol. 2, pp. 42ff.

24. Leviticus Rabba 34:3.

25. Sanhedrin 91b.

26. Maimonides, Mishneh Torah, Laws of Repentance 8–9; *Treatise on Resurrection*.

27. Schechter, "Geniza Specimens," p. 656.

28. Taanit 2a. Some versions say the key to childbirth rather than that to prosperity.

29. Schechter, "Geniza Specimens."

30. Sifre Deuteronomy 306.

31. Gershom G. Scholem, *Jewish Gnosticism, Merkabah Mysticism, and Talmudic Tradition* (New York, 1960).

32. See Kadushin, *Worship and Ethics*, p. 151. Fleischer ascribes the Kedusha to Essene prayers ("Antiquity of Prescribed Prayer," p. 434).

33. Mann, "Genizah Fragments," p. 301; Abraham Millgram, *Jewish Worship* (Philadelphia, 1971), p. 136.

34. Sifre Deuteronomy 49.

35. Shalom Spiegel, *The Last Trial* (New York, 1967).

36. Originally, there were twelve middle blessings. Numbers 14 and 15 were one and later were divided into separate paragraphs. See pages 179–80.

37. For more specific discussions of these concepts, see G. F. Moore, *Judaism* (Cambridge, 1946), vol. 2, pp. 279–397; Joseph Klausner, *The Messianic Idea in Israel* (New York, 1955).

38. Berachot 34b.

39. The same phenomenon occurs in the Passover Hagaddah, where Moses is mentioned only once when a verse is quoted, but never discussed as the prime mover of the Exodus. The text there continuously emphasizes "I—the Lord—and no other."

40. Schechter, "Geniza Specimens," p. 657.

41. Shabbat 116a.

42. Ibid.

43. Another explanation is that the two blessings were originally separate and that it was another blessing, the "curse of the heretics," that was

added. This seems to be the implication of the passage in Berachot 28b stating that Rabban Gamliel asked if there were any among the Sages who could frame that paragraph, and Samuel the Little did so. In that case, they then combined the two blessings concerning David and Jerusalem in order to retain the number eighteen; see Fleischer, "Antiquity of Prescribed Prayer," pp. 435–36. The talmudic passage, however, may mean not that a new blessing was added, but that an old one had to be reformulated in view of new realities.

44. *Mekilta*, ed. Lauterbach, vol. 2, pp. 113ff. See Reuven Hammer, "The God of Suffering," *Conservative Judaism*, Fall–Winter 1976–77.

45. In an article which came to my attention only after I had drawn these conclusions concerning the Amida as a prayer for redemption, Reuven Kimelman also makes the case for reading the Amida in that way and demonstrates how midrashic and early medieval literature utilized that interpretation; see Kimelman, "The Daily Amida and the Rhetoric of Redemption," *Jewish Quarterly Review* 79, no. 2–3 (1988–89), p. 165ff.

46. Avoda Zara 7b.

47. Berachot 10a.

48. "God of our fathers" refers to the first blessing, as does "shield of our salvation," reminding us of the phrase "protector (literally 'shield') of Abraham" and "savior." "Our lives" echoes the second blessing's "reviver"—the Hebrew root is the same in both. Similarly, "Your steadfast kindnesses" appears in the second blessing as "with steadfast kindness."

49. In the version of the Amida in Sifre Deuteronomy 343, *modim* is the last blessing mentioned. Louis Finkelstein believes this passage to be the earliest form of the Amida, and he interprets the word *modim* ("We thankfully acknowledge You") as a command to the congregation to prostrate themselves (*New Light From the Prophets* [New York, 1969], pp. 37ff.).

50. In Sotah 40a, five different prayers used by various Babylonian Amoraim are mentioned. Rav Papa then says, "Let us recite them all," and that is what happened. They were combined into the Modim d'Rabbanan—the *Modim* prayer of the Sages.

51. Sifre Numbers 42.

52. Rule Scroll of the Dead Sea sect, in *Megillat ha-Serakhim*, ed. Y. Licht (Jerusalem, 1965). See pp. 277–79: "May the Lord bless you from His holy habitation which will never prove false. . . . May He be gracious to you with all manner of blessing. May He bless you with all goodness and guard you from all evil. May He enlighten your heart with the knowledge of life and be gracious unto you with everlasting knowledge. May He lift the countenance of His steadfast kindnesses unto you for perpetual peace."

53. Sotah 7:6. The method of pronouncing the blessing was somewhat dif-

ferent in the synagogue in order to indicate the superior sanctity of the Temple. In the Temple it was recited as one blessing, the actual name of God—the Tetragrammaton—was pronounced, and the priests' hands were raised above their heads. In the synagogue, the blessing is recited as three separate parts, the word Adonai is substituted for God's name, and the priests' hands are level with their shoulders.

54. Y. Muffs, *Love and Joy*, p. 187.
55. Berachot 16b–17a.
56. Berachot 57b.
57. Shabbat 119b.
58. Following Muffs' translation, *Love and Joy*, p. 187.
59. Pesachim 117b.
60. Y. Berachot 4:6. See Jeffrey Hoffman, "The Surprising History of the Musaf Amidah," *Conservative Judaism*, Fall 1989, pp. 41–45.
61. "The day of rest lovingly/willingly, spontaneously"—Muffs, *Love and Joy*, p. 187.
62. Berachot 6a.
63. Jonathan A. Goldstein (*I Maccabees* [New York, 1976], p. 18) contends that the prayer was "probably composed in the reign of John Hyrcanus (134–104 B.C.E.)."
64. Robert Gordis, *A Faith For Moderns*, p. 265.

Chapter 10. Concluding Prayers

1. See Rashi's comment to Num. 29:35 and Sukkah 55b.
2. Sifre Deuteronomy 26.
3. Sanhedrin 38a.
4. Gerson D. Cohen, *Studies in the Variety of Rabbinic Cultures* (Philadelphia, 1991), p. 164.
5. See the discussion of the Kedusha on pages 139–41.
6. Sotah 49a.
7. Joseph Heinemann, *Prayer in the Period of the Tannaim and the Amoraim* [Hebrew] (Jerusalem, 1978), pp. 158ff.
8. See the discussion of the Kaddish in chap. 14.
9. The phrase "The Lord alone is God" also appears in the story of Elijah's encounter with the priests of Baal. When fire descends from heaven and the people are convinced that the Lord and not Baal is the true God, "all the people flung themselves on their faces and cried out: 'The Lord alone is God, the Lord alone is God' " (1 Kings 18:39). The phrase also concludes the confession of faith recited at the end of the Day of Atonement.
10. Taanit 4:2 records that "priests and Levites would go up to Jerusalem,

and the Israelites of the group would gather together in their cities and read the story of creation." Priests from different parts of the country were formed into groups who would serve in the Temple for a week at a time. The Israelites who remained behind would gather together at the time of the Temple service and read sections from Genesis. Heinemann suggests that the Alenu would have made a fitting conclusion to such readings, since it deals with the creation, and that this may have been its origin (*Prayer in the Period of the Tannaim and the Amoraim*, pp. 173ff.). The Hebrew of the first line refers to *yotzer bereshit* ("the maker of 'the beginning' [creation]"). This first line, with its reference to God as "Lord of everything," is also reminiscent of the first blessing before the Shema, where God is called "creator of everything"; see the discussion on pages 138–39. The fact that this prayer does not begin or end with a blessing is an excellent indication of its antiquity. It was written before the blessing formula had become the official expression of prayer and was so well ingrained that no attempt was made to alter it to fit the new pattern.

11. *Mekilta*, ed. Lauterbach, vol. 2, p. 60.
12. Ibid., p. 159.
13. Tamid 7:4.
14. Rosh Ha-Shanah 31a.

Chapter 11. Sabbath and Holidays

1. Shabbat 119a.
2. Genesis Rabba 11:8.
3. Berachot 57b.
4. Tamid 7:4.
5. Gerson D. Cohen, "The Song of Songs and the Jewish Religious Mentality," in *Variety of Rabbinic Cultures* pp. 3–18. "The Hebrew God alone was spoken of as the lover and husband of His people, and only the house of Israel spoke of itself as the bride of the Almighty" (p. 6).
6. *Mekilta*, ed. Lauterbach, vol. 2, p. 252.
7. Isaiah 54:4: Fear not, you shall not be shamed.
                Do not cringe, you shall not be disgraced.

   Psalm 42:12: Why so downcast, my soul,
                   why disquieted within me?

   Jeremiah 30:18: The city shall be rebuilt on its mound,
                   And the fortress in its proper place.
8. See Rashi to Shabbat 24b.
9. Louis Ginzberg, *Commentary on the Palestinian Talmud*, vol. 3 [Hebrew] (New York, 1941), p. 170.

10. Genesis Rabba 11:2.
11. Shabbat 119b.
12. Pesachim 106a.
13. Pesachim 118a. The prayer also features the frequent repetition of *kol*— "all" or "every"—leading up to the blessing that begins the recitation of the Shema, "Creator of all." See Porton, "Midrash Tefilla," and discussion above, page 139.
14. Berachot 33a. Lawrence A. Hoffman speaks of *havdalah* prayers, a category of blessings that are "the ritualized reminder of the Jewish system of categorization," dividing reality between the holy and the profane (*Beyond the Text* [Bloomington, Ind., 1989], p. 39).
15. Pesachim 103b–104a.
16. Berachot 8:5.
17. Genesis Rabba 11:2.
18. Ibid.
19. Pesachim 117a.
20. Tosefta Sukkah 3:2.
21. Pesachim 95b.
22. Pesikta d'Rav Kahana 52:8.
23. Arachin 10a–b.
24. Yoma 20a.
25. Taanit 28b.
26. Reuven Hammer, "On the Origin of the Partial Hallel," *Conservative Judaism*, Summer 1969.
27. Pesachim 117a. The reading of the Book of Esther on Purim is also considered a *mitzva* and is preceded by a similar blessing.
28. Ibid.
29. Reuven Hammer, "Two Liturgical Psalms."

Chapter 12. Garments of Prayer: Tallit and Tefillin

1. Menachot 43b.
2. See Ibn Ezra to Numbers 15:39.
3. Shabbat 118b. Rav Huna considered it a mark of his piety, deserving reward, that he "never walked four cubits bareheaded." See also Shabbat 156b.
4. See Jacob Milgrom, *The JPS Torah Commentary: Numbers* (Philadelphia, 1990), pp. 410ff. The Torah places the section concerning the fringes after the story of the spies. The spies fell victim to "scouting" after their own eyes (Num. 13:17, 13:21, 13:32). The fringes are intended to prevent one from following ("scouting after"—the Hebrew is the same) one's eyes and heart, and thus going astray, as did the spies and the Israelites who followed them (Num. 15:39).

5. Avot 3:18.
6. Menachot 43b; Sifre Numbers 115.
7. Sifre Numbers 115.
8. Menachot 43a.
9. Ibid; Sifre Numbers 115.
10. Menachot 44a; Sifre Numbers 115.
11. Sanhedrin 48b.
12. Gabriel Barkai, *The Hinom Slope: A Treasure Opposite the Walls of Jerusalem* [Hebrew] (Jerusalem, 1986).
13. Menachot 35b.
14. Song of Songs Rabba 8:4.
15. Berachot 6a.
16. Midrash Psalms 1:17.
17. *Guide for the Perplexed* 3.44.
18. On the intermediate days of the festivals, Chol Ha-Moed customs vary. In most places tefillin are not worn at all then, since these days are part of the festival. In other places they are worn during the early part of the service to indicate that the day is not a complete festival, but are removed beginning with the Hallel, which is a festival prayer.
19. Eruvin 96a.
20. Saul Tchernichovsky, *Poems* [Hebrew] (Tel Aviv, 1951). Translation mine—R.H.

Chapter 13. The Blessing After Meals

1. Tosefta Berachot 4:4.
2. Berachot 35a. See also Tosefta Berachot 6:1, which suggests a biblical derivation.
3. Sifre Deuteronomy 43.
4. Genesis Rabba 54:6.
5. Tosefta Berachot 6:1.
6. Berachot 7:3.
7. "When the First Berakah is recited after eating, the meal and the recitation of the berakah constitute a unitary entity in time, and the meal, as the occasion for the berakah, is then an element in an integrated religious experience. By the same token, the recitation of the First Berakah is an expression, through worship, of the experience of God's love represented by the meal" (Kadushin, *Worship and Ethics*, p. 70).
8. Louis Finkelstein, "The Birkat Ha-Mazon," *Jewish Quarterly Review* 19, no. 3 (1928–29), p. 220.
9. Midrash Psalms 31:8.
10. Berachot 48b.

11. The Talmud records that when Bethar was taken, "men, women, and children were slaughtered in it until their blood ran into the great sea." There was so much blood in the waters of nearby streams that the local non-Jewish inhabitants could enrich their soil "with the blood of Israel without using manure" for seven years (Gittin 57a). It also states that there were four hundred synagogues there, each with four hundred teachers, each of whom had four hundred pupils. All were slain by the enemy, wrapped in Torah scrolls, and burnt with them (Gittin 58a). Exaggeration aside, the destruction of Bethar had an enormous impact on Jewish history and on the collective Jewish memory. For these and other legends, see H. N. Bialik and Y. H. Ravnitzky, eds., *The Book of Legends / Sefer Ha-Aggadah* (New York, 1992). See also Chaim Raphael, *The Walls of Jerusalem* (New York, 1968), pp. 48ff.

12. As Louis Finkelstein points out, the blessing was instituted by the rabbis of Yavneh and is mentioned by such authorities as Eliezer ben Hyrkanos, who lived prior to Bar Kochba ("The Birkat Ha-Mazon," pp. 217, 221). See Berachot 48b.

13. Berachot 9:2.

14. Sanhedrin 6:4–5.

Chapter 14. Rites of Mourning

1. Berachot 58b. It is recited when seeing those with afflictions such as blindness, amputated limbs, or misshapen heads.

2. Berachot 59b.

3. Berachot 9:5.

4. Sifre Deuteronomy 32.

5. Steinberg, *A Believing Jew*, pp. 317ff.

6. Sifre Deuteronomy 307. See above, pages 133–34.

7. Ibid.

8. Megilla 4:3, Ketubbot 8b. Max Kadushin, *Worship and Ethics*, pp. 152ff.

9. Ketubbot 8b.

10. *Hamlet*, act 1, scene 2.

11. This translation follows the suggestion of Lawrence A. Hoffman that *yitbarach* ("blessed") is the last word of the second line and not the first of the third line. The seven words in the third line are a sevenfold explanation of its meaning. Such strings of praise words were characteristic of the "chariot mysticism" of the time, which is reflected in both the Kedusha and the Kaddish (see Hoffman, *Canonization of the Synagogue Service*, pp. 79–60). The usual division and translation of the Kaddish has the second line read: "May His great name be blessed forever and for all eternity." The third section then begins: "May the name of the Holy One, blessed is He, be blessed. . . ."

12. The list in the Mishna of those prayers requiring a minyan does not include the Kaddish. It was recited following study and was considered a prayer for the immediate revelation of the kingdom of God. David de Sola Pool calls it "a closing doxology" following a discourse based on the lesson of Scripture, which always closed on a note of messianic comfort (see de Sola Pool, *The Old Jewish-Aramaic Prayer—the Kaddish* [Leipzig, 1909], p. 8). Later it became associated with the act of sanctification of God's name, which does require a minyan (see Kadushin, *Worship and Ethics*, pp. 141–42).
13. Matt. 6:9–10.
14. Shabbat 119b.
15. *Machzor Vitry*, pp. 112ff.
16. See Abraham Z. Idelson, *Jewish Liturgy and Its Development* (New York, 1932), p. 87.
17. Rosh Ha-Shanah 17a.
18. Solomon B. Freehof, "Hazkarath Neshamoth," *Hebrew Union College Annual* 36 (1965), p. 183.
19. Ibid., p. 181.

Chapter 15. Getting Started

1. Berachot 40b.
2. Sanhedrin 106b.
3. Midrash Psalms 4:9.
4. Abraham Isaac Kook, *Orot Ha-Kodesh* [Hebrew] (Jerusalem, 1963–64); see the translations in Jacob Agus, *Banner of Jerusalem* (New York, 1946).
5. Y. Berachot 8:1.
6. Berachot 29b.
7. Emanuel Rackman, *One Man's Judaism* (New York, 1970), p. 336.
8. Judith Plaskow, *Standing Again at Sinai* (San Francisco, 1990), pp. 136–46.
9. Leo Baeck, *Essence of Judaism*, p. 92.
10. Berachot 29b.

Glossary

Many Hebrew terms are used in this book to refer to different parts of the prayerbook or practices of Jewish worship. The following glossary defines terms that are used frequently and will be helpful in understanding the discussion. More detailed definitions will be found where appropriate in the text itself.

ALENU—a prayer acknowledging God as the sole master of creation and voicing the hope for universal recognition of God and the establishment of His kingdom on earth. The name is the first Hebrew word of the prayer, meaning "It is [incumbent] upon us."

ALIYA—literally, "going up," referring to a person being called to recite blessings over the Torah when it is read. Three people are called up on weekdays, four on Rosh Hodesh (the new month), five on festivals, six on Yom Kippur (the Day of Atonement), and seven on the Sabbath.

AMIDA—from the word "standing." This is the central prayer of every service. Whenever the term "service" is used, it refers to the recitation of an Amida accompanied by other prayers. The name reflects the fact that this prayer is recited while standing. It is sometimes called *ha-tefilla* (*the* Prayer), because of its central importance, or the Shemoneh Esrei (the Eighteen), because of the eighteen benedictions of which it was originally composed. The actual number of benedictions within it varies with the occasion. On weekdays there are nineteen; on the Sabbath, seven.

AMORA (pl. Amoraim)—Rabbinic Sages who lived in the period following the compilation of the Mishna from 200 to 500 C.E. in the Land of Israel or in Babylonia. Their teaching forms the basis for the discussions in the Talmud and the later midrashim.

ARVIT or MAARIV—from the word "evening." Since the Hebrew day begins after sunset, this is actually the first service of the day.

BAKASHA—"request"; plural: *bakashot*. Those prayers in which God is asked to grant some request, be it spiritual or physical.

BARCHU—from the root meaning "to bless." This is the invitation by the leader of the service to begin the recitation of the Shema and its blessings by blessing God. It is recited in both the evening and morning services.

BERACHA—a blessing; plural: *berachot*. A specific formula which always contains the words *baruch ata Adonai* ("Blessed are You, O Lord"). *Berachot* are recited as part of the services, when performing a ceremonial *mitzva*, before and after eating, and when undergoing significant experiences or viewing unusual sights.

BIRCHOT HA-SHACHAR—"the blessings of the morning." A series of blessings and readings recited at the beginning of the morning service. Originally said at home, they are now part of the synagogue service.

BIRKAT HA-MAZON—the Blessing of Food. A series of blessings recited after eating a meal.

GAON (pl. Geonim)—the heads of the Babylonian academies of Sura and Pumbedita from the sixth to the eleventh century who were the highest authorities of Jewish Law during that time.

HAFTARAH—literally, "conclude." The section from the Prophets that is read to conclude the Torah reading.

HALLEL—"praise." A prayer consisting of a collection of psalms which is recited on special festival days as a sign of rejoicing.

HATIMA—the blessing that comes at the conclusion of a specific prayer. It blesses God and then describes the particular aspect of God's works that was the subject of the prayer.

HAVDALAH—"separation." The blessings recited at the conclusion of the Sabbath or holy day, blessing God for having distinguished between the sacred and the weekday. On the Sabbath, wine, spices, and a candle are used; on other days, only wine.

HODAYA—"thanksgiving." The act of thanking God and acknowledging His goodness and sovereignty.

KABBALAT OL HA-MITZVOT—"the acceptance of the yoke of the commandments." The act of pledging to observe all of God's commands. This is connected with the recitation of the second paragraph of the Shema.

KABBALAT OL MALCHUT SHAMAYIM—"the acceptance of the yoke of God's kingship." The act of pledging one's exclusive allegiance to God when reciting the Shema and at other times.

KABBALAT SHABBAT—"welcoming the Sabbath." A collection of psalms and special hymns concerning the Sabbath which is recited Friday evening prior to the Arvit service.

KADDISH—a prayer in Aramaic proclaiming the sanctity of God and praying for the speedy establishment of His kingdom. The name comes from the root meaning "holy." The prayer is chanted between sections of the service. One version of this prayer is recited by mourners.

KAVANA—literally, "intention." To recite prayers with *kavana* means to invest them with seriousness and meaning or to say them with the intention or purpose of fulfilling some obligation.

KEDUSHA—another form of the word "holy," referring to the responsive prayer substituted for the third blessing of the Amida when it is repeated aloud. It proclaims God's holiness in the words of the angels: "Holy, holy, holy."

KIDDUSH—a different form of the word "holy," referring to the prayer recited over wine in which the sanctity of the Sabbath or festival day is proclaimed.

KIDDUSH HA-SHEM—"the sanctification of the name of God." The act of causing others to praise God. This can be done through the recitation of prayers proclaiming His holiness, through good deeds, or through martyrdom.

KRIYAT HA-TORAH—the public reading of the Torah which is part of the service on the Sabbath, Monday, Thursday, and festivals.

MAARIV—*see* Arvit.

MAFTIR—the closing *aliya* given to the person who will read the Haftarah.

MEGILLA—"scroll," referring to the Book of Esther or to the books of Ruth, Ecclesiastes, Song of Songs, and Lamentations, which are read as part of the synagogue service on various holy days.

MIDRASH—interpretations of the Bible by the Sages (second century B.C.E.– fifth century C.E.) found either in the Talmud or in books of midrash. These books also include legends and stories of the lives of the Sages.

MINCHA—the afternoon service, frequently recited in the late afternoon just before Arvit. It can, however, be recited at any time during the afternoon. The word means "offering" and reflects the connection between prayer and the sacrificial system in the Temple.

MINYAN—"number," referring to the quorum required for the recitation of certain public prayers. The minimum number of ten adults is derived from biblical passages where ten constitutes a group. Whether women can be part of this quorum or not is a matter of dispute in modern Jewish life.

MISHNA—the collection of traditions of Jewish Law based on the teachings of the Tannaim (second century B.C.E.–second century C.E.), compiled by Rabbi Judah the Prince in 200 C.E. As the authoritative statement of Jewish tradition, it formed the basis for later discussions that resulted in the compilation of the Talmud.

MUSAF—the additional service, recited on the Sabbath, Rosh Hodesh (the New Month), and major festivals; in short, whenever an additional sacrifice was offered in the Temple.

PESUKEI D'ZIMRA—"the verses of song." The preliminary service before the recitation of the morning service, consisting of sections from the Book of Psalms and other sections of the Bible.

PETICHA—"opening." The blessing that comes at the beginning of a specific prayer. It proclaims God to be "king of the universe" and then describes His actions that will be the subject of the prayer.

PIYYUT—plural: *piyyutim*. Liturgical poetry.

SHACHARIT—the morning service, from the word meaning "dawn." It is made up of the Shema and the Amida.

SHALIACH TZIBBUR—the "messenger of the congregation." The person who leads the group in public prayer. It is sometimes abbreviated as *"shatz."* Professionals who perform this task are called *hazzanim* (cantors).

SHEMA—three paragraphs from the Torah that are recited at the Arvit and the Shacharit services every day, accompanied by blessings before and after. The title means "hear" or "listen," from the first word recited. It is sometimes called *kriyat shema*, the recitation of the Shema. The first paragraph of the Shema is recited at bedtime, and the first line is recited before death.

SHEMONEH ESREI—*see* Amida.

SHEVACH—"praise." The praise and glorification of God which is a major part of Jewish worship. All blessings are acts of praise.

SIDDUR—from the Hebrew word meaning "order." The book that contains the order of prayer for the Sabbath and weekdays as it has evolved from earliest times until today. In current usage, the Siddur also includes the festival prayers.

TACHANUN—prayers of penitence. The word means to request or implore. These form a part of the weekday morning and afternoon services.

TALLIT—the special garment to which fringes (tzitzit) are attached at each of the four corners, intended to remind the wearer of God's commandments.

TANNA (pl. Tannaim)—the early Sages who lived in the Land of Israel from the second century B.C.E. until the compilation of the Mishna in 200 C.E. Their teachings form the basis for that work and for the early midrashim.

TEFILLIN—"phylacteries"; singular: tefilla. Small boxes containing sections from the Torah which are attached to the arm and the head by straps and worn during daily Shacharit prayers.

TOSEFTA—a compilation of teachings that were not included in the Mishna as well as early commentaries upon them.

TZITZIT—the fringes attached to the four corners of a tallit.

YAHRZEIT—the anniversary of a death, commemorated by the mourner by the recitation of Kaddish and other prayers.

YIZKOR—"remember." Prayers commemorating the dead, recited on Yom Kippur and the last day of each festival.

Bibliography

1. For further reading

Burman, Daniel. *Praying with Understanding*. Jerusalem, n.d.

Donin, Hayim H. *To Pray as a Jew*. New York, 1980.

Dresner, Samuel. *Prayer, Humility and Compassion*. Philadelphia, 1957.

Elbogen, Ismar. *Jewish Liturgy: A Comprehensive History*. Philadelphia, 1993.

Garfiel, Evelyn. *The Service of the Heart*. New York, 1958.

Gordis, Robert. *The Ladder of Prayer*. New York, 1956.

Heinemann, Joseph. *Prayer in the Talmud*. Berlin, 1977.

Heschel, Abraham Joshua. *Man Is Not Alone*. Philadelphia, 1951.

————. *Man's Quest for God*. New York, 1954.

Holtz, Barry W. *Back to the Sources*. New York, 1984.

Idelsohn, Abraham Z. *Jewish Liturgy and Its Development*. New York, 1932.

Jacobs, Louis. *Hasidic Prayer*. New York, 1973.

————. *Jewish Prayer*. London, 1955.

Kadushin, Max. *Worship and Ethics*. Evanston, Ill., 1964.

Millgram, Abraham. *Jewish Worship*. Philadelphia, 1971.

Munk, Elie. *The World of Prayer*. New York, 1961.

Petuchowski, Jakob J., ed. *Understanding Jewish Prayer*. New York, 1972.

Plaskow, Judith. *Standing Again at Sinai*. San Francisco, 1990.

2. Other works consulted in preparing this volume

Abudraham, David. *Abudraham Ha-Shalem* (in Hebrew). Jerusalem, 1963.

Agus, Jacob. *Banner of Jerusalem*. New York, 1946.

Arzt, Max. *Joy and Remembrance*. New York, 1979.

Baeck, Leo. *The Essence of Judaism*. New York, 1948.

Baer, Yitzhak. *Avodat Yisrael* (in Hebrew). Jerusalem, 1937.

Barkai, Gabriel. *The Hinom Slope: A Treasure Opposite the Walls of Jerusalem* (in Hebrew). Jerusalem, 1986.

Bialik, H. N., and Y. H. Ravnitzky. *The Book of Legends/Sefer Ha-Aggadah.* New York, 1992.

Bickerman, Elias. "The Civic Prayer for Jerusalem." *Harvard Theological Review* 55 (1962).

———. *From Ezra to the Last of the Maccabees.* New York, 1962.

Buber, Martin. *Moses.* New York, 1958.

———. *Tales of the Hasidim.* 2 vols. New York, 1947.

Childs, Brevard S. *The Book of Exodus.* Philadelphia, 1974.

Cohen, Gerson D. *Studies in the Variety of Rabbinic Cultures.* Philadelphia, 1991.

Cohen, Naomi G. "The Nature of Shimon Hapekuli's Act." *Tarbitz* 52, no. 4 (1983).

Cohen, Shaye J. D. "Pagan and Christian Evidence on the Ancient Synagogue." In Levine, ed., *The Synagogue in Late Antiquity.*

de Sola Pool, David. *The Old Jewish-Aramaic Prayer—The Kaddish.* Leipzig, 1909.

Elbogen, Ismar. "Eighteen Benedictions." In *Universal Jewish Encyclopedia.* Vol. 4. New York, 1939.

———. "Studies in Jewish Liturgy." *Jewish Quarterly Review,* o.s. 18 (1906).

Fackenheim, Emil L. *What Is Judaism?* New York, 1987.

Finkelstein, Louis. "The Birkat Ha-Mazon." *Jewish Quarterly Review* 19, no. 3 (1928–29).

———. "The Development of the Amida." *Jewish Quarterly Review* 16 (1925–26).

———. *New Light from the Prophets.* New York, 1969.

———. *Pharisaism in the Making: Selected Essays.* New York, 1972.

Fleischer, Ezra. *Eretz-Israel Prayer and Prayer Rituals* (in Hebrew). Jerusalem, 1988.

———. "On the Antiquity of Prescribed Prayer in Israel" (in Hebrew). *Tarbitz* 59 (1990).

———. "Toward a Clarification of the Expression Poreis Al Shema." *Tarbitz* 41 (1972).

———. *The Yozer: Its Emergence and Development* (in Hebrew). Jerusalem, 1984.

Freehof, Solomon B. "Hazkarath Neshamoth." *Hebrew Union College Annual* 36 (1965).

———. "The Structure of the Birchos Hashachar." *Hebrew Union College Annual* 23 (1950).

Ginzberg, Louis. *Commentary on the Palestinian Talmud* (in Hebrew). 5 vols. New York, 1941.

———. *Gaonica* (in Hebrew). New York, 1919.

———. "Tamid: The Oldest Treatise of the Mishnah." *Journal of Jewish Lore and Philology* 1 (1919).

Glatzer, Nahum N. *Franz Rosenzweig: His Life and Thought.* New York, 1953.

Goldstein, Jonathan A. *I Maccabees.* New York, 1976.

Gordis, Robert. *A Faith for Moderns.* New York, 1960.

Greenberg, Moshe. *Biblical Prose Prayer.* Berkeley, Calif., 1983.

Hammer, Reuven. "The God of Suffering." *Conservative Judaism,* Fall–Winter 1976–77.

———. "On the Origin of the Partial Hallel." *Conservative Judaism,* Summer 1969.

———. "Two Liturgical Psalms: Salvation and Thanksgiving." *Judaism* 40, no. 4 (Fall 1991).

———. "What Did They Bless?" *Jewish Quarterly Review* 81, nos. 3–4 (January–April 1991).

Heinemann, Joseph. "Once Again Melekh Ha Olam." *Journal of Jewish Studies* 15 (1964).

———. *Prayer in the Period of the Tannaim and the Amoraim* (in Hebrew). Jerusalem, 1978.

———. *Studies in Jewish Liturgy* (in Hebrew). Jerusalem, 1981.

Heschel, Abraham Joshua. *God in Search of Man.* Philadelphia, 1956.

———. "Prayer." *Review of Religion,* January 1945.

———. *The Prophets.* Philadelphia, 1962.

Hoffman, Jeffrey. "The Surprising History of the Musaf Amidah." *Conservative Judaism,* Fall 1989.

Hoffman, Lawrence A. *Beyond the Text.* Bloomington, Ind., 1989.

———. *The Canonization of the Synagogue Service.* Notre Dame, Ind., 1979.

Idelsohn, Abraham Z. *Jewish Liturgy and Its Development.* New York, 1932.

Jager, Walter. *Paideia.* New York, 1943.

Josephus. *Antiquities of the Jews.*

———. *Wars of the Jews.*

Kadushin, Max. *The Rabbinic Mind.* New York, 1952.

Kaplan, Mordecai M. *The Meaning of God in Modern Jewish Religion.* New York, 1937.

Kaufmann, Yehezkel. *The Religion of Israel.* Chicago, 1960.

Kievel, Herman. *The High Holy Days.* New York, 1959.

Kimelman, Reuven. "The Daily Amida and the Rhetoric of Redemption." *Jewish Quarterly Review* 79, nos. 2–3 (1988–89).

———. "Psalm 145 and the Liturgy." *Proceedings of the Rabbinical Assembly* 54 (1992).

———. "The Shema and Its Blessings." In Levine, ed., *The Synagogue in Late Antiquity.*

Klausner, Joseph. *The Messianic Idea in Israel.* New York, 1955.

Kohler, K. "The Origin and Composition of the Eighteen Benedictions."

In Petuchowski, ed., *Contributions to the Scientific Study of Jewish Liturgy.*

Kook, Abraham Isaac. *Orot Ha-Kodesh* (in Hebrew). Jerusalem, 1963–64.

Leibreich, Leon J. "An Analysis of U-Ba'Le-Ziyyon in the Liturgy." *Hebrew Union College Annual* 21 (1948).

Levine, Lee I., ed. *Ancient Synagogues Revealed.* Jerusalem, 1981.

———, ed. *The Synagogue in Late Antiquity.* Philadelphia, 1987.

Licht, Y., ed. *Megillat Ha-Hodayot* (in Hebrew). Jerusalem, 1951.

———, ed. *Megillat Ha-Serakhim* (in Hebrew). Jerusalem, 1965.

Liber, M. "Structure and History of the Tefilah." *Jewish Quarterly Review* 40 (1949).

Lieberman, Saul. *Hellenism in Jewish Palestine.* New York, 1950.

———. "Light on the Cave Scrolls from Rabbinic Sources." *Proceedings of the American Academy of Jewish Research* 20 (1951).

———. *Tosefta Ki-Fshutah* (in Hebrew). New York, 1955.

Machzor Vitry (in Hebrew). Nuremberg, 1923; reprinted New York, n.d.

Maimonides, Moses. *The Guide for the Perplexed.* 2 vols. Chicago, 1974.

Malinowski, Bronislaw. *Magic, Science and Religion.* New York, 1954.

Mann, Jacob. "Changes in the Divine Service of the Synagogue Due to Religious Persecutions." *Hebrew Union College Annual* 4 (1927).

———. "Genizah Fragments of the Palestinian Order of Service." *Hebrew Union College Annual* 2 (1925).

Marmorstein, A. "The Oldest Form of the Eighteen Benedictions." *Jewish Quarterly Review* 34 (1943–44).

Milgrom, Jacob. *The JPS Torah Commentary: Numbers.* Philadelphia, 1990.

Moore, George Foote. *Judaism.* Cambridge, 1946.

Muffs, Yochanan. *Love and Joy.* New York, 1992.

Petuchowski, Jakob J. "The Creation in Jewish Literature." *Judaism* 28, no. 3 (Summer 1979).

———. *Theology and Poetry.* London, 1978.

———, ed. *Contributions to the Scientific Study of Jewish Liturgy.* New York, 1970.

Porton, Bezalel. "Midrash Tefilla: The Literary-Ideological Continuum from Pesukei d'Zimra to Alenu." *Tarbitz,* not yet published.

Pritchard, James B., ed. *Ancient Near Eastern Texts.* Princeton, N.J., 1955.

Rackman, Emanuel. *One Man's Judaism.* New York, 1970.

Raphael, Chaim. *The Walls of Jerusalem.* New York, 1968.

Reif, Stefan C. "Liturgical Difficulties and Geniza Manuscripts." In S. Morag, ed., *Studies in Judaism and Islam.* Jerusalem, 1981.

Rosenzweig, Franz. *The Star of Redemption.* New York, 1970.

Sarason, Richard S. "Religion and Worship." In Jacob Neusner, ed., *Take Judaism, For Example.* Chicago, 1983.

Schechter, Solomon. "Geniza Specimens." *Jewish Quarterly Review,* o.s. 10 (1898).

Schiffman, Lawrence H. "The Dead Sea Scrolls and the Early History of Jewish Liturgy." In Levine, ed., *The Synagogue in Late Antiquity.*

Scholem, Gershom G. *Jewish Gnosticism, Merkabah Mysticism, and Talmudic Tradition.* New York, 1960.

Simon, Ernst. "On the Meaning of Prayer." In Jakob J. Petuchowski, ed., *Understanding Jewish Prayer.* New York, 1972.

Soloveitchik, J. B. "Thoughts on Prayer" (in Hebrew). *Ha-Darom* 47 (1979).

Spiegel, Shalom. *Amos and Amaziah.* New York, 1957.

———. *The Last Trial.* New York, 1967.

———. "On Medieval Hebrew Poetry." In Louis Finkelstein, ed., *The Jews: Their History, Culture, and Religion.* Philadelphia, 1960.

Steinberg, Milton. *Basic Judaism.* New York, 1947.

———. *A Believing Jew.* New York, 1951.

Talmon, S. "Order of Prayers of the Sect from the Judean Desert" (in Hebrew). *Tarbiz* 29 (1960).

Towner, W. S. "The Modulation of a Biblical Formula." *Catholic Biblical Quarterly* 30 (1968).

Vermes, Geza. "The Decalogue and the Minim." In Matthew Black and Georg Fohrer, eds., *In Memoriam Paul Kahle.* Berlin, 1968.

Zeitlin, Solomon. "The Morning Benediction and the Readings in the Temple." *Jewish Quarterly Review* 44 (1953–54).

———. "The Shemoneh Esreh: An Historical Study of the First Canonisation of the Hebrew Liturgy." *Jewish Quarterly Review* 54 (1963–64).

Index

About the Author

REUVEN HAMMER received his rabbinic ordination and a doctorate in theology from the Jewish Theological Seminary of America, and a doctorate in education from Northwestern University. After serving as a congregational rabbi for fifteen years, he made *aliya* to Israel together with his wife, Raḥel, an artist, and their five children. Since 1973 he has taught Jewish studies and special education at various Israeli institutions. As dean of the Jewish Theological Seminary–Jerusalem Campus and founding director of the Seminary of Judaic Studies, he has supervised the training of hundreds of American, Israeli, and South American rabbinical students. A former president of the Rabbinical Assembly of Israel, he currently serves as its *Av Bet Din L'Giyur,* the head of the rabbinic court for conversion. His articles on popular and scholarly topics have appeared in numerous periodicals and newspapers in both Hebrew and English. He is the author of *Sifre: A Tannaitic Commentary on the Book of Deuteronomy,* which received the National Jewish Book Award as the outstanding work of scholarship of 1987.